March to Independence

THE INDEPENDENCE TRILOGY

Spark of Independence:
The American Revolution in the Northern Colonies, 1775–1776

United for Independence:
The American Revolution in the Middle Colonies, 1775–1776

March to Independence:
The American Revolution in the Southern Colonies, 1775–1776

A JOURNAL OF THE AMERICAN REVOLUTION BOOK

MARCH *TO* INDEPENDENCE

THE REVOLUTIONARY WAR IN THE SOUTHERN COLONIES, 1775–1776

MICHAEL CECERE

WESTHOLME
Yardley

© 2021 Michael Cecere

Maps by Tracy Dungan. © 2021 Westholme Publishing

Westholme Publishing, LLC
904 Edgewood Road
Yardley, Pennsylvania 19067
Visit our Web site at www.westholmepublishing.com

ISBN: 978-1-59416-368-5
Also available as an eBook.

Printed in the United States of America.

CONTENTS

List of Maps

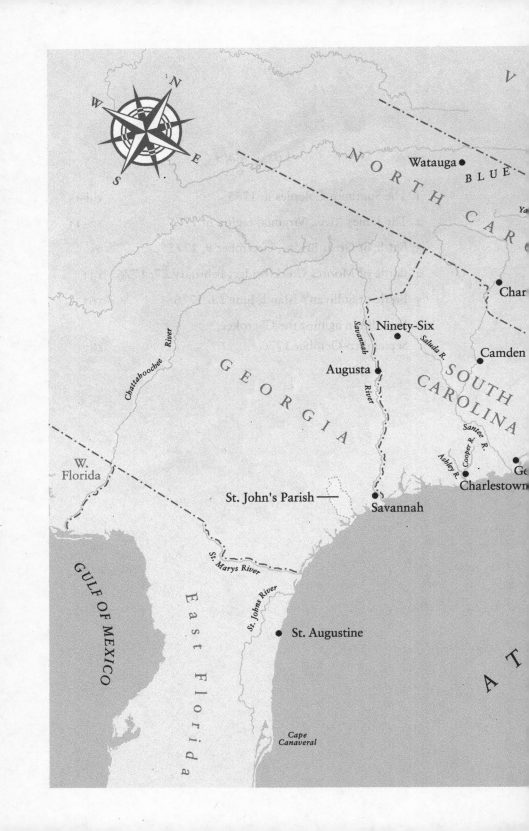

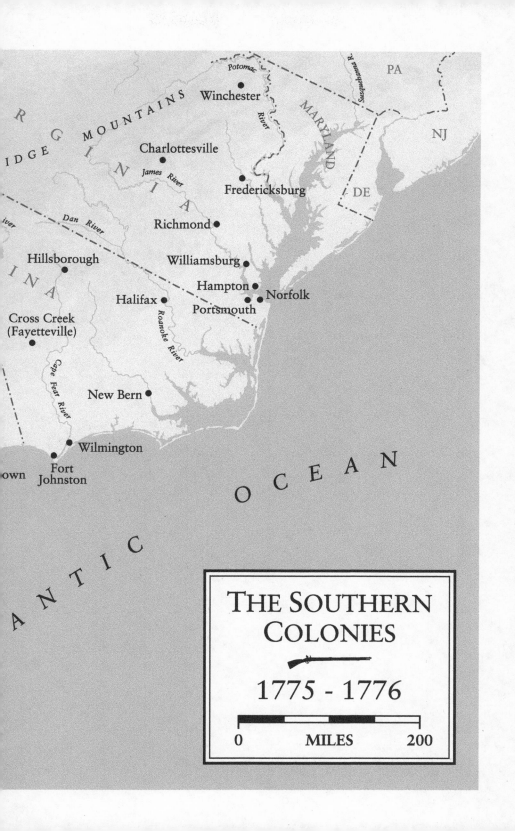

THE SOUTHERN COLONIES

1775 - 1776

0   MILES   200

Winchester

Charlottesville

Fredericksburg

Richmond

Hillsborough

Williamsburg

Halifax

Hampton
Portsmouth

Cross Creek
(Fayetteville)

New Bern

Wilmington

Cross
Town Johnson

INTRODUCTION

The Southern Colonies on the Eve of the Revolution

I T IS UNIVERSALLY UNDERSTOOD THAT THE REVOLUTIONARY WAR in America began in Lexington, Massachusetts, on April 19, 1775, when the "shot heard around the world" triggered a bloody engagement between Massachusetts minutemen and British redcoats. The bloodshed at Lexington and Concord—goes the thinking—prompted the other American colonies to join Massachusetts in a long war for independence that initially centered in New England in 1775, then in the mid-Atlantic states from 1776 to 1779, and finally in the southern states from 1780-1781.

Setting aside the complex political issues of 1775, the progression of the Revolutionary War did, as far as large military engagements go, seem to unfold in a sort of regional pattern from the north to the south (with frequent conflict in the western frontier after 1775). However, by compartmentalizing the war into separate theaters of action during distinct periods of time, we tend to overlook the events that occurred in each region outside of their prescribed time period.

For instance, a search of scholarship on the Revolutionary War in the South will produce a number of fine works on the war in that region from 1778 (when the British captured Savannah) through 1781 (ending with Yorktown). Some focus on particular battles like Cowpens or Yorktown while others look at the war in general in the South or in a particular southern state for that time period (or a portion of that time period).

The consequence of placing so much attention on the war in the South from 1778 onward is that people assume that nothing happened in the southern states *before* 1778. There is a dearth of writing on the Revolutionary War in the South prior to 1778.

At the time of its occurrence, the American Revolution was not the singular movement coordinated by the Continental Congress, as it is often viewed, but rather thirteen separate revolutions within each rebellious colony. Circumstances, necessity, and choice ultimately brought the colonies closer together, but the realities of the age also meant that each colony was often isolated from the other at important times and in important ways. To better understand and appreciate the American Revolution, it is essential to understand what occurred in each individual American colony.

This work attempts to address the lack of attention on the southern colonies in the early part of the Revolutionary War by focusing on the significant events that occurred in Virginia, North Carolina, South Carolina, Georgia, and Florida during the sixteen months from the outbreak of war in April 1775 through the summer of 1776 when independence was declared. Readers will discover that the story of the American Revolution and the Revolutionary War in the southern colonies was a bit more eventful and complex than they realized.

VIRGINIA

In 1775 the population of Virginia, the largest of Britain's North American colonies, numbered over half a million people, approximately 40 percent of whom were enslaved.[1] Tobacco production drove Virginia's economy and its society. Virginians shipped hundreds of thousands of pounds of tobacco to England and Scotland annually and prospered as a result.[2] Virginia and Maryland tobacco accounted for nearly a million pounds sterling in export revenue in 1770 and dwarfed the next most valuable export commodity produced in all of the colonies, flour.[3]

Virginia's reliance on the production of tobacco influenced its development and settlement. Large tracts of cultivated land were necessary to meet the ever-growing demand for tobacco. As a result, few large towns or cities developed in Virginia, despite the Old Dominion's head start in settlement in 1607. Norfolk, situated on the Elizabeth River and within sight of Hampton Roads, was Virginia's largest city with several thousand inhabitants. Williamsburg, the capital of Virginia with just two thousand residents, was closer to a small town than a city and second in population to Norfolk.[4] Within Williamsburg, however, assembled some of America's greatest Revolutionary leaders: Patrick Henry, Thomas Jefferson, George Washington, Peyton Randolph, George Mason, and Richard Henry Lee, just to name a few. It is impossible to overstate the contribution these Virginians made to the formation of the United States.

NORTH CAROLINA

North Carolina's population in 1775 was approximately 240,000, with about a quarter of the population enslaved.[5] A large number of North Carolinians were settled in the interior counties of the colony by 1775 where cash crops were more difficult to grow and get to market. As a result, North Carolina was significantly less affluent than either Virginia or South Carolina, which was the chief exporter of the third most valuable colonial commodity, rice.

Like Virginia, there were no large settlements to speak of in North Carolina, although Wilmington was a busy port on the Cape Fear River and New Bern was the capital. A significant rift existed between those colonists who lived in the eastern part of the colony, some of whom were large land and slave owners, and those who lived a more subsistence lifestyle in the interior of the colony. In fact, in 1771, bloodshed erupted between North Carolinians when disgruntled colonists from the backcountry, dubbed regulators, rose up in opposition against corrupt local authorities. Governor William Tryon led militia from the eastern counties to confront the defiant regulators and crushed their ill-planned uprising.

Tryon moved on to govern New York, and most of the regulators were pardoned after pledging loyalty to the crown, but the animosity between eastern and western colonists in North Carolina remained just under the surface.

SOUTH CAROLINA

Over 150,000 people lived in South Carolina in 1775, well over half of whom were enslaved.[6] South Carolina broke the pattern of most cash crop–oriented colonies by having the fourth largest city in the American colonies, Charlestown. It was through Charlestown that the very valuable commodities of South Carolina plantations and farms in the lowcountry, rice and indigo, were exported. The production of these exports was the result of the hard work of the colony's large and growing slave population, which easily surpassed the White population of South Carolina.

Reliance on the forced labor of over half the population made free, White South Carolinians vulnerable to, and hypervigilant toward, any possibility of a slave insurrection. This constant concern, and their economic dependence on trade with Great Britain, did not dampen South Carolina's determination to resist Parliament's unconstitutional policies toward the American colonies. This determination, however, was not shared by all free South Carolinians. Many of those who lived in the backcountry of South Carolina strongly resented the gentlemen planters of the lowcountry, who profited immensely from the cultivation of rice and indigo raised largely by slave labor and who held all of the political power in the colony. A regulator movement similar to that in North Carolina had also developed in South Carolina in the 1760s, and on the eve of the Revolutionary War the resentment and distrust of the lowcountry gentlemen that spawned this movement lingered among many colonists in the backcountry.

GEORGIA

Georgia's population of nearly forty thousand people in 1775 (more than one third of whom were enslaved) was spread along its short coastline and the southern bank of the Savannah River.[7] Savannah, located just a few miles from the mouth of the river, was the principal town of the colony, and rice and indigo were its principal exports.

Georgia's small population made its inhabitants particularly vulnerable and constantly concerned about the many Creek and Cherokee Indians who lived just to the west and north of them. An annual trade with Indian leaders for furs, in exchange for gunpowder, shot, and firearms, helped keep a fragile peace, but as more colonists arrived to settle in Georgia, encroachment upon Indian land occurred regularly. This source of conflict was partially addressed in 1773 when Georgia's royal governor, James Wright, signed a treaty with the Creek Indians in Augusta, conveying two million acres of land to Georgia to erase a mounting trade debt the Indians had accrued with colonial traders.[8] Although the ceded land reduced the frequency of further encroachment for the time being, it did not halt all bloodshed on the frontier. Several bloody encounters, initiated by members of both sides, occurred after the treaty was signed.[9] The Creek and Cherokee Indians remained a powerful force (and potential threat), and a large number of settlers in Georgia's backcountry valued Britain's military might and protection more than they opposed Parliament's colonial policies that upset their fellow Georgians in the coastal region, who were farther away from and thus less likely to be attacked by the Indians.

EAST FLORIDA

On the eve of the Revolutionary War, East Florida, with a population of approximately three thousand nonnative people, over one third of whom were enslaved, was easy to overlook.[10] Although the fortified town of St. Augustine could boast of being the oldest permanent European settlement in North America, the province of East Florida had seen limited growth over its nearly two hundred years of existence. A British colony for just over a decade (the result of Spain's decision to support France in the Seven Years' War) the settlers and slaves of East Florida grew indigo as their chief export.[11] They also produced a small amount of wooden planks and traded with the Indians for furs. It was a tenuous existence for many in a difficult region full of alligators, insects, and Indians. Such challenges were likely the reason that a majority of East Florida's small English population lived in or adjacent to St. Augustine.

Unlike the thirteen American colonies to the north, East Florida had no elected assembly. Government authority rested in the hands of the royal governor and several appointed officials. Patrick Tonyn, a retired British officer and veteran of the Seven Years' War, was the governor of East Florida on the eve of the Revolutionary War.

With no elected assembly to challenge Governor Tonyn or Parliament's flawed policies, and a tiny population of colonists that were heavily dependent on Great Britain for protection and trade, there was little chance that the uproar and unrest so prevalent in the other colonies would occur in East Florida.

As spring took firm hold in the southern colonies in April 1775, a sense of impending conflict existed, fostered by weekly reports in the newspapers of British military preparation and activity. There were also, however, occasional reports from London that gave hope that reconciliation between Great Britain and her colonies was still possible.

Although most colonists desired reconciliation, they also understood that by the spring of 1775 the likelihood of such a development was slim. Twelve colonies had come together in Philadelphia a few months earlier (in the fall of 1774) and hammered out an agreement to boycott British goods and eventually embargo their own goods to Britain if the dispute continued for another year. The agreement was an impressive display of colonial unity among the very different British colonies, but it also covered disagreements among colonial leaders about just how far they should go to resist Parliament and the king's ministers. In 1774 economic measures were the extent to which colonial unity had been achieved. As the days passed in April 1775 and the British occupation of Boston continued, few knew how their fellow colonists would react if the conflict with Great Britain turned violent. The answer to that question was revealed in the weeks following the bloodshed at Lexington and Concord.

Part I
1775

One

Spring

It had already been a very eventful spring when the sun rose in Virginia on April 19, 1775. A month earlier, Patrick Henry had famously declared, at the Second Virginia Convention in Richmond, that he would take "Liberty or Death" in the decade-long dispute with Great Britain over Parliament's attempt to extend greater authority over the American colonies. The passage of Henry's resolution in late March 1775, which called for Virginia to improve its "posture of defense," prompted a number of counties to form volunteer companies. There was no great sense of urgency, however, in the days and weeks that followed Henry's speech. In fact, conflicting reports from England simultaneously foretold of reconciliation and war.

Hundreds of miles separated Virginia from Massachusetts, so when fighting erupted on Lexington Green early that morning, Virginians remained unaware of the bloodshed for ten days. It was an incident that occurred in Williamsburg, Virginia's capital, just two days after Lexington and Concord, which actually threw the colony into an uproar.

In the early morning hours of April 21, twenty armed men from the HMS *Magdalen* (6 guns, 30 crew) landed at Burwell's Ferry on the James River and rapidly marched to Williamsburg, four miles away.[1] Their orders, at the behest of Governor John Murray, the fourth earl of Dunmore, were to seize a supply of gunpowder stored in the powder magazine in the center of Williamsburg and transport it back to their ship. Lord Dunmore explained his rationale behind this provocative act in a letter to his superiors in England:

> The series of dangerous measures pursued by the people of this colony against government, which they have now entirely over-turned and particularly their having come to a resolution of rais-ing a body of armed men in all of the counties, made me think it prudent to remove some gunpowder which was in a magazine in this place where it lay exposed to any attempt that might be made to seize it, and I had reason to believe the people intended to take that step.[2]

Forty-five-year-old Lord Dunmore had been Virginia's royal gov-ernor for four years; it was a post he grudgingly accepted in lieu of his brief governorship of New York, which was taken away from him in 1771 by the British ministry. Dunmore's disappointment in his transfer to Virginia gradually abated and, like many of the Old Dominion's landed gentry, he saw opportunities in the vast tracts of land to the west. In fact, just four months prior to the seizure of gun-powder in the capital, Lord Dunmore had returned triumphantly to Williamsburg from an expedition against the Shawnee Indians that secured Virginia's land claims all the way to the Ohio River. The House of Burgesses praised the governor for his accomplishment and he was briefly the toast of Williamsburg. Much had changed in Vir-ginia over the ensuing four months and the events of April 21, 1775, ignited a firestorm of controversy for the governor.

Hoping to remove the gunpowder in secret and avoid a confronta-tion, the small British naval detachment from the *Magdalen* entered the capital in the predawn hours unnoticed. Armed with a key to the magazine provided by Lord Dunmore, they quickly loaded fifteen half barrels of gunpowder onto a wagon and started back to their ship.

At some point in the operation the British detachment was discovered and the alarm spread throughout town, but not before they escaped to their ship with the powder. Lord Dunmore recalled that, "Drums were then sent through the city, [and] the independent company got under arms."[3] Anxious city residents, many of them armed with muskets and fowlers, gathered at the courthouse, directly across from the magazine, in the dim light of dawn to learn what had happened.[4]

A few hundred yards from the courthouse, at the Governor's Palace, Lord Dunmore heard the commotion created by the agitated crowd. He reported to the British ministry after the incident that, "All the people assembled and during their consultation continued threats were brought to my house that it was their resolution to seize upon or massacre me and every person found giving me assistance if I refused to deliver the powder immediately into their custody."[5]

Luckily for Dunmore, Peyton Randolph, Virginia's Speaker of the House of Burgesses and probably the most respected man in Virginia, as well as several other city leaders, were able to calm the irate crowd gathered at the courthouse and prevent them from marching on the Governor's Palace. Randolph lived within sight of the powder magazine and county courthouse and probably noticed the commotion out his window within minutes of the alarm. A portly man of fifty-four years who had served as attorney general prior to becoming Speaker of the House of Burgesses in 1766, Randolph was the closest thing to Virginia royalty there was. Moderate in his views compared to the likes of Patrick Henry or Richard Henry Lee, Randolph's stature in Virginia extended to the Continental Congress, where he was selected to preside over both the first and second Continental Congresses until his untimely death in the fall of 1775.

After a tense meeting with the capital's inhabitants, during which a formal address to the governor was drafted, Speaker Randolph led a small delegation of the city's leaders to the governor's residence to deliver the address. It expressed the city's alarm at the removal of the gunpowder from the public magazine and asserted that the powder magazine remained the best place to store the gunpowder, especially given recent talk of possible slave insurrections. The address concluded with a polite request that Governor Dunmore explain his reasons for removing the powder and that it be immediately returned to the magazine.[6]

Realizing the precarious situation he was in, Governor Dunmore admitted to Lord Dartmouth, Britain's secretary of state for the colonies, that "With their armed force at a little distance . . . I thought proper, in the defenceless state in which I [found] myself, to endeavour to soothe them and answered verbally to the effect that I had removed the powder (lest the Negroes might have seized upon it) to a place of security from whence when I saw occasion I would at any time deliver it to the people."[7]

Dunmore further explained that he had the powder removed before dawn "to prevent any alarm," and that "he was surprised to hear the people were under arms on this occasion, and that he should not think it prudent to put the powder into their hands in such a situation."[8]

When the delegation that delivered the address departed from the governor's palace, Lord Dunmore was uncertain whether his explanation had defused the crisis. To his great surprise and relief, Williamsburg's leaders convinced the assembled crowd at the courthouse that the governor's response was satisfactory and they peacefully dispersed.[9] The situation remained calm until evening when a new report spread through the city that a detachment of British marines had landed and were marching on Williamsburg.[10] Benjamin Waller, a prominent attorney in the city, recalled that the residents "expressed great uneasiness and went with their Arms to the Magazine to guard it, but soon dispersed except a few who acted as patrole that Night."[11] Although the reported landing of British marines proved to be false, the armed Virginians who gathered at the magazine to challenge the marines demonstrated a degree of resistance to British authority that had rarely been seen in Virginia.

The following day, Lord Dunmore sparked another uproar when he lost his temper and unleashed a verbal tirade against the colonists. Mayor John Dixon, like most of Williamsburg, learned of Dunmore's outburst secondhand and noted the impact it had on the capital's inhabitants: "The Inhabitants appeared to be in perfect tranquility til a Report was spread by his Excellency's throwing out some threats respecting the Slaves, when there seemed to be great uneasiness but nothing more was done but doubling the usual Patrole."[12]

Dixon's recollection of Dunmore "throwing out some threats" was a reference to the governor's chance encounter with Dr. William Pasteur. Dr. Pasteur reported that he met the highly agitated governor on the street the morning after the powder was seized and that Dunmore "seemed greatly exasperated at the Peoples having been under Arms."[13] Doctor Pasteur assured the governor that Williamsburg's residents realized the rashness of their actions and regretted it, but Dunmore would not be placated and unleashed a tirade in response. Pasteur recalled that

> His Lordship then proceeded to make use of several rash expressions and . . . swore by the living God that if a Grain of Powder was burnt at Captain Foy or Captain Collins, [Dunmore's aide and the captain of the *Magdalen*] or if any Injury or insult was offered to himself, or either of them, that he would declare Freedom to the Slaves, and reduce the City of Williamsburg to Ashes. His Lordship then mentioned setting up the Royal Standard, but did not say that he would actually do it, but said he believed, if he did he should have a Majority of white People and all the Slaves on the side of Government, that he had once fought for the Virginians, and that, by GOD, he would let them see that he could fight against them, and declared that in a short Time, he could depopulate the whole Country.[14]

Reports of Dunmore's volatile outburst and rash threats spread quickly through Williamsburg, surprising no one and reinforcing a growing belief among many that Dunmore cared little for their safety or their interests.

This view was further supported by a letter from London (printed in the local gazettes on the day of the powder incident) that claimed that Lord Dunmore had willfully exaggerated the unrest in Virginia in 1774 in a letter to his superiors in London in late December in order to alarm the British ministry into action. The London correspondent who revealed Dunmore's letter noted that "A scene of greater confusion, misrule, and injustice, cannot be conceived, than is described in a letter of Lord Dunmore's dated Dec. 24, as is now prevailing in the province of Virginia."[15]

The negative characterization of Virginia that Dunmore's December letter to the ministry presented outraged many colonists.[16] Clearly Governor Dunmore viewed the colonists, and their opposition to Parliament's policies, with contempt and disdain, and the feeling of the colonists toward Dunmore was becoming mutual.

Had Virginians been aware of the contents of a letter Lord Dunmore wrote to Lord Dartmouth on May 1, 1775, they would have been even angrier. Declaring the unrest in Virginia over the seized gunpowder an "insurrection" caused by the "rebellious spirit" of the people, Dunmore reported that "parties of armed men were continually coming into town from the adjacent counties . . . offering fresh insults," and that "2,000 armed men" in Fredericksburg were preparing to march on the capital to force him to return the powder.[17] Dunmore noted that since he could not "make any effectual resistance" against such an overwhelming force, he had sent his wife and children to a British warship in the York River out of fear for their safety. Dunmore was determined, however, to remain in the capital to assert royal authority, and he expected city officials to intervene to stop the marchers from Fredericksburg from entering Williamsburg.[18] Dunmore informed Lord Dartmouth that if the magistrates and loyal Virginians did not "repair to my assistance," he would consider "The whole country in an actual state of rebellion and myself at liberty to annoy it by every possible means, and that I shall not hesitate at reducing their houses to ashes and spreading devastation wherever I can reach."[19]

Dunmore confidently concluded his letter to Lord Dartmouth by asserting that if just a small body of British troops were sent to Virginia with a number of extra muskets and ammunition, "I could raise such a force from among Indians, Negroes and other persons as would soon reduce the refractory people of this colony to obedience."[20]

Luckily for Lord Dunmore, his views and proposals in his letter to Lord Dartmouth remained undisclosed to the public.

That was not the case concerning the news of the seized gunpowder in Williamsburg, which spread quickly throughout Virginia and reached Fredericksburg, one hundred miles to the north, on April 24, the same day that the Spotsylvania Independent Company mustered for drill. Captain Hugh Mercer dispatched messengers to neighboring counties and called for a general muster of militia companies in Fredericksburg on Saturday, April 29. Their intention was to form a mounted corps of light horse militia to ride to Williamsburg and recover the stolen gunpowder.[21]

Riders were also sent to Williamsburg to confirm and update the news from the capital. Mann Page Jr. and two others reached Williamsburg on April 27 and were informed that Peyton Randolph and the city leaders of Williamsburg had the situation well under control. In fact, Speaker Randolph, aware of the volatile temper of Governor Dunmore, was alarmed to learn of the militia's planned march to Williamsburg and urged the riders to return to Fredericksburg as quickly as possible to halt the march. Mann Page carried back with him a letter written by Speaker Randolph thanking the militia for their assistance but assuring them that it was not needed and might only make matters worse.[22]

Page returned to Fredericksburg at almost the same time that an express rider from the north with the first news of the bloodshed in Massachusetts (Lexington and Concord) passed through town and alarmed everyone.[23] British troops had reportedly fired without provocation upon the Massachusetts militia, killing six and wounding four others.[24] A second account claimed that 4,000 colonial militia had surrounded a brigade of British troops (1,000 strong) in Lexington and had killed 150 regulars (redcoats) at a loss of 50 of their own men.[25] Clearly, something significant had occurred in Massachusetts, and the troops assembled in Fredericksburg must have wondered if the events to the north were in any way related to their own crisis in Virginia.

Undoubtedly anxious about the news from Massachusetts, an officer's council from fourteen volunteer companies (representing six

hundred mounted men) listened intently as Speaker Randolph's letter
was read aloud. A debate on whether to proceed to Williamsburg
followed. Peyton Randolph's views held tremendous weight with
those assembled, and after much discussion it was agreed to heed his
plea and cancel the march to the capital. Instead, the officer's council
publically condemned Lord Dunmore for his actions and pledged to
reassemble at a moment's notice to defend their rights or those of
any sister colony that was unjustly invaded.[26]

Patrick Henry was surprised and disappointed when he learned
that the volunteers gathered in Fredericksburg had cancelled their
march on the capital. A week earlier, Henry had confided to two
friends that Dunmore's seizure of the powder was a fortunate circumstance that would awaken and animate the public:

> You may in vain talk to [the people] about the duties on tea, etc.
> These things will not affect them. They depend on principles, too
> abstracted for their apprehension and feeling. But tell them of the
> robbery of the magazine, and that the next step will be to disarm
> them, you bring the subject home to their bosoms, and they will
> be ready to fly to arms to defend themselves.[27]

The news from Fredericksburg suggested that the animated spirit
Henry expected in the people had already waned.

It seemed only fitting that after ten years of heated rhetoric in opposition to the British ministry's misguided colonial policies, thirty-
nine-year-old Patrick Henry would be the one to lead armed men
into Williamsburg. The son of a middling tobacco farmer in central
Virginia, Henry did not have the family pedigree to advance auto-
matically in Virginia politics. He had to earn his advancement, and
he did so through his extraordinary oratory and keen mind, which
led him to the House of Burgesses in 1765 to represent Louisa
County, northwest of Richmond. He immediately established a rep-
utation in the assembly as a firebrand when he authored a number
of bold resolutions against the Stamp Act.

There was no turning back from that point, and for most of the
next decade Patrick Henry was the recognized leader of Virginia's

opposition to Parliament. He served with Peyton Randolph, George Washington, and several other prominent Virginians as a delegate to the First Continental Congress in 1774 and was set to return to Philadelphia in May. Henry is probably best remembered, however, for the speech he delivered just a month before the seizure of the gunpowder. His fiery "Liberty or Death" speech at the Second Virginia Convention in Richmond, which called on Virginia to better prepare itself for war, and the convention's subsequent adoption of Henry's position, is what prompted Lord Dunmore to seize the gunpowder in the magazine in Williamsburg.

Discouraged by the cancellation of the march from Fredericksburg but determined to lead troops to the capital, Henry delayed his journey to Philadelphia to attend the Second Continental Congress and, instead, rode to the small town of Newcastle to meet with the Hanover county committee and the independent company.[28] In the late afternoon of May 2, Henry delivered a powerful address to the volunteers that inspired them to proceed with their march on Williamsburg. Reinforced by volunteers from nearby counties, Henry and approximately 150 men reached Doncastle's Ordinary, about sixteen miles north of Williamsburg, on May 3 and encamped there.[29]

Fearful that Henry and his men could appear in the capital at any moment, Dunmore hastily prepared for battle. Captain George Montagu, the commander of the recently arrived warship HMS *Fowey* (20 guns, 130 crew) rushed 43 men armed with swords, cutlasses, and bayonets (but no muskets) to the governor's residence and threatened to bombard Yorktown if the detachment was confronted or harassed on its march to Williamsburg.[30] The sailors joined Dunmore's tiny force of armed servants at the governor's palace. Dunmore also placed cannon before the palace and swore to fire on the town should Henry's troops dare enter.[31]

Henry dismissed several appeals from Williamsburg's leaders to end the march, but when Carter Braxton arrived in camp and proposed to ride to Williamsburg to obtain payment for the powder, Henry agreed to await the outcome of his efforts. With the help of Thomas Nelson Sr., the respected president of the governor's council, Braxton returned on May 4 with a bill of exchange for 330 pounds

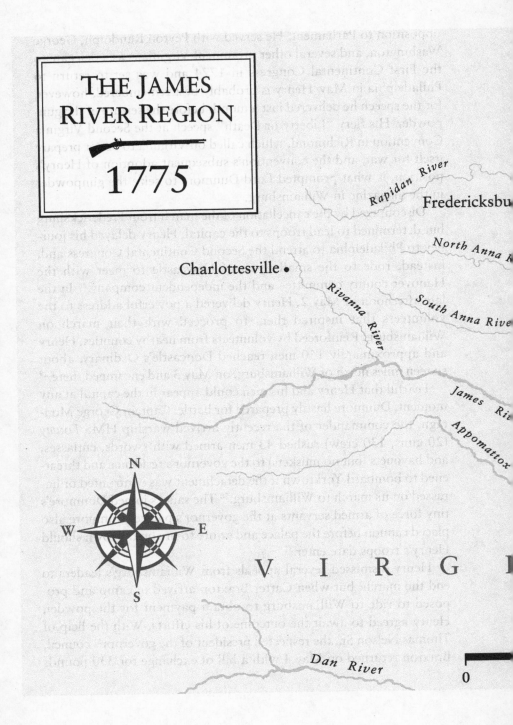

THE JAMES
RIVER REGION

1775

Rapidan River

Fredericksbu

North Anna R

Charlottesville •

Rivanna River

South Anna Rive

James Riv

Appomattox

N

W   E

S

V I R G I

Dan River

0

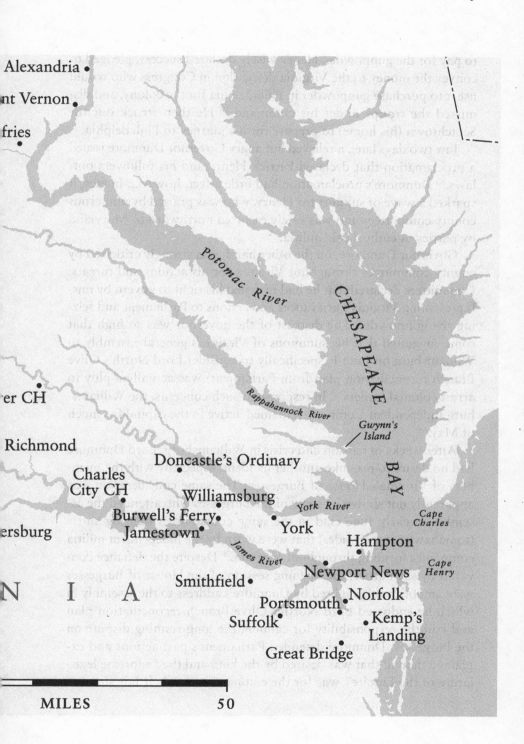

Alexandria

nt Vernon

fries

Potomac River

CHESAPEAKE

Rappahannock River

Gwynn's
Island

er CH

Richmond

Doncastle's Ordinary

Charles
City CH

Williamsburg

BAY

Burwell's Ferry

York River

Cape
Charles

ersburg

Jamestown

York

James River

Hampton

Cape
Henry

Smithfield

Newport News

Portsmouth

Norfolk

N I A

Suffolk

Kemp's
Landing

Great Bridge

MILES   50

to pay for the gunpowder. Henry wisely declared success, pledged to convey the money to the Virginia delegation in Congress who would use it to purchase gunpowder in Philadelphia for the colony, and dismissed the troops under his command.[32] He then struck out for Scotchtown (his home) to prepare for his journey to Philadelphia.

Just two days later, a relieved but angry Governor Dunmore issued a proclamation that declared Patrick Henry and his followers outlaws.[33] Dunmore's proclamation had little effect, however. In fact, it sparked a wave of support for Henry, who was praised by numerous county committees and was safely escorted northward to Maryland by parties of enthusiastic militia.

Governor Dunmore, on the other hand, was strongly criticized by county committees throughout Virginia for his actions and threats. Committees declared that he had forfeited his right to govern by misrepresenting Virginia's grievances and actions to Parliament and seizing the gunpowder. The distrust of the governor was so high that some suggested that his summons of Virginia's general assembly to Williamsburg on June 1 (specifically to consider Lord North's Olive Branch reconciliation plan from Parliament) was actually a ploy to arrest colonial leaders.[34] In response to such concerns, the Williamsburg Independent Company remained active in the capital for much of May.[35]

After weeks of tension and crisis in Williamsburg, Lord Dunmore had no desire to provoke another incident, especially with the members of Virginia's House of Burgesses. The same consideration was apparently not shown by some of the burgesses who attended the assembly in early June clad in the same coarse linen hunting shirts (tomahawks at their sides) that were worn by the independent militia companies forming throughout Virginia.[36] Despite the defiance conveyed by such attire, the opening session of the House of Burgesses went smoothly, highlighted by Dunmore's address to the assembly in which he endorsed Lord North's Olive Branch reconciliation plan and laid the responsibility for calming the long-running dispute on the burgesses. Dunmore defended Parliament's past actions and explained that all that was desired by the king and the "supreme legislature of the Empire" was for the colonies to pay their fair share of the burden of operating the empire.[37] In fact, Lord North's plan called for the colonists to decide for themselves what amount to contribute annually to the operation of the empire.[38]

The House of Burgesses responded to Dunmore's address within days and asserted that the crisis of the last decade was all the fault of the British ministry and their unconstitutional policies, begun in 1765 and carried to the present.[39] The burgesses also took a swipe at Dunmore for consistently misleading the ministry about the situation in Virginia: "However strangely this Country may have been misrepresented, we do solemnly avow the firmest and most unshaken Attachment to our most gracious Sovereign and his Government, as founded on the Laws and Principles of our excellent Constitution."[40]

The house assured Dunmore that they would fully consider Lord North's reconciliation plan and respond as soon as possible, but the assembly's resolutions of approval for the proceedings of both the First Continental Congress and the 2nd Virginia Convention bode ill for Lord North's Olive Branch plan.[41] Many Virginians viewed North's plan for what it was, an effort to split the colonies, and Speaker Randolph wanted to delay consideration of it out of fear of undermining the Continental Congress, who were themselves considering Lord North's plan.[42] Unity among the colonies was crucial, and Peyton Randolph, along with most of his fellow burgesses, was determined to maintain it. He was assisted in these efforts by a new crisis at the powder magazine that seized everyone's attention in the capital.

On the night of June 3 a party of young men broke into the Williamsburg powder magazine to retrieve weapons. A blast from a spring-loaded musket showered them with shot. Pellets struck one youth in the arm and shoulder, seriously wounding him, and another lost two fingers on his right hand.[43] The city was once again alarmed, and many were outraged when they learned that spring guns (set to fire by a trip wire) had been secretly placed in the magazine. Alexander Purdie's gazette declared that "had any person lost his life, the perpetrator or perpetrators, of this diabolical invention, might have been justly branded with the . . . title of MURDERERS!"[44] John Pinkney's gazette pointed a finger straight at Dunmore.[45]

The spring guns proved to be an ineffective deterrent, and a large crowd gathered at the magazine two days later to cart away muskets and other military stores. A report then spread through the city on June 6 that a party of marines and sailors from the *Fowey* were marching to the governor's palace.[46] When members of the governor's council approached Dunmore to request that he order the landing party to return to their ship, he professed surprise that they were coming and agreed that, if they were, he would send them back.[47] While this occurred, the Williamsburg Independent Company mustered at the magazine, "determined to attack the said Marines and Sailors, if they should come."[48] Alas, the landing party did not arrive, and it is unclear whether they were ever sent. What is clear is that Lord Dunmore had had enough of the disorder.

A degree of calm settled upon the capital on Wednesday, June 7, prompted in part by Governor Dunmore's newfound cooperative attitude (he granted a house committee access to the powder magazine to inspect what was left inside). The House of Burgesses even passed a resolution of thanks to the governor for his service against the Indians on the frontier in 1774.[49]

In the evening, Lord Dunmore walked across town unmolested to visit one of his strongest supporters, John Randolph, Virginia's attorney general and brother of Speaker Peyton Randolph. There is no record of what they discussed, but it is likely that Dunmore either learned of or informed Randolph that the Virginia gazettes were going to print more damning commentary on Dunmore's December 24 letter to Lord Dartmouth. A letter from a correspondent in London who was privy to Dunmore's letter reached Virginia in early June and painted Lord Dunmore in the worst possible light:

Extract from a Letter from London
Dunmore . . . proceeded warmly to recommend to lord Dartmouth that some men of war [ships] should be stationed in Chesapeake Bay, to prevent the Virginians from carrying on any external trade, except with this country, and that all communication might be cut off between them and the northern colonies . . . . [Dunmore] . . . observed that the COUNCIL, as well as the HOUSE OF

BURGESSES, and almost EVERY PERSON OF FORTUNE AND CONSID-
ERATION IN THE COLONY except the ATTORNEY GENERAL [John
Randolph], were [as] deeply engaged as the inferior planters in
factious associations and plans of resistance, great outrages and
disorders would soon take place among them, from the want of
regular distribution of law; and therefore he strongly urged the
king's ministers, as a sure method to increase their disorders, and
which . . . could not fail to produce petitions from the RICH, pray-
ing for protections of [Parliament], that his majesty would, without delay, order HIMSELF, and all the other EXECUTIVE OFFICERS
of Virginia, to withdraw from thence.⁵⁰

The London correspondent concluded with the suggestion that
Lord Dunmore was a chief cause of the ongoing political crisis. "Can
you therefore, my dear sir, wonder that [the ministry] perseveres in
their ruinous and despotic system of American politics?"⁵¹

Given all of the unrest that had occurred to date and that was sure
to follow after the publication of this letter, Dunmore decided that it
was time to withdraw to the safety of the *Fowey*. Early in the morning of June 8, the governor and his family (who had returned to the
palace), accompanied by Captain Foy and his wife and a few of Dunmore's household servants, left the palace and made their way to the
British schooner *Magdalen*, anchored in Queen's Creek. From there
they sailed to the York River where Dunmore and his party transferred to the larger *Fowey*, anchored off of Yorktown.

NORTH CAROLINA

The bloodshed at Lexington and Concord on April 19, 1775, occurred roughly a month after North Carolina's royal governor, Josiah
Martin, wrote to General Thomas Gage in Boston requesting a supply of arms and ammunition.⁵² Like Lord Dunmore, thirty-eight-
year-old Governor Martin had been the royal governor of North
Carolina since 1771. It fell to the retired lieutenant colonel of the
British army to lead the colony in the aftermath of the Battle of Alamance in 1771. Martin's predecessor, William Tryon, defeated approximately two thousand regulators at Alamance who rebelled
against the frequent corruption of local officials and complacency of

the eastern elite. The crushing defeat of the poorly organized regulators to Governor Tryon reaffirmed political control of North Carolina among the tidewater gentlemen of the east. Governor Martin's fair treatment of the defeated regulators, however, gradually earned the respect of many, but the events of late 1774 and early 1775 had him concerned.

Governor Martin explained to General Gage that the "hostile preparations" of the New Englanders over the winter and the "plan of resistance" of the Virginians convinced him to "support his Majesty's Government in this Province to which the contagion of their ill example has already reached."[53] Martin expressed confidence that with the aid of the king's loyal subjects in North Carolina, many of whom were Scottish Highlanders in the interior of the colony, he could "maintain the Sovereignty of this Country to the King," provided of course that his supporters were properly armed.[54]

Two weeks after he wrote to General Gage (and two weeks before Lexington and Concord) Governor Martin discovered that his boast to keep North Carolina loyal may have been premature. The North Carolina Provincial Convention, made up of representatives from most of the colony's counties and towns, gathered in the capital of New Bern to respond to the acts of the First Continental Congress the previous fall and to select delegates to return to Philadelphia in May. Governor Martin issued several proclamations from his imposing residence in New Bern, declaring the convention an illegal assembly and demanding that its members disband. The delegates ignored him and strongly endorsed the Continental Association (boycott and embargo) adopted by the Continental Congress in October 1774.[55] The convention also returned its delegation of William Hooper, Joseph Hewes, and Richard Caswell to Congress with their thanks and rebuked the governor for his unconstitutional attempt to prevent his Majesty's subjects from peacefully assembling in the convention.[56]

Governor Martin described the actions of the convention to Lord Dartmouth in London and speculated that "The Spirit of the Convention here . . . has been inflamed by the Communication of the Proceedings of a like monstrous Body lately assembled in Virginia."[57] Martin was of course referring to Virginia's second convention in

Richmond that was held in late March where Patrick Henry delivered his "Liberty or Death" speech. Governor Martin added, though, that an attempt by the North Carolina Convention to raise volunteer militia companies in every county the way they were doing in Virginia was rejected by the delegates in New Bern.[58]

In his next letter to Dartmouth, written on the day after the fighting at Lexington and Concord but over two weeks before word of the conflict reached North Carolina, Governor Martin dismissed the North Carolina Convention as not representative of the sentiment of most inhabitants in the colony: "Ten of the 34 Counties of this Province sent no Delegates to this late Convention, in many others the Committees consisting of 10 or 12 Men took upon themselves to name them and the rest they were not chosen . . . but one twentieth part of the people, notwithstanding every act of persuasion was employed by the Demagogues."[59]

Governor Martin also confidently assured Dartmouth that North Carolinians, particularly those in the western part of the colony, would remain loyal.

I have received the fullest assurances of their [the inhabitants of the western counties] devotion to His Majesty and of their readiness to support me in maintaining the constitution and Laws of their Country upon all occasions, and I have no doubt that I might command their best services at a word on any emergency. This, My Lord, affords me the higher satisfaction, for as these Counties are by far the most populous part of the Province, I consider I have the means in my own hands to maintain the sovereignty of this Country to my Royal Master in all Events.[60]

"Firmness and resolve against the seditious mob was what was called for now," added Martin. "Any concessions of the Parent Country at this time will only invigorate the distemper with which these Members of the British Empire are afflicted."[61]

Governor Martin's bold assertions were soon put to the test. Word of the fighting in Massachusetts reached New Bern on May 6 and created an uproar.[62] James Davis proclaimed in his weekly gazette that "The Sword is now drawn, and God knows when it will be sheathed."[63] Governor Josiah Martin informed Lord Dartmouth in London that

> The Inhabitants of this Country on the Sea Coast, are for the most part infected with the ill spirit that prevails in the adjacent Provinces of Virginia and South Carolina, whose extravagancies they are copying be arming men, electing officers and so forth. In this little Town [New Bern] they are now actually endeavoring to form what they call Independent Companies under my nose & Civil Government becomes more and more prostrate every day.[64]

Governor Martin's focus on the inhabitants along the coast was an important distinction. Support for the patriot or rebel cause was strong in the eastern portion of North Carolina, but farther west in the interior, where large numbers of Scotch Highlanders had recently settled and where many regulators maintained their resentment of the tidewater establishment that had long governed North Carolina, support for royal authority remained strong. Governor Martin asserted that he could easily raise thousands of men to fight from "the interior Counties of this Province, where the People are in General well affected."[65] His dilemma was that he could not properly arm them.

Martin did not have such loyal support in New Bern, however, and with tensions high in the days following the news of Lexington, he felt compelled to act on reports that the New Bern committee planned to seize several large cannon that sat upon the grounds of his residence.[66] Although these weapons were old and used mostly for ceremonies, they were still functional and, thus, dangerous to anyone who faced them. Governor Martin ordered the cannon dismounted from their carriages on May 22, leaving them inoperable as well as difficult to move or transport.

When the inhabitants of New Bern discovered Martin's actions, a committee, led by attorney Abner Nash, who Governor Martin considered the "principal promoter of sedition" in the colony, arrived at the governor's residence to request an explanation for his actions.

Governor Martin, like Governor Dunmore in Virginia a month earlier, offered a plausible but untruthful explanation. He explained, "I had dismounted the Guns, and laid them on the ground because the carriages were entirely rotten and unserviceable and incapable of bearing the discharge of them on the King's birthday," which Martin was preparing to celebrate on June 4, with the usual fanfare of cannon fire.[67] This fabricated explanation seemingly satisfied the committee. Governor Martin disdainfully recalled that Mr. Nash announced that he was persuaded and "retired with his mob" with a bow. Martin confessed to Lord Dartmouth in his report of the incident that, although the carriages were indeed in poor condition and in need of repair, "my principal object in throwing [the cannon] off the carriages . . . was to make the removal of them more difficult."[68]

Although Governor Martin had little to fear from revealing his motives a month after the incident to Lord Dartmouth, in the days following the affair he and his family remained quite vulnerable in New Bern. Concerned that they could be seized or harmed by a mob at any moment, Martin sent his family to New York by ship on May 29. He then traveled to Fort Johnston, near the mouth of the Cape Fear River (about twenty-five miles downriver from Wilmington) where the fort and a British sloop of war, HMS *Cruizer* (8 guns, 60 crew), commanded by Captain Francis Parry, offered some protection.[69]

While Governor Martin made his way to Fort Johnston, county committees began to react to the news of Lexington and Concord. The inhabitants of Mecklenburg County in the western part of the colony (which Martin thought was firmly loyal to the king) adopted perhaps the boldest measures of any county.

The Mecklenburg Resolves were adopted in the town of Charlotte on May 31, 1775. They defiantly asserted that the king's proclamation in February of that year (which declared that the American colonies were in an actual state of rebellion) placed them out of the authority of the king. This meant that all laws and commissions derived under the authority of the king and Parliament (such as Governor Martin's authority as governor) were annulled and vacated. In other words, the inhabitants of Mecklenburg County declared that

British authority over the colonies was forfeited because of the king's false characterization of the colonies in his February proclamation.[70] The resolves went on to call upon provisional congresses in all of the colonies to assume the legislative and executive powers of government and for North Carolina leaders to better organize the militia that was being raised throughout the colony.[71] The Mecklenburg Resolves appeared to many to be nothing short of a declaration of independence.

Although it would be over a year before the American colonists adopted a similar position with the Declaration of Independence, Governor Martin's flight from the capital in late May did signify the cessation (or abandonment) of royal rule in North Carolina, at least for the time being. Whether this was a temporary or permanent development remained to be seen.

SOUTH CAROLINA

Heavily dependent on British trade and the British navy to protect their valuable exports of rice and indigo, South Carolina's leaders nevertheless rallied to Boston's defense a year before Lexington and Concord upon learning of the closure of Boston Harbor in 1774. In July of that year, a provincial congress assembled in Charlestown selected Christopher Gadsden, Thomas Lynch, Henry Middleton, Edward Rutledge, and John Rutledge to represent South Carolina in the First Continental Congress in Philadelphia. It also created a committee of correspondence to keep apprised of developments in the colonies and better coordinate colonial actions.

In January of 1775 the South Carolina Provisional Congress met again and endorsed the First Continental Congress's plan of association (boycott and embargo of Great Britain). At that same January meeting, South Carolina's leaders "recommended . . . to all of the inhabitants of this Colony, that they be diligently attentive in learning the use of arms; and that their officers be required to train and exercise them at least once a fortnight" (every two weeks).[72] These actions occurred more than two months before the Second Virginia Convention recommended that each county in Virginia raise just one company of volunteer militia and three months before the bloodshed at Lexington and Concord.

The measures adopted by the provisional congress were not universally supported in South Carolina, however. A large number of loyalists in the backcountry resisted calls to support Congress's nonimportation association. The inhabitants of South Carolina's backcountry were vastly different from those who lived in the lowcountry (tidewater) of the colony, where the cultivation of rice and indigo created fortunes for a select few. Many settlers in the backcountry were transplants from colonies to the north who had traveled down the Great Wagon Road in the years following the French and Indian War. German, Dutch, Scotch, Irish—they held different backgrounds and religious beliefs, but most had one thing in common: a deep resentment for the South Carolina gentlemen of Charlestown and the lowcountry who controlled colonial politics and economics and who had long treated the backcountry with disdain. Thus, support for the militant measures of the leaders of Charlestown was much weaker in the backcountry.

Forty-five-year-old William Moultrie glossed over this difference when he recalled in his memoirs that within a month of the provincial congress in January 1775, "a military spirit pervaded the whole country; and Charleston had the appearance of a garrison town; everything wore the face of war."[73] Moultrie, the son of a prominent physician, married into wealth and property in 1749. He was a prosperous planter, colonial legislator, and militia commander who saw action against the Cherokee in the early 1760s. By 1774 Moultrie had risen to the rank of colonel in the militia, but more impressively, he was selected as one of South Carolina's delegates to the First Continental Congress, an appointment that he declined in order to remain in South Carolina.

With the long-serving sixty-five-year-old Lieutenant Governor William Bull unable to take any significant action to stem the deterioration of royal rule, and the newly appointed governor, William Campbell, yet to arrive in South Carolina, there was very little royal resistance to the actions of South Carolina's provisional congress.

A few days before the fighting in Massachusetts erupted, letters from the British ministry in London to the royal governors of Virginia, North Carolina, South Carolina, Georgia, and East Florida were intercepted and read by a secret committee in Charlestown. They revealed that, despite talk of a reconciliation plan from Parliament that appeared to remove one of the primary objections of the colonists, that of taxation without representation (by allowing each colony to determine for itself the amount of revenue it would send to the British treasury annually and how it would be collected), Parliament's real intention was to coerce the colonies into obedience.[74]

At about the same time the letters were intercepted, Lord North's conciliatory plan, which did nothing to relieve the suffering colonists of Massachusetts, appeared in the newspapers. As in Virginia, it was viewed by many as a ploy to divide the colonies and was dismissed as such. Henry Laurens, who would preside over the Continental Congress in a few years, observed to his son John (a future aide-de-camp to General George Washington) that "The people of this province are alarmed by Lord North's conciliatory plan which they conceive is intended more effectually to enslave them."[75] A prosperous merchant, slave trader, and planter, the fifty-one-year-old Laurens had command experience of militia during the French and Indian War and nearly two decades of experience in the colonial legislature. He informed his son John in the spring of 1775 that a number of people about Charlestown "have removed all the provincial Muskets, Bayonets, etc. which belong indeed to themselves, from the public Armory to places more accessible to themselves & they have also taken into their possession all the Gun powder which was in the public Magazines Besides."[76]

This action was done, ironically, on the evening of April 21, the same day that Lord Dunmore in Virginia had gunpowder seized in Williamsburg. A secret committee of five appointed by the president of the provincial congress, Charles Pinckney, coordinated the seizure of gunpowder and arms from several locations.[77] They gathered over 1,500 pounds of gunpowder, 800 stands of arms, 200 cutlasses, and an assortment of other military equipment.[78]

William Moultrie recalled in his memoirs that it was not so much Lord North's devious Olive Branch proposal that provoked the ire of South Carolina's leaders in April 1775 as it was the determination "of England to coerce America," expressed in the intercepted letters to the southern royal governors. The letters directed the governors "to prepare such Provincial forces as they could, to co-operate when the [British forces] should come."[79] In other words, while Parliament publically expressed its desire for a peaceful settlement through its Olive Branch plan, it was secretly planning to expand its coercive measures to the southern colonies.

The news of Lexington and Concord reached Charlestown on May 8 and validated the suspicions of many.[80] Henry Laurens lamented to his son in London that "The Sword of Civil War was drawn in the environs of Boston on the 19th of April."[81] He wrote a more detailed letter a week later that declared,

> We will go forth & be ready to Sacrifice our Lives & fortunes in attempting to Secure [our] Freedom & Safety. . . . The daily & nightly Sound of Drums & Fifes discover a Spirit in the people to make all possible resistance against that arbitrary power complained of. . . . In a word, the people are resolved to do all in their power to resist against the force & Stratagems of the British Ministry.[82]

Alexander Innes, secretary to Governor William Campbell, arrived in Charlestown ahead of Governor Campbell and reported to Lord Dartmouth in London that "Nothing less is talked of than storming Boston, and totally destroying the British Troops. Violent resolutions have since been proposed in the Committee here, but the moderate party have so far prevailed."[83]

Innes added that the provincial congress, which had been called to meet again on June 1, 1775, in response to the bloodshed of Lexington and Concord, was expected to raise two thousand troops and that a loyalty test (to the American cause) and new association had already been framed. "Those not in support will be forced from the colony," wrote Innes, and "a report from London that the Ministry has proposed to grant freedom to such Slaves as should desert their Masters and join the King's troops . . . has raised a great ferment."[84] Innes speculated that two British regiments in South Carolina would put things right in the colony and go far to restore the morale of the king's friends, "who are not a few . . . [and] are in the lowest state of despondency."[85]

No such morale problem existed among the king's opponents, who styled themselves Whigs. Henry Laurens reported about two weeks after the news of Lexington and Concord that "In this Colony an amazing readiness is Shewn by the people to contribute all in their power to the common cause—indeed a few of us have very hard work to restrain the zeal & ardour of the many."[86]

One group that demonstrated significant zeal in its resistance to Parliament was Charlestown's general committee, which publically blamed British troops for the commencement of civil war in America with their actions in Massachusetts and declared that it was necessary to put South Carolina into "a state of security against any attack by British arms."[87] The committee accused the British ministry of encouraging both a slave rebellion and Indian attacks upon the defenseless frontier and asserted that the British ministry had resolved to "quell the American troubles by arms [rather than] laws of reason and justice."[88]

William Moultrie remembered that the people of South Carolina at this time were greatly alarmed and anxiously awaited the decisions of their provincial congress. "They saw that a war was inevitable, [recalled Moultrie] and that it was to be with the country which first planted them in America, and raised them to maturity; a country with which they were connected . . . by custom, and by manners; by religion; by laws; and by language; a country that they had always been taught to respect."[89]

With little money, arms, ammunition, generals, armies, or fleets, continued Moultrie, South Carolina's provincial congress, "determined upon a defensive war."[90] Several ships were sent to the West Indies to procure gunpowder, and two regiments of infantry comprised of five hundred men each along with a smaller three-hundred-man regiment of mounted rangers were authorized by the provincial congress.[91] Moultrie was tapped to command the second regiment. He recalled that "the military ardor was so great, that many more candidates presented themselves from the first families in the Province, as officers . . . than were wanted; everyone was zealous in the cause."[92] The 1st Regiment was commanded by Colonel Christopher Gadsden, and the rangers of the 3rd Regiment were led by Lieutenant Colonel William Thomson.[93] Two company commanders in South Carolina's new military establishment, Captain Francis Marion and Captain Peter Horry, were destined for fame for their wartime service while two others, Charles Cotesworth Pinckney and Thomas Lynch, would make their mark in politics.

South Carolina's efforts to bolster its military were largely successful in the summer of 1775. They had to turn away volunteers for the officer corps, and recruitment of the rank and file was strong.

Into this situation arrived Governor William Campbell on June 18. Born in Scotland, the forty-five-year-old governor had previously served as a captain in the Royal Navy and then as royal governor of Nova Scotia. It was in his service in the navy, while posted in America, that he met his wife, Sarah Izard, the daughter of a prominent South Carolina planter. After his departure from the navy and seven years of service as Nova Scotia's governor, Campbell and his wife desired to return to South Carolina. He managed to gain an appointment as governor in 1773. Delayed by a voyage back to England, Campbell arrived in Charlestown on June 18, 1775. He was greeted at the wharf by a company of militia grenadiers and escorted into town, passing more militia, artillery, and light infantry companies. Henry Laurens, who witnessed the procession, speculated that "I am Sure he must have Seen Such improvement in these new Troops as would, if the Times were other wise, have filled him with Surprize & pleasure."[94] Laurens added that "you would be astonished if you were to See the advances we have made in military exercises."[95]

Colonel Moultrie noted that Governor Campbell, who was well acquainted with several officers of the provincial troops, "told them we were doing wrong, that he was in hopes all matters would be adjusted."[96] Although he opposed the measures taken by the provincial congress, Governor Campbell was wise enough not to act on or express his opposition publically. He even gave commissions to the volunteer companies that were forming as a gesture of support, but in a letter to General Thomas Gage in Boston, written two weeks after his arrival in Charlestown, Governor Campbell revealed his true thoughts.

It was with equal Surprize, & concern, I found the People of this
Province did not yield to any of their Northern Brethren in the violence of their measures, & contempt for all Legal Authority. The
Provincial Congress had been sitting about a Fortnight before my
Arrival, & had come to several Resolutions of a very daring, &
dangerous nature . . . . Your Excellency can hardly conceive a
more distress'd & or embarras'd situation than the one I am at
present in.[97]

The irony of Campbell's last statement was undoubtedly not lost on
General Gage, who sat with his bloodied and battered troops in Boston
in a most distressful situation following the Battle of Bunker Hill.

Thirty-three-year-old William Henry Drayton, a leader in South
Carolina's provincial congress and member of the secret committee
that coordinated the seizure of arms and powder in April, believed it
would not be long before South Carolina joined Massachusetts in
war. Like most of South Carolina's leaders, Drayton was born into
wealth and privilege, the son of a prominent planter. Drayton studied
in England and upon his return to the colony married well. He was
elected to the colonial legislature in 1765, but his conservative views
and opposition to the nonimportation of British goods in 1769 cost
him his seat. Drayton's views changed considerably upon Parliament's passage of the Intolerable Acts in 1774, and he was elected to
South Carolina's provincial congress the following year, quickly
emerging as a leader in that body.

Convinced that war would soon fall upon South Carolina, Drayton noted on July 3 that "Peace, Peace, is now, not even an Idea. A
civil War, in my opinion, is absolutely unavoidable. We already have
an Army & a treasury. . . . In short a new Government is in effect
erected."[98]

That government was the provincial congress in which Drayton
served, and when it was not in session, a new council of safety,
formed in mid-June and headed by Henry Laurens, assumed the gov-
erning powers of the colony.

Governor Campbell was unable to prevent any of it and sullenly
watched royal authority evaporate. At the end of July he informed

General Gage that "all legal Government is now at an end," and he lamented that South Carolina as well as Georgia had been abandoned by the British administration.[99] Captain Edward Thornbrough of the HMS *Tamar* (16 guns, 100 crew), the lone British warship stationed in South Carolina (which was often referred to as the *Tamer*), concurred with Governor Campbell. He informed Admiral Samuel Graves in Boston that "this place is now in an actual State of Rebellion."[100]

GEORGIA

The news of Lexington and Concord had a significant impact on Georgians in May 1775. Prior to the bloodshed in Massachusetts, a large number of Georgians opposed the efforts of the Continental Congress in 1774 in support of Massachusetts. Like most of their fellow colonists, Georgians disagreed with many of Parliament's colonial measures over the past decade, but they refused to send a delegation to Philadelphia for the First Continental Congress in 1774, and when they learned of Congress's boycott and embargo on Great Britain, a large number of Georgians refused to join the effort. An appreciation of their own weakness against the dangers posed by the Indians to the west and north as well as British forces to the south in East Florida and the powerful British navy, which could sail unchallenged all along Georgia's exposed coast, were just some of the factors behind the reluctance of many Georgians to join in opposition to Great Britain.[101] Economic considerations (many Georgians relied on trade with Britain for their livelihood) and support for Governor James Wright, whose fourteen-year stewardship as royal governor was marked by peace and prosperity for most Georgians, were other factors.[102]

Fifty-nine-year-old James Wright was born in London but raised in South Carolina where his father served as chief justice of the colony. Wright studied law in England and practiced it in South Carolina, eventually becoming attorney general of the colony. In 1760, he was appointed royal governor of Georgia and over the next fifteen years oversaw the rapid expansion and prosperity of the colony. Wright prospered along the way, amassing over twenty-five thousand acres of land on eleven plantations, upon which over five hundred enslaved persons labored.[103]

Governor Wright opposed efforts to hold a provincial congress in Savannah in January 1775 and was relieved when only five of twelve parishes (counties) sent representatives.[104] Many merchants and traders opposed the strong economic sanctions imposed by the Continental Congress, and many others were undecided on how Georgia should proceed.[105]

Although Georgia's rump provincial congress did select delegates in January to attend the next Continental Congress in May, they declined to approve the Continental Association adopted by the Continental Congress the previous fall. Georgia's embarrassed delegates to Congress delayed their journey to Philadelphia as a result and explained their absence and the failure of Georgia to support the continental association in a letter to Congress two weeks before the fighting in Massachusetts erupted. The delegation wrote,

> Truth forbid them to call their Proceedings [in January] the Voice of the Province, there being but five out of twelve Parishes concerned, and . . . they [lacked] strength sufficient to enforce [the association]. They found the Inhabitants of Savannah not likely soon to give Matters a favorable Turn. The Importers were mostly against any Interruption and the Consumers very much divided. There were some of the latter virtuously for the Measures, others strenuously against them, but more who called themselves Neutrals than either.[106]

Interestingly, not all of the congressional delegates from Georgia delayed their attendance. A week before the fighting at Lexington and Concord, Dr. Lyman Hall of St. John's Parish in Georgia arrived in Philadelphia to attend the Congress that was scheduled to meet in May. Fifty-one-year-old Dr. Hall was actually born in Connecticut, where he became a Congregationalist minister. He abandoned the ministry for medicine and moved to St. John's Parish (present-day Liberty County) in Georgia in 1760. Hall emerged as a leading proponent of colonial opposition to the British Parliament in St. John's Parish and was a natural choice as a delegate to attend the Second Continental Congress. He attended, however, not as a representative of Georgia but as one from St. John's Parish and brought with him an address from the inhabitants of his community that proclaimed their strong support for the Continental Association and their frustration that the rest of Georgia would not act to support such measures: "As we of this Parish are a Body detached from the Rest of this Province by our Resolutions, and sufficiently distinct by local Situation, large enough for particular Notice, adjoining a particular Port, and in that Respect, capable of conforming to the General Association . . . we . . . hope you will not condemn the Innocent with the Guilty."[107]

As a result of Dr. Hall's efforts, the prohibition of trade with Georgia imposed by Congress for their refusal to join the Continental Association did not extend to St. John's Parish.[108]

The situation and sentiment in Georgia changed considerably in the spring of 1775 upon news of the bloodshed at Lexington and Concord, which reached Georgia around the middle of May. Henry Laurens of neighboring South Carolina observed on May 22 that "Georgia is, notwithstanding all of the flattering accounts of Governor [James] Wright, in commotion."[109] Laurens noted the decision of St. John's Parish to send their own delegate to Philadelphia and reported that "last Week the Magazine under the Nose of . . . Governor [Wright] was Stripped of all the public Store of Gun powder. I am well assured [concluded Laurens] that at Savanna there is a large majority of the Inhabitants ready to participate in the measures of their American Brethren."[110]

The change of heart among many Georgians was not necessarily all the result of the bloodshed in Massachusetts. Some grudgingly embraced the rebel cause out of concern over the economic impact Congress's ban on commerce with Georgia would have on them.

In June, Lieutenant William Grant of the armed schooner HMS *St. John* (6 guns, 30 crew) arrived in Georgia for a brief stop and reported to Admiral Samuel Graves in Boston that "This Colony being like all others through America is in Anarchy and Confusion. . . . In short it is with the utmost difficulty that publick officers can now do their duty."[111] Two weeks before Grant's letter, on the eve of the king's birthday, "some notorious people" spiked and overturned several cannon overlooking the Savannah River in Savannah.[112]

Governor Wright blamed instigators from South Carolina and called forth several militia officers to inquire whether they would defend him should South Carolinians attempt to seize him as a hostage.[113] John Stuart, the fifty-six-year-old superintendent of Indian affairs in the southern colonies, had already fled Charlestown for Savannah and was now forced to flee Savannah for the safety of Lieutenant Grant's ship because of accusations that he sought to instigate the Indians on the frontier against the colonists.[114] Scottish born, Stuart arrived in Charlestown at age thirty and soon married. He served on the frontier as a militia captain during the French and Indian War and befriended many Cherokee including Attakullakulla, the Little Carpenter, who saved Stuart from a party of hostile Cherokee. In 1762 Stuart was named British superintendent for the Southern Indian Department and over the years established strong relations with Indian leaders in the South, earning the respect and appreciation of many southern colonists as well. That respect evaporated, however, when rumors circulated in the spring that Stuart had encouraged the Indians to attack settlers on the frontier. Threatened with imprisonment or worse, he fled to Savannah and then to the safety of the *St. John* in the Savannah River, which eventually took him to St. Augustine.

Governor Wright's appeal for support from Georgia's militia leaders went unheeded, and by summer it appeared that more and more Georgians were siding with the rebellious South Carolinians. Lieutenant Grant, aboard the *St. John*, reported that a number of canoes full of armed men (from South Carolina) were assembled near the mouth of the Savannah River in June, apparently waiting to seize a shipload of gunpowder intended for the Indian trade that was due to arrive any day. A number of leaders of the "disaffected party" in Georgia, reported Grant, attempted to pass his schooner by boat to link up with the South Carolinians, but the British naval officer intervened to prevent their juncture, and both groups dispersed. The next morning, however, a number of armed men appeared on the beach, hoisted the American Liberty flag on a lighthouse and fired a musket "across us out of the bushes."[115] Lieutenant Grant recorded in the ships log that there was "No Doubt but [the shot was fired] with an intention to Kill somebody on board" his vessel.[116]

Near the end of June, Governor Wright requested more assistance from Admiral Graves in Boston, explaining that the armed schooner under Lieutenant Wright was simply not powerful enough to deal with the growing threat in Georgia. "Pardon me, Sir, for saying that an armed schooner will be of little use, or anything less than a sloop of war of some force."[117]

Unfortunately for Governor Wright, his letter never reached Admiral Graves. The secret committee in Charlestown intercepted it and replaced it with a forgery that claimed that the situation in Georgia was well under control. "It gives me the highest pleasure to acquaint you," wrote the forgers, "that I now have not any occasion for any vessel of war, and I am clearly of opinion that his Majesty's service will be better promoted by the absence than the presence of vessels of war in this port."[118]

With mounting turmoil and tension in the colony, the Second Georgia Provincial Congress (this time comprised of representatives from nearly all of Georgia's parishes) met in Savannah on July 4, 1775, and finally agreed to adhere to the Continental Association of 1774. They also wrote to Governor Wright to request him to declare a day of fasting and prayer for a peaceful resolution of the crisis in British America (which he reluctantly did while at the same time rejecting the legality of the provisional congress). The provincial congress also sent one last petition to the king in hopes of swaying him to intervene on behalf of the colonists.[119]

One of the things the provincial congress did early in its second session was to write to the Continental Congress as soon as Georgia's delegates had been selected and the association approved. The letter sought to soften any hard feelings toward Georgia and introduced its delegates who, except for Lyman Hall (who was already in attendance), would not arrive in Philadelphia until September. The letter assured Congress that Georgia had had a change of heart and would now faithfully support the American cause:

Some Parishes that upon former Occasions seemed rather reluctant and even Protested against our Proceedings have manifested a very Laudable Zeal upon this Occasion, [noted the committee

tasked with writing the letter]. Several Gentlemen in this Place
that have been hitherto neutral or declared against America, now
Speak of the Proceedings of Parliament, as Illegal and Oppressive.
We flatter ourselves for the future You may look upon Us as an
United People. . . . We have already Resolved strictly to adhere to
the Continental Association, and are heartily disposed Zealously
to Enter into every measure that your Congress may deem necessary for the Saving of America.[120]

All told, the measures of the Georgia Provincial Congress were
rather mild compared to their neighbors to the north. Reconciliation
with Britain was still paramount to most delegates, so although they
agreed to abide by the Continental Association, they also appealed
directly to the king (bypassing the Continental Congress, which had
come to speak for all of the other colonies). Governor James Wright,
although concerned about incidents of lawlessness in his colony such
as the seizure of arms and gunpowder, remained in Savannah as a
symbol of royal authority. Just how much actual authority he still
held, however, was debatable.

EAST FLORIDA
With a small population of just a few thousand mostly loyal colonists
who were almost totally dependent on trade with Great Britain, the
British inhabitants of East Florida had no intention of jeopardizing
their economic lifeline with England by supporting the Continental
Association of 1774 or even sending delegates to the Continental
Congress in Philadelphia. In fact, the economic disruption caused by
the rift between Britain and the colonies created an opportunity for
many of the colonists in Florida, who strove to supply some of the
embargoed colonial exports (like indigo and lumber) to England and
her Caribbean colonies.[121]

Economic necessity and opportunism were not the only reasons
the colonists of East Florida refused to support their fellow colonists
to the north, however. Peaceful relations with the nearby Creek and
Seminole nations, who desired British trade goods (particularly gunpowder and shot) and expected them annually, was essential for the
outnumbered British colonists on the east coast of Florida. If the

supply of those trade goods, which came almost exclusively from Britain, was stopped, conflict with the indigenous people would surely follow.

So it is not surprising that, given their relative isolation from the other American colonies and their heavy dependence on trade with Great Britain, the colonists of East Florida had little interest in joining the efforts of the colonists to the north and greeted the news of Lexington and Concord with relative indifference.

They could not, however, completely isolate themselves from the growing conflict. Disappointed at their refusal to join the Continental Association, the American Congress in Philadelphia restricted trade to both East and West Florida (as well as the Canadian provinces) in May 1775.[122] This had some impact on East Florida but nothing close to the impact that trade restrictions with Britain would have had. Additionally, as tensions mounted in the north and both sides prepared for war, a steady stream of loyalist refugees arrived in St. Augustine. One of the first to arrive was Indian Superintendent John Stuart, who had fled Savannah.[123]

Upon his arrival Stuart replied to a letter from the South Carolina Provincial Congress placing him under suspicion for working to encourage the Indians on the frontier to rise up against the colonists. Stuart adamantly denied that orders from Britain to raise up the Indians existed and further declared that he had no inclination to do such a thing.[124]

Although Governor Patrick Tonyn was firmly in control of St. Augustine and East Florida, thanks to the support of an overwhelmingly loyalist population, he was still concerned that the colony might be attacked by rebellious colonists from Georgia and the Carolinas. The fifty-year-old governor was born in Ireland and served in the British army in Germany during the Seven Years' War, where he rose to the rank of lieutenant colonel. Tonyn was granted thousands of acres of land in East Florida for his service and was appointed royal governor of that colony in 1774. As such, he wielded significant power, thanks to the nonexistence of a colonial legislature in East Florida.

Tonyn informed Lord Dartmouth in early July that "Common fame has blown it about, that the Carolina people intend to visit this province. I am therefore, preparing to put everything in the best state of defence."[125] With the solid stone walls of the Spanish-built Fort Castillo de San Marcos for protection and the bulk of the British 14th Regiment (over 250 officers and men) garrisoned at St. Augustine, the capital of East Florida was relatively secure.[126] Governor Tonyn worried about his limited supply of gunpowder, but a large shipment from England was expected any day.[127] While he waited, he had engineers sketch maps of the roads, swamps, and defiles between St. Augustine and Georgia and inspect the fort in order to "make them repent of their excursion, in case it takes place."[128] He expressed his doubt that the Carolinians would actually come, however, contending that "they will surely have enough, for the present, to engage their attentions at Home."[129]

Two

Summer

T HE SUMMER OF 1775 WITNESSED SEVERAL SIGNIFICANT EVENTS
and developments that widened the rupture between Great
Britain and her American colonies. On June 14, the Continental Congress took steps to form the Continental Army and the next day appointed George Washington of Virginia to command it. Within days
of his appointment, one of the bloodiest battles of the entire war
erupted in Massachusetts upon Breed's Hill (misidentified as Bunker
Hill ever since), further widening the rift between the two sides and
signaling a full-scale war in New England. In the American southern
colonies, blood had not been shed, nor a gunshot even fired, but tensions rose and everyone was aware of the events to the north.

VIRGINIA
The House of Burgesses expressed shock and dismay at Governor
Dunmore's flight from Williamsburg on June 8. The representatives
both criticized his action and assured him that they desired order as
much as he did. More importantly, they insisted that he and his family were in no danger.[1]

Governor Dunmore replied that the "commotions among the People and their menaces and threats," and the unsupportive conduct of the burgesses which often countenanced "the violent and disorderly proceedings of the People, were the chief cause of his flight."[2] The governor was also upset with the threats directed at the king's forces on June 6th and the apparent usurpation of his executive authority by the House of Burgesses when they instructed the independent militia company to guard the magazine.[3]

Dunmore stated that he was willing to work with the assembly to resolve the dispute and proposed several measures that would alleviate the crisis, but the House of Burgesses had no interest in Dunmore's proposals.[4] Without the governor, the House of Burgesses was unable to conduct any significant business, so by the end of June it adjourned, never to meet as burgesses again.

Speculation in late June about the possible arrival of two thousand British troops in Virginia prompted the residents of Williamsburg to appeal for assistance from the surrounding counties.[5] They hoped to add 250 men to reinforce their own volunteer militia companies to better protect the city.[6]

As far as Lord Dunmore was concerned, Williamsburg was already a fortified city. He wrote as much in a letter to Lord Dartmouth near the end of June: "A constant guard is kept in Williamsburg relieved every day from the adjacent Counties, and that place is become a Garrison, the pretense of which is the Security of the Person of their Speaker, who because he has been Chairman of the Congress, it is reported, (in order to inflame), that Government is anxious to Seize him."[7]

Dunmore also noted (no doubt with a great deal of frustration) that "Guards likewise Continually mount at the Town of York opposite to which the Men of War [on which Dunmore was staying] lie, and thro' out the whole Country the greatest attention is paid to these Military preparations and a universal appearance of War is put on."[8]

Dunmore's expectation of hostilities with the "rebels" prompted him to send his wife and children back to England in late June aboard the *Magdalen*. Despite protests from Virginians that Dunmore's decision was an overreaction, the arrival in Williamsburg of militia troops from as far as the piedmont of Virginia (some eighty miles away) in July added to the warlike atmosphere in the capital and suggested that Dunmore's concerns might be valid. Purdie's *Virginia Gazette* announced that all of the volunteers were "ready to take a crack with any ministerial troops that may be sent to molest us."[9]

The Virginian troops that gathered in Williamsburg were not the only ones ready to fight. Riflemen from Frederick and Berkeley Counties, in the northwest corner of Virginia, eagerly answered the call of the Continental Congress to reinforce the New England army posted outside of Boston. The Continental Congress authorized the formation of ten independent rifle companies from Pennsylvania, Maryland, and Virginia on June 14, hoping that their rifles, which were more accurate than smoothbore muskets, would be a difference maker on the battlefield. Captain Daniel Morgan and Captain Hugh Stevenson were selected by their respective counties to command Virginia's two rifle companies. They set out for Boston by mid-July and three weeks later joined their fellow Virginian, General George Washington, who had been appointed by Congress to command the Continental Army.

While Virginians throughout Virginia prepared for conflict, Lord Dunmore remained aboard the *Fowey*, anchored off of Yorktown, and dutifully reported to Lord Dartmouth in England on the deteriorating (and increasingly militant) situation in the colony: "A great number of people, horse and Foot, from various parts of the country have flocked to Williamsburg, armed and accoutered, and wearing uniforms. . . . They have made a Barrack of the Capital . . . and they have taken possession of the Park [adjoining the Governor's Palace]."[10]

Dunmore reported that in his absence his residence in Williamsburg (the governor's palace) had been broken into a second time and that the intruders "broke open every lock . . . and carried off a considerable number of arms."[11] The governor himself was nearly carried off in early July in an encounter with a party of militia at his farmhouse (Porto Bello) on Queen's Creek, just a few miles outside of Williamsburg. Dunmore described the incident to Lord Dartmouth:

I happened . . . to go in the [*Fowey's*] barge, to a Farm (my own
property) about Seven miles from Williamsburg. . . . And Just after
Captain Montague and I had done dinner . . . we were informed
by my Servants that a body of men in Arms were Seen advancing
directly to the House. . . . We had but just time to get into our
boat and escape.[12]

Two carpenters who accompanied Dunmore's small party in
search of a new ship mast were seized by the militia, and the "rebels"
fired upon one of the governor's servants as he fled in a canoe, but
the governor and the rest of his party escaped unharmed.[13] Aggrieved
by this incident, Dunmore expanded his complaints to Lord Dartmouth to include the increasingly provocative actions of the militia
posted in Yorktown: "We have now a Camp of these People behind
the Town of York, not half a Cannon-Shot from the Ships; and the
men are Continually parading in arms along the Shore Close to us,
and at night we hear them challenge every boat or person that approached them."[14]

One of the things that had the militia on alert were reports of
British landing parties robbing local inhabitants of livestock and
other provisions. The militia was determined to halt these raids, and
to demonstrate their resolve a large detachment of troops at Yorktown forcibly detained a landing party from the HMS *Otter* (16
guns, 100 crew). The detention of the landing party prompted a midshipman from the *Otter* to go ashore to investigate. He reported,

I walked up to their camp, which consisted of a few pales [fences]
covered with leaves, and found two hundred rebels round our
men, whom they had been informed belonged to the *Otter*; and
at my arrival [the rebels] vowed, that if they caught any belonging
to the Fowey man of war, they would never let them go. I enquired
into the reason why they detained the men, and was asked to
whom they belonged; I answered to the King. The Captain of the
Guard then asked me if I belonged to the *Otter* and [whether] any
of the men or officers would venture on shore again. I told him,
that both officers and men would, if they were ordered, come on
shore to [do their] duty. They said they hoped they would behave

themselves well, or they would get something they did not like. I replied that if saying they belonged to the King was impertinent, it was the answer they must always expect. Thus you see, [concluded the midshipman] that the people of York, in Virginia, are worse than at Boston.[15]

Lord Dunmore had reached a similar conclusion about the colonists, noting in a letter to Lord Dartmouth that they were "lawless ruffians" who displayed open rebellion:

The People of Virginia manifest open Rebellion by every means in their power, and they declare at the Same time that they are his Majesty's Most dutyfull Subjects . . . and that as designs have never been formed against my person, but that I may, whenever I please return to my usual Residence without the least danger; notwithstanding that my own Servants are prevented from passing with provisions which is thus cut off from me & denied to me, my people have been Carried off by the guard, while my house has been a third time rifled, and is now entirely in the possession of these lawless Ruffians.[16]

Captain Charles Scott of Cumberland County, a veteran of the French and Indian War and future brigadier general in the Continental Army, may have actually agreed with Dunmore's characterization of the militia in Williamsburg as "lawless ruffians." Selected by the officers in the capital to command this mixed force of volunteer militia, Scott faced the enormous challenge of instilling a degree of discipline in the largely untrained and untried troops—now 250 strong and encamped near the capitol in a wooded grove.[17]

While Captain Scott struggled to maintain order among the troops in Williamsburg, Virginia's leaders met for a third time in convention in Richmond with the singular purpose of raising "a sufficient armed Force . . . under proper Officers for the Defence and protection of this Colony."[18] George Mason, a key member of the committee charged with drafting a plan to achieve this, described the enormous challenge that confronted the delegates:

This is hard duty, and yet, we have hitherto made but little progress. . . .This will not be wondered at when the extent and importance of the business before us is reflected on—to raise forces for immediate service—to new model the whole militia— to render about one-fifth of it fit for the field at the shortest warn- ing—to melt down all the volunteer and independent companies into this great establishment—to provide arms, ammunition, &c.,—and to point out ways and means of raising money, these are difficulties indeed![19]

Nearly a month passed before the convention finished its work. Their plan called for two regiments of regular (full-time) soldiers raised for one year's service. Patrick Henry was selected to command the first regiment of over five hundred men.[20] Colonel William Wood- ford, of Caroline County, was given command of the second regiment, which comprised approximately 475 men.[21] He was a prosperous, forty-one-year-old planter with some political experience but, more importantly, military command experience under Colonel George Washington during the French and Indian War. Much would fall on Woodford's shoulders in the coming months.

The regular troops were not the only soldiers ordered to Williams- burg; hundreds of minutemen were ordered to march to the capital as well. They comprised a second tier of Virginia's new military es- tablishment. The convention authorized sixteen battalions of min- utemen, each comprised of five hundred troops. These men were drawn from the ranks of the militia and were "more strictly trained to proper discipline" than the ordinary militia. The last tier of Vir- ginia's new military establishment was the traditional county militia who were instructed to hold private musters every two weeks, except in the winter.[22]

While the Third Virginia Convention spent much of the summer organizing the colony's military force and establishing a set of regu- lations for the new troops (Articles of War), Lord Dunmore sought to strengthen his meager forces in opposition to the rebellious Vir- ginians. Dunmore sailed out of the York River aboard the *Otter* in mid-July and anchored off of Norfolk in the Elizabeth River. The

Otter was joined by the HMS *Mercury* (20 guns, 130 crew), which had arrived from New York to replace the Boston-bound *Fowey*.[23]

By August, two companies of British regulars from the 14th Regiment at St. Augustine (amounting to over ninety officers and men) joined Lord Dunmore off of Norfolk.[24] Alexander Purdie's *Gazette* informed its readers of their arrival and speculated about their intentions:

> Lord Dunmore reviewed his 60 body-guardsmen, lately arrived from St. Augustine . . . at Gosport and we hear, that he daily expects an additional reinforcement, of 40 more soldiers, from the same place. His Lordship it is said, as soon as they arrive, and when joined by the marines from the *Mercury* and *Otter* men of war, and a number of other select friends in different places, intends coming round to York town; from whence, if not prevented, it is likely he will pay us a visit in this city [Williamsburg], although he cannot expect the same cordial reception as on former occasions, but will probably be received with such illuminations &ct. as may make him forget his way to the palace.[25]

Mr. Purdie then made a stern declaration:

> The good people of Virginia now consider Lord Dunmore as their mortal enemy, and will no longer brook the many insults they have received from him, which are daily repeated; and the "damn'd shirtmen," as they are emphatically called by some of his minions . . . will make [them regret] before long, their ill-timed, base, and ungenerous conduct.[26]

Although Dunmore acknowledged in a letter to Lord Dartmouth on August 2 that the newly arrived British troops were too few to restore order in this "distracted colony," he confidently declared, "[Were] I speedily supplied with a few hundred more [troops] with Arms, Ammunition and the other requisites of War, and with full powers to act . . . I could in a few months reduce this Colony to perfect Submission."[27]

Both sides busily prepared for armed conflict.

NORTH CAROLINA

A brief period of calm settled over North Carolina in the days following Governor Martin's arrival at Fort Johnston in early June. With his family safely onboard a ship heading to New York, the governor was free to focus on reestablishing some degree of royal rule in the colony. Nearly two weeks passed, however, before he acted forcefully.

The respite in activity extended to Governor Martin's adversaries in the colony, many of whom met in their local county committees but took no coordinated action. An intercepted letter from Governor Martin and a stern proclamation in mid-June snapped North Carolina's leaders back to action. Martin's letter to Henry White in New York requested several items that suggested the governor intended to take the field against those he now considered rebels in the colony. "I shall be extremely obliged to you if you can contrive to send me, with the royal standard I mentioned to you some time ago . . . a good tent and markee, of the size of the Colonel's tent in the Army, with a tent-bed to fit the boot of it, and furniture, viz: mattress, bolster and pillows."[28]

Three days after he wrote this letter, Governor Martin issued a stern proclamation which amounted to a cease and desist order to anyone circulating "false and seditious reports against the King and his government."[29]

In Philadelphia, North Carolina's congressional delegation, concerned that their fellow colonists back home were not doing enough to prepare for the escalating conflict with Britain, penned an address to the several committees of safety in the colony. It outlined the defensive measures the other colonies were taking and noted that "North Carolina alone remains an inactive Spectator of this general defensive Armament."[30] The delegates accordingly urged their constituents to stockpile gunpowder and be in readiness to better defend themselves.

There was actually little need for such an address, as many committees in North Carolina had already taken steps to secure what gunpowder they could and better organize their militia.[31] Some went further and created patrols to confiscate all arms from free and enslaved Blacks, fearing that Governor Martin would encourage them to fight on his side.[32]

At Fort Johnston, the governor assembled his privy council on June 25 to discuss the state of the colony and what should be done with the dilapidated fort. He began with a strong indictment of the rebellious North Carolinians:

> The seditious Combinations that have been formed, and are still forming in several parts of this Colony and the violent measures they pursue in compelling His Majesty's Subjects by various kinds of intimidations, to subscribe to Associations, inconsistent with their Duty and allegiance to their Sovereign . . . and the late most treasonable publication of a Committee in the County of Mecklenburg explicitly renouncing obedience to His Majesty's Government and all lawful authority whatsoever are such audacious and dangerous proceedings, and so directly tending to the dissolution of the Constitution of this Province, That I have thought it indispensably my Duty to advise with you on the measures proper to be taken for the maintenance of His Majesty's Government, and the Constitution of this Country, thus flagrantly insulted and violated.[33]

The council offered no specific course of action for Governor Martin but did affirm that his actions thus far were completely justified. As for what to do with Fort Johnston, which was in very poor condition and destitute of troops and gunpowder, the council recommended that Governor Martin write to General Gage in Boston for assistance.[34]

Martin immediately did so, requesting ten thousand stand of arms for the loyalist North Carolinians he was convinced would rally to him when called. He also asked for six brass six-pound cannon and enough ammunition for the cannon and muskets.[35] Governor Martin then wrote to Lord Dartmouth in London to update him on affairs in the colony. He confidently stated that, if he were properly reinforced, he could hold North Carolina for the king and explained, "Reason and argument can never restore the just power and authority of Government in America. The People now freely talk of Hostility toward Britain in the language of Aliens and avowed Enemies."[36] He added, "In charity to [the colonists] and in duty to my King and country, I think myself bound [to observe] that the rod of correction cannot consistently with the good interest of either, be longer spared."[37]

Perhaps in anticipation of the "correction" that Governor Martin called for, North Carolina's committees began to act. Calls for a new provincial congress grew out of the need for a more unified opposition to Governor Martin. Although the Wilmington Committee of Safety did not hesitate to require that "every white man capable of bearing arms . . . shall [by July 10] enroll himself in one of the two companies" and sign the association or else be considered "inimical to the common cause of America," it still sought guidance from a more centralized power in the colony.[38] A week after issuing its decree on militia service, the committee in Wilmington urged that another provincial congress be held:

> Our situation here is truly alarming, the Governor collecting men, provisions, warlike stores of every kind, spiriting up the back counties, and perhaps the Slaves, finally strengthening the fort with new works, in such a manner as may make the Capture of it extremely difficult. In this Situation Sir, our people are Continually clamouring for a provincial Convention. . . . We have a number of Enterprising young fellows that would attempt to take the fort, but are afraid of having their Conduct disavowed by the Convention.[39]

Wilmington's appeal was unnecessary; a call to meet in congress in Hillsborough on August 20 began circulating in the colony three days earlier.[40]

The Wilmington Committee of Safety, aware through Governor Martin's intercepted letter of his intention to erect the king's standard and "lead the disaffected . . . against the friends of American Liberty," forbade further communication with the governor at Fort Johnston on July 10.[41] To enforce this measure, militia were deployed under Colonel Robert Howe to cut off access to Fort Johnston by land.[42] Forty-three-year-old Colonel Howe was a prosperous planter and member of the colonial legislature who was well acquainted with Fort Johnston, having commanded a garrison of militia there just a few years earlier. Howe had also commanded North Carolina troops in the French and Indian War and Governor Tryon's artillery at the Battle of Alamance, so he was one of North Carolina's most experienced military leaders.

Feeling the pressure and having little ability to defend the fort, Governor Martin abandoned Fort Johnston for the safety of the *Cruizer*, anchored just off the fort, in mid-July. He explained his decision to Lord Dartmouth:

> The continual reports of the People designing to make themselves Masters of Fort Johnston, & Captain Collet's [the fort's commander] just and well grounded Representations that he would not pretend to hold the place with only three or four men that he could depend upon against a multitude said to be collecting to attack it, determined me to dismount the Artillery that is considerable in value, and to lay it under cover of the Cruizer's Guns. I have also . . . withdrawn what little remained of the Garrison, with the shot, and movable Stores.[43]

Although the eighteen- and nine-pounder cannon tubes, which numbered thirty pieces, lay somewhat secure along the shore protected by the cannon of the *Cruizer*, Fort Johnston was left abandoned and exposed.[44] Governor Martin thus watched helplessly early in the morning of July 18 when fire erupted in the fort.[45] Approximately five hundred militia under Colonel Howe and Colonel John Ashe had marched to the fort and, over the course of a day, burned it down. The justification offered by the Wilmington Committee of Safety was that the fort's commander, John Collett, had prepared the fort for the reception of reinforcements who were "to be employed in reducing the good people of this province to a slavish submission to the will of a wicked and tyrannic Minister."[46] Governor Martin was infuriated at the "wanton malice" displayed by the militia parties as they burned everything in and around the fort, but explained to Lord Dartmouth his rationale for not firing upon the militia while they destroyed the fort: "These proceedings however to the last degree violent, extravagant and provoking, I did not think My Lord of consequence sufficient to justify me in commencing hostilities against the People so long as they forebore to touch the King's Artillery, as I had no men to land I could do it with so little effect, and as all the material damage that the Fort could sustain had been effected in the night by persons yet undiscovered."[47]

It is doubtful that, even if Governor Martin had ordered the *Cruizer* to fire upon the militia onshore, it would have been very effective, for the ship's captain reported a week later to Admiral Graves in Boston, "If I am attacked my chief dependence is on Swivels and small arms, my Deck being so weak in some parts as I doubt whether it bear much firing even with the three Pounders, our heaviest Metal."[48] Fortunately for Captain Parry, his ship and crew were not tested.

While Fort Johnston lay in ruins, counties and towns throughout North Carolina held elections to select delegates for a new provincial congress to meet in Hillsborough on August 20.[49] The county committees were also warned in the end of July by the Wilmington Safety Committee that Governor Martin was attempting to raise loyalist support in the backcountry and might even travel there, so they should "keep a strict lookout, and if possible, arrest him in progress," if he were so brazen as to leave the safety of his British warship.[50]

Governor Martin was indeed working to raise loyalist support, but he did so from the safety of the *Cruizer* in the Cape Fear River. On August 8, he issued a fiery and lengthy proclamation condemning the treasonous actions of the various county committees. He also declared the provincial congress that was to meet in Hillsborough an unconstitutional assembly and instructed all government officials, including county magistrates and sheriffs, to bring to justice the leaders of any "Treasons and Traitorous Conspiracies."[51] The proclamation had little effect, in part because few people ever read or heard it. Committees throughout the colony took measures to intercept and destroy most copies, and no newspaper in the colony dared to print it.[52]

Despite these efforts to suppress dissent, North Carolina was far from united in its opposition to Governor Martin and British authority. Those of the more rebellious persuasion dominated most county safety committees, and many resorted to harsh tactics to compel support, or at least acceptance, of their cause. They were not always persuasive, however, and Governor Martin counted on this loyalist resistance to survive until help arrived from Britain.

The provincial convention or congress that met in Hillsborough on August 20 was nearly two hundred strong with representatives from all thirty-five counties and every borough town of North Carolina.[53] Presided over by Samuel Johnston, it began by declaring that, although their allegiance to the king remained, they were bound by the acts of both the Continental Congress and provincial congress because, "in both they are freely represented by persons chosen by themselves."[54] The delegates also agreed to pay North Carolina's portion of the cost of the Continental Army (which had been formed in June by the Continental Congress).[55] On the fifth day of the provincial congress, the delegates condemned Governor Martin's recent proclamation as "false, Scandalous, Scurrilous, malicious, and seditious Libel," worthy of being burnt by the common hangman.[56]

In September the provincial congress met and authorized the formation of two, five-hundred-man regiments of regular (full-time troops) to be paid for by the Continental Congress (who had offered to assume the cost of them earlier in the summer).[57] The 1st Regiment was commanded by Colonel James Moore and the 2nd Regiment by Colonel Robert Howe.[58] The provincial congress also authorized six battalions of minutemen (with five hundred men in each battalion) and arranged to pay for the significant cost of all these new troops by printing paper bills in the amount of sixty thousand pounds (dollars).[59] A number of other measures were taken during the first week of September, all with the intention to better prepare for the armed conflict with Governor Martin and Great Britain that everyone sensed was coming.

SOUTH CAROLINA

Like Governor Martin in North Carolina, Governor Campbell in neighboring South Carolina (who had not yet fled Charlestown for the protection of the *Tamar* offshore) believed that a large number of loyalists inhabited the backcountry. Reliable men like Colonel Thomas Fletchall, a prominent militia leader in the Ninety-Six district of the colony, who informed the South Carolina Council of Safety in late July, "I . . . do utterly refuse to take up arms against my King."[60] Major Joseph Robinson from the Camden district was another back-country loyalist with influence among his neighbors. Working with Fletchall, Robinson drafted a counter association in July that declared that the king had done nothing to forfeit his right to their allegiance and they therefore refused to take up arms against him.[61] While it was not certain that such a stance ensured that Fletchall and Robinson would fight against the Whigs if the time came, Governor Campbell believed these loyal men only awaited encouragement in the form of British ships, supplies, and troops to come forward and help suppress the rebellion.[62] Campbell reported to Lord Dartmouth in mid-July that "The intolerable Tyranny and Opposition used by the Committees in enforcing their Mandates, has already given Offense to the moderate of their Party; and has stirred up such a Spirit in the back Parts of this Country, which is very populous, that I hope it will be attended with the best Effects."[63]

Fort Charlotte, a frontier post on the Savannah River about thirty miles southwest of the trading settlement of Ninety-Six, held approximately a ton of gunpowder and several cannon. In late June, two companies of mounted rangers under the command of Major James Mayson seized the fort from its caretaker, a lone British captain and his family.[64]

Leaving one company behind to garrison the fort, Major Mayson proceeded to Ninety-Six with some of the captured gunpowder and Captain Moses Kirkland's company of rangers. It was an unfortunate choice for Mayson because Captain Kirkland, disgruntled at being overlooked for higher command by the provincial congress (for which he partially blamed Major Mayson) and harboring loyalist sentiments, called upon a party of loyalist militia gathered near Ninety-Six to march there to arrest Mayson and recapture the powder. Before the two hundred loyalist militia arrived on July 17, Kirkland's company, with his encouragement, dissolved. The loyalists took possession of both Major Mayson and the gunpowder, releasing Mayson after a few hours. [65]

A few weeks after this incident, Kirkland made his way into Charlestown and met with Governor Campbell. He no doubt gave Campbell reason to hope that loyalist support in the backcountry was strong, and Kirkland returned to the interior with several militia commissions signed by Campbell.[66]

Reports of strong opposition in the South Carolina backcountry to the provincial congress and the Continental Association led William Henry Drayton and the Reverend William Tennent, at the behest of the provincial congress, to travel there to "Explain to the people, the causes of the present disputes between Great Britain and the American Colonies, and to endeavor to persuade them to sign the association."[67]

They met with little success at first, discovering that many of the German settlers were convinced they would lose their lands if they rose against their king.[68] At a meeting at Colonel Thomas Fletchall's residence with some of the principle loyalist leaders in the backcountry, including Joseph Robinson, Patrick Cunningham, and Thomas Brown of Georgia, Drayton and Tennent realized that it was impossible to persuade all but Fletchall from their loyalist stance and even Fletchall was doubtful. Tennent reported to the council of safety after the meeting, "We soon found the unchangeable malignity of their minds . . . [and] found that reasoning was vain with those who were fixed by Royal emoluments."[69]

Over the next few weeks a campaign of words ensued between Drayton and Tennant and their loyalist opponents. Colonists gathered to hear both sides present their arguments. Drayton described one such encounter to the council of safety in late August:

> We arrived here yesterday and met with Col. Fletchall, Kirkland, the two Cunninghams, and Brown. By the contrivances of [these men], very few people met us . . . not above 250. . . . The most perfect good order prevailed with the people, who heard us with much attention. But Kirkland treated the Congress, the Committee, the Council, and ourselves with the highest insolence. . . .

Imagine every indecency of language, every misrepresentation, every ungenerous and unjust charge against the American politics that could alarm the people, and give them an evil impression of our designs against their liberties and the rights of Great Britain . . . and you will not exceed what we heard as well from Kirkland. . . . Brown loudly declared that when the King's troops arrived, he would join them against us, and he hoped every other person in these parts would do the same.[70]

When he learned at the end of August that Moses Kirkland and others had taken the field under arms and were raising a force to attack Fort Charlotte, William Henry Drayton moved to counteract the threat, ordering hundreds of Whig militia to take the field. The time for persuasion had passed and coercion was to be applied to eliminate the loyalist threat in the backcountry.[71] Drayton marched to Ninety-Six with over a hundred troops and four swivel guns. Nearly a hundred Georgians soon joined them, bringing their total to over two hundred troops.[72] An expected engagement with Fletchall, Cunningham, and Brown (Kirkland had abandoned the field when he was specifically targeted for arrest by Drayton) failed to transpire when the loyalists failed to appear at Ninety-Six.

With his force rapidly growing to nearly a thousand men, Drayton next issued a proclamation threatening military action against those who remained obstinate in their refusal to comply with the continental association, declaring in mid-September, "I shall march and attack, as public enemies, every person in arms, or to be in arms . . . in opposition to the measures of Congress [and will] prosecute military measures with the utmost rigor.[73]

Drayton's threats and actions convinced a number of loyalist-leaning colonists, including Colonel Fletchall, to proclaim their neutrality in mid-September and sign an agreement dubbed the Treaty of Ninety-Six that established a tenuous truce in the backcountry between Whigs, loyalists, and neutrals.[74] Several important loyalist leaders, however, including Joseph Robinson and Patrick Cunningham, refused to sign the document and remained hostile to the council of safety and provincial congress.

While events in the backcountry temporarily ended in disappointment for Governor Campbell, a promising development for him was
the refusal of Alexander Cameron, the deputy superintendent of Indian affairs, to support the Continental Association. Scottish-born
Alexander Cameron had immigrated to the American colonies some-
time in the 1730s or 1740s. His service in the French and Indian War
brought him in frequent contact with the Cherokee, with whom he
developed many acquaintances, and he even married a Cherokee
woman. Cameron settled upon a two-thousand-acre land grant on
the South Carolina frontier awarded to him for his service in the war
and caught the attention of fellow Scotsman John Stuart, the British
superintendent of the Southern Indian Department, who named
Cameron principle agent and then deputy superintendent in 1768.[75]
Cameron's influence with the Cherokee Indians was significant, and
the South Carolina Council of Safety desired to swing him to the
Whig cause, but Cameron would have none of it and retained his
loyalty to Britain. When it appeared he might be arrested by the
council for his stance, he retreated into Cherokee country, alarming
the council of safety further with fears that he would encourage the
Cherokee to support the British and launch attacks on the frontier.[76]

Around the same time these events unfolded in the backcountry,
a supply of 5,200 pounds of gunpowder in over 250 casks and kegs
was transferred from Georgia to South Carolina.[77] It was a portion
of approximately 12,700 pounds of gunpowder that colonists from
both Georgia and South Carolina had seized near the mouth of the
Savannah River from the ship *Phillipa*.[78] The powder was originally
meant to be used in Georgia as part of the annual Indian trade to
stay on good terms with the Indians to the west. Another portion of
the gunpowder was meant for St. Augustine.[79] Instead, it was seized
before it reached Savannah. A delegation from the South Carolina
Council of Safety persuaded the Georgia Provincial Congress to loan
five thousand pounds to South Carolina who then shipped four thousand pounds of it to Philadelphia for the use of the Continental
Army.[80]

While South Carolina and Georgia successfully expanded their
gunpowder stocks, Admiral Graves in Boston fretted to his superiors

in the British Admiralty about his inability to better assist the southern colonies. "I transmit Copies of [letters] I have received from the Governors of South and North Carolina to shew their Lordships how pressing they are for an additional number of ships and small Vessels to be stationed within their Governments."[81] Graves added, "I enclose the Copy of a Letter from Sir James Wright, Governor of Georgia. It gives me much satisfaction that as his Majesty's Service would not admit of my sending a sloop to Savannah according to their Lordships Orders, the King's Affairs in that Colony have not suffered thereby."[82]

Admiral Graves had been duped by the forged letter that the South Carolinians had sent in place of Governor Wright's original letter that appealed for help!

Complicating matters further, the two sloops that were stationed in the Carolinas were in need of relief and repair. Graves reported that the *Cruizer* was in need of extensive repairs while the *Tamar* lacked an assortment of ship's stores and provisions. Neither could be spared at the moment, however, so they had to remain at their posts until relief arrived from Britain in the form of additional naval vessels.[83]

While no help was forthcoming to the British governors in the southern colonies, South Carolina continued to bolster its gunpowder stocks. In August, Captain Clement Lempriere sailed out of Charlestown with a crew of thirty aboard the armed sloop *Commerce* in search of gunpowder. They had planned to sail to the Bahamas but learned of a British ship that was due at St. Augustine with a large supply of gunpowder, so Captain Lempriere made his way toward Florida. His bold efforts led to the capture of six tons of gunpowder for South Carolina. Accounts vary as to how Captain Lempriere achieved this, but deception and surprise most assuredly played a key role. Arthur Middleton, a future signatory of the Declaration of Independence from South Carolina, learned about the raid soon after it occurred and shared the good news with William Henry Drayton:

Our Admiral and his crew have behaved like heroes; they have lightened Capt. Loftres of six tons of the needful [gunpowder];

they surprised a superior crew, and took it out of the vessel lying at anchor within a mile of the castle of [St.] Augustine; ten soldiers were on board, but luckily had no arms with them; in short, Providence favored us in all points of winds, seas, tides, etc.[84]

Governor Patrick Tonyn in St. Augustine provided a more detailed account of the raid from the perspective of the British. The ordnance ship full of gunpowder and shot arrived off of St. Augustine on August 3 but was too heavy to cross the sandbar. Tonyn recounted to General Gage in Boston what occurred next:

The 4 [of August] the Provincial Vessel was sent to lighten the Brig, to bring as much powder out of her as she could stow. The Vessel returned the 5 [of August] with two hundred ninety three barrels of Gunpowder, the Brig being sufficiently lightened. The 6 [of August] being calm the Brig could not come into Port. The 7 [of August] in the morning at low water, a Sloop which was taken for a Negro Vessel, run on board the Brig, boarded with twenty six Men armed, took away a hundred and eleven barrels of the Kings powder and some for the Merchants here. More powder would have been taken, but ten Soldiers were on board, as labourers without arms, to get the Ordnance stores out of the Brig; they grew angry, and began to plot, to seize some of the Pirates arms to drive them out of the Brig. The Pirates took alarm [and] evacuated the Brig in confusion.[85]

Governor Tonyn added, "The instant I heard of this villainy, the provincial Vessel was equipped, with eight pieces of small ordnance [swivel guns] an officer and 30 Privates of the 14th Regiment, and sailed in pursuit of the Pirates."[86] Their pursuit was unsuccessful.

At about the same time many in South Carolina were celebrating Captain Lempriere's success, a pair of particularly brutal incidents occurred in Charlestown that highlighted the divide that existed among the colonists. A gunner posted at Fort Johnson, which sat on the shore of James Island and guarded the entrance to Charlestown Harbor, was tarred and feathered for his insolent speech.[87] Governor

Campbell described the gunner's "insolent speech" as "expressions of loyalty."[88] Whatever the cause, the unfortunate soul was tarred and feathered and then paraded throughout Charlestown, stopping a number of times at the homes of suspected Tories, where he was forced to drink to their damnation, terrifying the inhabitants in the homes, who feared they would be next unless they abandoned their loyalty to the British government (or in some cases neutrality in the dispute).

In another incident that severely rattled Governor Campbell, Thomas Jeremiah, a free Black who was himself a slave owner and an accomplished harbor pilot in Charlestown, was hanged and burned in Charlestown for suspicion of inciting a slave rebellion.[89] Governor Campbell described the incident to Lord Dartmouth:

> Yesterday under colour of Law, they hanged, & burned, an unfortunate Wretch, a free Negroe of considerable property, one of the most valuable, & useful Men in his way, in the Province, on suspicion of instigating an Insurrection, for which I am convinced there was not the least grounds. I could not save him My Lord! The very reflection Horrows My Soul! I have only the comfort to think I left no means untried to preserve him. They have now dipt their hands in Blood, God Almighty knows where it will end, but I am determined to remain till the last extremity.[90]

The brutality of both of these incidents foreshadowed the tragic times ahead for South Carolina.

Throughout August several officers of the 1st and 2nd Regiments traveled to North Carolina and Virginia to recruit for their units while others remained in Charlestown to organize and train new recruits.[91] Governor Campbell estimated on August 19 that near eight hundred men, "consisting of Vagabonds and Thieves from all Countries," were quartered in barracks in Charlestown.[92] They were more than a match for any force Governor Campbell could then muster, despite the arrival on September 7 of the armed ship *Cherokee* (6 guns, 50 crew) from England, so he maintained his reserved approach toward the situation in South Carolina as best he could.[93]

His efforts were apparently not good enough, for in September the governor became ensnared in a trap. William Moultrie, the commander of the 2nd South Carolina Regiment, recalled in his memoirs that two men posing as loyalists from the backcountry attempted to draw out Governor Campbell's true sentiments in conversation and partially succeeded. When Campbell's views were reported to the safety council, they demanded to see Campbell's official correspondence, which he refused to reveal. The council considered arresting Campbell but decided against such a provocative move on questionable evidence. Campbell made his way aboard the *Tamar* on September 14 to confer with Captain Thornbrough and then returned to his residence in Charlestown.[94] A few hours later, a party of thirty sailors from the *Tamar* dismounted all of the cannon at Fort Johnson.[95] They did so just ahead of a provincial detachment of 150 men under Lieutenant Colonel Isaac Motte that landed on James Island from Charlestown.[96] Two grenadier companies and Francis Marion's light company were selected for the mission by Colonel Moultrie. Captain Barnard Elliott, who commanded one of the grenadier companies, described the operation in his diary:

> About Eleven OClk at Night March'd from the Barracks with all possible silence to Gadsden Wharf where they embarked on board the Carolina & Georgia Packet, when they had set sail, Col. Motte called the Officers down into the Cabin & informed them, that his Orders were to take possession of Fort Johnson, that tho' there were but few Men in Garrison, there, he was informed a reinforcement had been thrown in from the *Tamar*.[97]

Elliot then described the outcome of the operation in his next entry:

> About an hour after we set sail [from Gadsden's wharf] we crossed the harbor & came to an Anchor near the opposite shore not far from Captain Stone's landing, it was with much difficulty that we disembarked, as we had but two small boats we could not land above fifteen men at a time, the Vessel being near half a Mile from the Shore & a long muddy flat, over which we partly dragged the

boats, & then waded through the Water up to our Middles. . . .
Pinckney's Granadiers were ordered first to land & possess themselves of the sea beach, to cover us in case any foes should offer
to Oppose our landing, as soon as his company was landed Captain Elliott's Granadiers, embarked from on board the Vessel in
the small boats, Col. Motte landed in One & Captain Elliott in
the other, by this time the day began to dawn.[98]

Motte's plan of attack was bold but unnecessary. No resistance
was offered from the small garrison in the fort, and the gates were
open. Captain Elliott recorded in his diary that "When Lieut Mouatt
came up to the Glaces [with the forlorn hope detachment] he found
the Gates open, and rushed in with his detachment & took possession of the Garrison making prisoners of the few men within."[99]
Along with the fort and a handful of men, the provincials seized the
fort's cannon, which numbered over twenty guns ranging from
twenty-six- to nine-pounder cannon. All were dismounted, but they
had not been spiked which meant they could be repaired and reused.
Lieutenant Colonel Motte learned from the fort's commander that
he and his men had entered the fort just two hours after the British
sailors who damaged the guns had departed.[100]

Despite the damage to the cannon, the operation was considered
a success, and more importantly, no shots had been fired and no casualties inflicted. Governor Campbell could not be sure, however, if
that would remain the case, so he withdrew with the Great Seal of
the Province (but without his wife who remained in their residence
in Charlestown) to the safety of the *Tamar* the next day.[101]

GEORGIA

Like his counterparts in the South, Governor James Wright felt under
siege in July 1775. However, unlike the other governors, there was
no British warship to flee to in the Savannah River or off the coast
of Georgia, nor was there an immediate need to flee. The schooner
St. John (6 guns, 30 crew) had been in the area earlier but returned
to St. Augustine, and Admiral Graves in Boston (who had been misled by the forged letter the South Carolina secret committee had sent
in place of Governor Wright's original letter) believed there was no

need to send a warship to Georgia. Thus, Governor Wright could only watch helplessly as armed men from both South Carolina and Georgia in several boats waited near the mouth of the Savannah River to ambush and seize gunpowder aboard the *Phillipa*. Governor Wright's helplessness extended to shore when he learned in July that, "a Great Many People were taking & Carrying away some of the [King's] Guns, Carriages, Shot, etc."[102] No doubt many of these items found their way aboard an armed schooner that "the Liberty Men" were fitting out [the armed sloop *Commerce*].[103]

Wright reported that that very vessel played a role in capturing the *Phillipa*.[104] The 12,700 pounds of gunpowder the colonists seized was a substantial amount for such a small colony, but that did not stop the Georgia Provincial Congress from only offering three thousand pounds of the powder to South Carolina when their delegation arrived in mid-July, hat in hand.[105] They eventually agreed to loan five thousand pounds of powder after their neighbors to the north balked at Georgia's original offer.

About two months after the *Phillipa* was seized, another large shipment of gunpowder, over 250 barrels on the *Rainer*, the bulk of which was meant to be the annual gift to the Indians to maintain the peace, was seized once again by the Liberty Men and brought to Savannah in triumph.[106]

While Georgia's Liberty Men had success building up their gunpowder stocks, the colony's delegation to the Continental Congress finally appeared in Philadelphia and presented themselves to Congress in mid-September. Prior to their arrival, Georgia was represented in Congress by a single delegate, Dr. Lyman Hall, appointed by the colony months after he arrived in Philadelphia to represent his local parish.[107] He returned to Georgia in early August, however, so for six weeks Georgia had no representation in Congress. On September 13, the president of the Georgia Provincial Congress, Archibald Bulloch, along with John Houstoun and Dr. John Zubly, stepped forward in Congress to present their credentials.[108]

John Adams recorded his impressions of the delegates in his diary on September 15:

Dr. Zubly is a Native of Switzerland, and a clergyman of the Independent Perswasion . . . He speaks, as it is reported, Several
Languages, English, Dutch, French, Latin, etc. Is reported to be a
learned Man. He is a Man of a warm and zealous Spirit. Houstoun is a young Gentleman, by Profession a Lawyer, educated
under a Gentleman of Eminence in South Carolina. He seems to
be sensible and spirited, but rather inexperienced. Bullock is
cloathed in American Manufacture.[109]

It is hard to interpret the brevity of Adams's description of
Archibald Bulloch. As the president of the Georgia Provincial Congress, he was likely the leader of the delegation, and although wearing American-made clothing in the fall of 1775 was surely a mark of
support for the cause, the fact that this observation was the extent
of Mr. Adams's remarks on Bulloch is curious.

Two weeks later in a new diary entry, Adams elaborated on his
views of Bulloch. They came after Adams and his cousin Sam
(Adams) were dinner guests of Bulloch and Houstoun. Following a
carriage ride in Bulloch's new phaeton, Adams recorded this additional observation of the former president of Georgia's Provincial
Congress: "He is a solid, clever Man."[110] Three days before this dinner, Mr. Bulloch and Mr. Houstoun had paid a visit to John and Sam
Adams in their quarters. John Adams described the visit in his diary:

In the Evening Mr. Bullock and Mr. Houstoun came into our room
and smoked and chatted, the whole Evening. Houstoun and [Sam]
Adams disputed the whole Time in good Humour. They are both
Dabbs at Disputation I think. [Houstoun] a Lawyer by Trade is
one of Course, and Adams [Sam] is not a Whit less addicted to it
than the Lawyers. The [question] was whether all America was
not in a State of War, and whether We ought to confine ourselves
to act upon the defensive only. He was for acting offensively next
Spring or this fall if the Petition [the Olive Branch petition the
Continental Congress sent to the King in July] was rejected or neglected.[111]

The topic of conversation included the state of Georgia and South Carolina, of which the Georgians gave a melancholy account. Adams continued in his diary:

[The Georgians] say that if 1000 [British] regular Troops should land in Georgia and their commander be provided with Arms and Cloaths enough, and proclaim Freedom to all the Negroes who would join his Camp, 20,000 Negroes would join it from the two Provinces in a fortnight [two weeks] . . . . They say, their only Security is this, that all the King's Friends and Tools of Government have large Plantations and Property in Negroes. So that the Slaves of the Tories would be lost as well as those of the Whiggs.[112]

Fortunately for the slave-owning colonists of Georgia (and unfortunately for the enslaved) there was little chance of any British force arriving in the fall of 1775 to rally the Tories of Georgia to action. A frustrated Governor Wright, who had requested that a British warship be sent to Georgia months ago, was puzzled by the lack of action by Admiral Graves and the British navy. All Wright and his supporters could do was endure the actions of their rebellious fellow Georgians, who primarily focused on acquiring gunpowder but in one instance brutally assaulted Thomas Brown, an avowed loyalist from Augusta, who was severely beaten, tarred and feathered, and scalped and had his feet burned by a mob when he refused to sign a loyalty oath to their cause and shot one of his assailants.[113] Embittered by this attack, Brown eventually recovered and fled to South Carolina to take up with loyalists there; determined more than ever to fight for the crown as soon as the chance appeared.

EAST FLORIDA

Governor Tonyn had spent the early part of the summer preparing for a rumored possible attack by colonists from the Carolinas and had little to show for his efforts. In mid-July two companies of the 14th Regiment, totaling approximately ninety officers and men, sailed for Virginia at the urgent request of Governor Dunmore. Then, in early August, Captain Clement Lempriere appeared off the sandbar in command of the rebel sloop *Commerce* and managed to steal nearly six tons of gunpowder from the recently arrived supply ship *Betsy*. Governor Tonyn was furious at the loss and expressed his anger in a proclamation in mid-August that vowed to punish those responsible for the theft of 111 barrels of the king's gunpowder as well as another 400 pounds of powder owned by a private merchant.[114] Tonyn included a brief description of the crime in his proclamation: "A Sloop Commanded by one Clement Lempriere run alongside [the *Betsy*] and in a Hostile and violent manner instantly boarded her with Twenty six Men; some armed with Muskets and Bayonets fixed, others with Swords and Pistols and . . . in an audacious and Piratical like manner opened the Hatches and took out [the gunpowder]."[115]

The governor offered a reward of two hundred pounds sterling to anyone who could apprehend Lempriere and pardons to any of Lempriere's crew who stepped forward to identify their fellow sailors.

Captain Lempriere's successful raid did more than deny St. Augustine valuable gunpowder; it also apparently spooked Governor Tonyn into realizing how vulnerable St. Augustine was, for in early September General Thomas Gage in Boston reached out to Admiral Graves on Tonyn's behalf:

> By letters I have lately received from Governor Tonyon, he acquaints me, that he has great Apprehensions for the Safety of St. Augustine, and therefore begs any Succor that can be given him, I have some Time ago Ordered three Companies of the 16th Regiment [in Pensacola] to him, and am told by General Grant that a Small Vessel will secure the Harbour, a large Ship not being able to pass the Bar, and I hope you will be able to give this Assistance. The Rebels have Seized one Ship with Ammunition bound to St. Augustine, and Governor Tonyon is under apprehensions of others expected there.[116]

Governor Tonyn also wrote to Admiral Graves in September in hopes of convincing the admiral to transfer at least one of the two warships stationed in the Bahamas, either the sloop *Savage* (8 guns, 60 crew) or the *St. John* to St. Augustine. Both ships "Harbour at

[New] Providence, out of the way of action, in perfect quiet," complained Tonyn, "when His Majesty's service calls for their assistance in these Seas."[117]

Tonyn placed some of the blame for the loss of gunpowder in the rebel raid in August on Lieutenant William Grant of the *St. John*, who was supposed to return to St. Augustine from Georgia in July. Governor Tonyn asserted,

> I had intelligence that armed Cruisers, were out from Carolina, to intercept, some Merchant Ships, coming to this Place, with Ordnance stores for His Majesty's Garrison, and Powder for the Merchants. I intended upon their appearance, the *St John* should go out to protect them [the merchant ships] until the wind permitted them to come into the Harbour. If Mr. Grant had returned, an act of Piracy which happened off this Bar, would not have been committed.[118]

To bolster his argument for naval support, Governor Tonyn added, "A [rebel] cruiser of considerable force, I am informed, is to be stationed, from Saint Marys River, the north boundary of this Province, to intercept whatever vessels, may be bound [here]."[119] It was to be commanded by Tonyn's nemesis, Captain Lempriere.

In early October Governor Tonyn, with a great deal of relief, acknowledged the arrival of the schooner, *Saint Lawrence* (6 guns, 30 crew), writing to Admiral Graves that "She will be of great use to this Province, I am very thankfull to you for this mark of your attention to His Majesty's service in this Province. I shall endeavor to make the service here, as agreeable to Captain [John] Graves as possible."[120]

With another detachment of troops from the 14th Regiment (sixty men) heading to Virginia to reinforce Lord Dunmore, Governor Tonyn was in great need of reinforcements himself. General Gage in Boston had transferred three companies of the 16th Regiment posted in Pensacola to St. Augustine, but those troops had not arrived yet, and there was concern Gage's orders had miscarried, so the arrival of the missing companies could still be weeks away. With less than

one hundred officers and men of the 14th Regiment fit for duty in
St. Augustine and another twenty men posted along the coast essentially as lookouts, the arrival of the *Saint Lawrence* provided some
much-needed firepower for Governor Tonyn.[121]

Three

Fall

T HE SITUATION IN THE FALL OF 1775 IN MASSACHUSETTS WAS one of stalemate between the British army in Boston and the American army outside of it. While General Washington's troops did not conduct a siege in the classical sense of digging trenches ever closer to the enemy to eventually overpower them or force their surrender, his troops did keep the city cut off by land and the British cooped up in Boston. General William Howe replaced General Thomas Gage as commander of British forces in America, and the British navy exacted some revenge for an incident in the summer on the coast of Maine (then part of Massachusetts) that cost them a ship; they burned the town of Falmouth (today Portland, Maine) to the ground in October. Other than these incidents, however, the British were relatively inactive in the fall of 1775.

The Americans, however, were anything but. Colonel Benedict Arnold embarked on an epic march through the wilderness of Maine to strike at Quebec, departing in September and arriving in November. A second prong of this attack on Canada was led by General

Richard Montgomery, who marched into Canada via New York and pushed his way through Montreal to Quebec. Despite some severe hardships suffered by Arnold's troops, the expedition looked promising by the end of November. It was undoubtedly strange to consider that the Americans were the ones on the offensive in late 1775, not the British. This was not the case, however, in every colony.

VIRGINIA

Over four months had passed since the Battles at Lexington and Concord, and although royal authority had effectively collapsed in Virginia with Governor Dunmore's flight from Williamsburg in June, combat and bloodshed had not yet occurred in the colony. Hundreds of Virginia riflemen had joined their fellow Virginian, George Washington, in Massachusetts, and together they had seen combat outside of Boston, but the troops in Virginia had yet to fire a shot in anger.

This changed in late October in Hampton when Captain Matthew Squire of the HMS *Otter* attempted to burn the town of Hampton to the ground. Squire was retaliating for the loss of one of his tenders, which had run aground near Hampton nearly two months earlier. Most of the crew of the stranded tender were detained by the local militia and the vessel stripped of its equipment and burned. Captain Squire, who was one of the few on the tender to escape, was furious about the incident and demanded that the vessel and the stolen items onboard it be returned.[1]

The Hampton Committee forwarded Captain Squire's demand to Williamsburg with a plea for assistance. One hundred volunteers marched to Hampton the next day to reinforce the local militia.[2]

The arrival of the reinforcements from Williamsburg bolstered the spirits of Hampton's inhabitants and prompted the town committee to belligerently refuse Captain Squire.[3] He angrily responded by blockading Hampton and seizing any vessel that sailed from its harbor. A stalemate ensued for the next five weeks.

Across the water at Norfolk, Lord Dunmore waited impatiently aboard a ship in the Elizabeth River for more British assistance. Two small detachments of British regulars from the 14th Regiment at St. Augustine, numbering a little over one hundred men, had arrived in August and September, but they were far too few to help Dunmore regain control of the colony. He had to settle instead on using this small force for a number of raids to seize weapons and gunpowder in the countryside of Norfolk and Princess Anne County.

Captain Samuel Leslie, the ranking officer of the 14th Regiment in Virginia, led the first raid on October 12, and recalled,

> I landed the 12th of [October] at 11 o'Clock at night about three miles from hence with Lieut. Lawrie, two Serjeants, & forty rank and file of the 14th Regiment, and after marching three miles into the country in search of Artillery we found in a wood nineteen pieces of cannon, some of them twelve, others nine, six & three pounders; seventeen of which we destroyed, & brought off two, and then returning to our boats we reimbarked without the least opposition. Lord Dunmore accompanied us upon this expedition.[4]

Several other raids followed over the next two weeks, all of which were unopposed, leaving Captain Leslie with an abundance of confidence, which he expressed in a letter to General Howe in Boston. "Many great guns, small arms, & other implements of war have been taken since by small parties, so that there has been in all at least seventy seven pieces of ordinance [cannon] taken & destroyed since my Detachment arrived here without the smallest opposition, which is a proof that it would not require a very large force to subdue this Colony."[5]

Dunmore also offered an assessment of the impact of the raids on both the rebels and the friends of government to his superior, Lord Dartmouth. "I can assure your Lordship that landing in this manner has discouraged exceedingly the Rebels, and has raised the Spirits of the friends of Government so much that they are offering their Services from all quarters."[6]

The growing confidence of Lord Dunmore and his supporters generated by the successful raids was tempered by events across the James River in late October. While Dunmore had employed the 14th Regiment to seize arms and ammunition against virtually no opposition, Captain Matthew Squire's blockade of Hampton had continued into late October and had expanded to include small landing parties that seized provisions, livestock, and occasionally slaves. The inhabitants of Hampton were furious but resolute in their refusal to return the seized military stores that Squire demanded and prepared for a possible attack on their town by partially blocking the harbor channel with scuttled vessels. Within Hampton, a mixed force of Virginia regulars, minutemen, and local militia waited to see if Captain Squire would act on his threat to punish the town. The answer arrived on October 26.

Early that morning Captain Squire's small flotilla was spotted in the channel of the Hampton River at the location of the scuttled vessels. An eyewitness observed that, "There appeared off the mouth of Hampton river a large armed schooner, a sloop, and three tenders, with soldiers on board, and a message was received at Hampton, from Captain Squire, on board the schooner, that he would that day land and burn the town; on which a company of regulars and a company of minute-men . . . aided by a body of militia, were . . . called together on the occasion."[7]

Accounts differ as to which side fired the first shot, but the first engagement of the Revolutionary War in Virginia occurred that day in Hampton. Governor Dunmore, who was not present but probably received a detailed account of the battle from Captain Squire, claimed that George Nicholas, the son of Treasurer Robert Carter Nicholas and the commander of the company of regulars, fired first from shore at one of the tenders as it made its way up the Hampton River. Only then, according to Dunmore, did the tenders return fire.[8]

Another account of the engagement claimed that two volleys of musket fire from the British tenders were the first shots fired and were answered by rifle fire from Captain [George] Lyne's minute company. One of the tenders answered with a four-pound cannon and then "began a pretty warm fire from all the tenders." The account continued, "Captain Nicholas, observing this, soon joined about 25 of his men. The fire of our musquetry caused the tender nighest to us to sheer off some distance."[9]

The heated engagement lasted over an hour but caused few, if any, casualties. The decks of the British ships were raked by rifle and musket fire from shore, and the British crews responded with cannon, swivel, and musket fire.

Although nightfall ended the fighting, both sides remained active. Under cover of darkness and a driving rain the British returned to the sunken obstructions and worked to create a passage through the channel while the rebels strengthened their breastworks on the town wharf and anxiously waited for reinforcements from Williamsburg. Colonel William Woodford of the 2nd Virginia Regiment marched all night with a company of Culpeper Minutemen to reach Hampton by morning and assume command of the rebel forces.

In a letter to his friend Thomas Jefferson, John Page, a prominent member of the Committee of Safety, provided a detailed account of the resumption of combat the following day. His source was probably Colonel Woodford:

> Col. Woodford accompanied Captain Buford's rifle company through a heavy rain to Hampton and arrived about 7 a.m. When the Col. Entered the Town, having left the Rifle Men in the Church to dry themselves, he rode down to the River, took A view of the Town, and then seeing the Six Tenders at Anchor in the River went to Col. Cary's to dry himself and eat his Breakfast. But before he could do either the Tenders had cut their Way through the Vessel's Boltsprit which was sunk to impede their Passage and having a very fresh and fair Gale had anchored in the Creek and abreast of the Town.
>
> The People were so astonished at their unexpected and sudden Arrival that they stood staring at them and omitted to give the Col. the least Notice of their approach. The first Intelligence he had of this Affair was from the Discharge of a 4 Pounder. He mounted his Horse and riding down to the Warf found that the People of the Town had abandoned their Houses and the Militia had left the Breast Work which had been thrown up across the Wharf and street. He returned to order down Captn. Nicholas's Company [of regulars] and Buford's [riflemen] and meeting Nicholas's, which had been encamped near Col. Cary's he lead them pulling down the Garden Pails [fence] through Jones's Gar-

den under Cover of his House, and lodged them in the House directing them to fire from the Window which they did with great Spirit. He then returned and lead Buford's Company in the same manner under Cover of Houses on the other Side of the Street placing some in a House and others at a Breast work on the Shore.

Here he found the Militia had crowded in, and incommoded the Rifle men. He therefore ordered them off and stationed them with Captn. Lynes on the back of the Town to prevent a surprise, by an Attack of Regulars who it was said had landed at Back water. Captn. Barron with the Town Militia and Part of Nicholas's Company were stationed at the Breast Work on the Wharf and across the Street. The Fire was now general and constant on both Sides. Cannon Balls Grape Shot and Musket Balls whistled over the Heads of our Men, Whilst our Muskets and Rifles poured Showers of Balls into their Vessels and they were so well directed that the Men on Board the Schooner in which Captain Squires himself commanded were unable to stand to their 4 Pounders which were not sheltered by a Netting and gave but one Round of them but kept up an incessant firing of smaller Guns and swivels, as did 2 Sloops and 3 Boats for more than an Hour and 1/4 when they slipt their Cables and towed out except the Hawk Tender a Pilot Boat they had taken some Time before from a Man of Hampton, which was [captured].[10]

Lord Dunmore confirmed much of Page's account in a report to Lord Dartmouth.[11]

The rebellious Virginians had held their ground under heavy fire and had even inflicted a handful of casualties upon the British raiding force. Accounts in the newspapers lauded the conduct of the troops. They all "acted with a spirit becoming freemen and Americans, and must evince that Americans will die, or be free!" boasted one correspondent to Pinckney's *Virginia Gazette*.[12]

The two-day conflict at Hampton marked a significant milestone in Virginia, the first spilling of blood between the two sides. A threshold was crossed at Hampton, one that had been crossed in Massachusetts six months earlier, and there was no stepping back from it.

The Revolutionary War had reached Virginia, and in the weeks that followed it only intensified.

Days before the fighting at Hampton, the Virginia Committee of Safety decided to send assistance across the James River to Norfolk, and upon the return of Colonel Woodford to Williamsburg at the conclusion of fighting at Hampton those plans proceeded. They called for Woodford to cross the James River at Jamestown with his regiment of 2nd Virginians and five companies of the Culpeper Minute Battalion, approximately 660 men in all. Once across the river they were to march to Norfolk and confront Lord Dunmore and his small force of British regulars, sailors, marines, Tories, and runaway slaves.[13]

Supply problems and the sudden appearance of several British vessels off Jamestown, which obstructed the ferry crossing, delayed Woodford's departure and led to a series of ship-to-shore engagements between the British sailors and Virginia riflemen guarding the shore. Posted at Jamestown and Burwell's Ferry to guard possible landing spots, a company of Virginia riflemen under Captain John Green provided very effective opposition to the enemy ships. The accuracy and long range of the rifles compensated for the absence of cannon along the shore, and Captain Green's men were particularly effective at keeping the enemy ships at bay.[14]

By mid-November Colonel Woodford successfully crossed the James River a few miles upriver at Sandy Point where it narrowed. Woodford's subsequent march to Great Bridge, which lay approximately ten miles south of Norfolk, shifted everyone's attention to that part of Virginia, and Dunmore's ships sailed back down the James River as a result.

Ever since the repulse of Captain Squire's squadron at Hampton, which Lord Dunmore viewed as an "overt act of rebellion," the governor longed for a chance to strike the rebels. The efforts of his naval squadron off of Jamestown proved ineffectual, and he was frustrated. Dunmore vented some of his frustration in a written proclamation that "raised the King's standard," but he withheld its release out of concern over his shortage of arms, powder, and troops. He had confessed to Lord Dartmouth a month earlier that the primary cause of his reluctance to declare an open rebellion in Virginia and raise the king's standard (as many loyal Virginians urged him to do) was that he did not have the means to defend his supporters or crush the rebels. He did not want his supporters, many of whom had remained quiet, placed in the position of declaring themselves for the king when they were still vulnerable to assault and abuse from the rebels.[15]

The situation seemingly improved for Dunmore in mid-October with his successful raids around Norfolk, but the engagements at Hampton and near Jamestown were setbacks, and Dunmore continued to hesitate. He needed a significant victory to seize upon, and on November 14 he and his troops produced such a victory when they routed a detachment of rebel militia at Kemp's Landing.

Governor Dunmore explained the events that led up to the battle to Lord Dartmouth:

> I was informed that a hundred and twenty or thirty North Carolina rebels had marched into this colony to a place called the Great Bridge, about ten miles from hence and a very strong post, in order to join some of ours assembled not far from thence. This I was determined not to suffer. I accordingly embarked in the night in boats with all of the 14th regiment that were able to do duty, to the amount of 109 rank and file, with 22 volunteers from Norfolk. The Carolina people had fled the evening before, but hearing at the Bridge that there were between three and four hundred of our rebels assembled at a place called Kemp's Landing nine or ten miles from the Bridge, I was then determined to disperse them if possible.[16]

Captain Samuel Leslie, who commanded the British regulars with Dunmore, described what followed:

> After directions had been given to erect a kind of wooden fort to secure the pass [over the Great Bridge], we proceeded nine or ten miles farther to Kemp's landing where we were informed there were three or four hundred of the rebels ready to receive us, under the command of a Colonel Lawson. When we arrived within sight of Kemps landing our advance guard was twice fired upon by the

rebels, who had concealed themselves in very thick woods on the left of the road, but upon our rushing in among them they were very soon totally routed.[17]

The inexperienced and undoubtedly nervous rebel militiamen had fired too soon, exposing their position without inflicting any damage to Dunmore's advance guard. Dunmore acknowledged that his troops were surprised by the ambush but recovered quickly and routed the rebels.[18] Captain Leslie credited the militia's precipitous flight through difficult terrain (which hampered pursuit) as the primary reason most of them escaped.[19]

Initial accounts from the rebel side described a much different engagement, one in which the militia stood bravely, inflicted losses on the enemy, but were eventually overwhelmed and forced to retreat.[20] Within two weeks, however, the uncomfortable truth became apparent; the Virginians had been routed. John Page, who received accounts of the battle as a member of the Committee of Safety, provided a critical account of the battle to Thomas Jefferson in Philadelphia: "Two hundred of the Militia of [Princess Anne County] were as judiciously disposed of in Ambush as could be, and the Ministerial Tools fell into it very completely, but were so faintly attacked, that although the advanced Guards were thrown into Confusions, They with little or no Loss gained a compleat Victory. Not a tenth Part of the Militia fired. They fled in a most dastardly manner."[21]

The Battle of Kemp's Landing was a humiliating defeat for the Virginians and an important victory for Lord Dunmore. He seized upon his success to finally issue his proclamation:

> I have thought fit to issue this my Proclamation . . . in Virtue of the Power and Authority to ME given, by His Majesty, determine to execute Martial Law, and cause the same to be executed throughout this Colony: and to the end that Peace and good Order may the sooner be restored, I do require every Person capable of bearing Arms, to resort to His Majesty's STANDARD, or be looked upon as Traitors to His Majesty's Crown and Government, and thereby become liable to the Penalty the Law inflicts upon such Offences; such as forfeiture of Life, confiscation of Lands, &c.

&c. And I do hereby further declare all indentured Servants, Negroes, or others (appertaining to Rebels,) free that are able and
willing to bear Arms, they joining His Majesty's Troops as soon
as may be, for the more speedily reducing this Colony to a proper
Sense of their Duty, to His Majesty's Crown and Dignity.[22]

Governor Dunmore had thrown down the gauntlet, declared martial law, and offered freedom to slaves and indentured servants of rebellious Virginians who agreed to fight for him. Virginia was in
full-scale rebellion, and Lord Dunmore meant to crush it and restore
royal rule.

North Carolina
In North Carolina, Governor Martin, aboard the HMS *Cruizer* in
the Cape Fear River, presented a bleak picture to officials in London
in mid-September. The provincial congress had just adjourned after
raising two regiments of regular troops as well as several minute battalions of militia. The congress also adopted a loyalty pledge, and
zealous adherents to it intimidated many colonists to comply who
otherwise would not. Governor Martin reported that these actions
by the rebellious colonists, coupled with the lack of support from
Great Britain, significantly demoralized North Carolina's loyalists:
"The spirits of the loyal and well affected to Government droop and
decline daily; they despair, my Lord, of succor and support, and for
the preservation of their persons from insult, and their property from
confiscation, which has been threatened to those who do not join in
all the measures of the seditious Committees. They indignantly and
reluctantly yield to the overbearing current of revolt."[23]

Martin confessed that "given their circumstances, I know not how
to blame; it is the combined influence of self-preservation and interest
to which they submit."[24] He added that the congresses, conventions,
and committees now wielded complete authority in North Carolina,
and "lawful Government is completely annihilated."[25]

Ten days after Martin penned these observations, several casks of
gunpowder and shot were discovered buried in his garden (under a
patch of cabbages) and hidden in his cellar at New Bern. Much was
made of the discovery of Martin's "infernal magazine," but the gov-

ernor dismissed the incident as the work of servants who simply sought to keep the items out of the hands of the mob.[26]

As autumn took hold of the region, North Carolina resembled a militarily mobilized country, with county committees raising and supplying troops and sending them to their muster stations. Governor Martin was powerless to prevent these developments and expressed his frustration at his weakness, as well as the lack of support from Britain, in another letter to Lord Dartmouth. Although his correspondence contained much of the same information as his earlier ones, it did include one alarming observation: "I have heard too My Lord with infinitely greater surprise and concern that the Scotch Highlanders on whom I had such firm reliance have declared themselves for neutrality."[27]

If this were true, it was a serious blow to Governor Martin's hopes of eventually regaining control of the colony with loyalist support. He reminded Lord Dartmouth that seven months had passed since he first requested assistance from General Gage in Boston and wistfully hoped that the Scots would rediscover their loyalty when British support finally did arrive.[28]

In the absence of any royal authority and the adjournment of the provincial congress, a provincial council of safety assumed the reins of government in North Carolina. Cornelius Harnett Jr. of Wilmington presided over the council, which oversaw the implementation of the provincial congress's many resolutions and added a number of its own. Harnett was a native of North Carolina and a successful merchant from Wilmington with over twenty years of legislative experience in the colonial assembly. In accepting the appointment he became North Carolina's de facto chief executive.

North Carolina's regular troops were recruited, deployed throughout the eastern part of the colony, and provided for with food, pay, and clothing while adjustments were made to the minute battalions to address a shortage of recruits in some counties.[29] Cannon were repaired and remounted and small arms collected throughout the colony to better arm all of the troops.[30]

Governor Martin finally received some good news on November 11 when a lookout aboard the *Cruizer* spotted the approach of a

British warship and two transports.[31] The armed sloop HMS *Scorpion* (14 guns, 100 crew), commanded by Captain John Tollenmach, arrived to relieve the *Cruizer*.[32] Governor Martin's pleasure at the *Scorpion*'s arrival (it was nearly twice the size of the *Cruizer*) was tempered by the realization that its arrival was the extent of assistance he could expect from the British navy for the immediate future.[33]

The *Scorpion* was to replace the *Cruizer*, which was ordered back to Boston to refit, but Governor Martin believed that, with winter closing in, the *Cruizer* was in no condition to make the voyage to Boston. He suggested to Lord Dartmouth that the *Cruizer* instead remain in North Carolina for the winter and sail to Boston when conditions improved in the spring. If the ship remained in North Carolina, wrote Martin, it could be "usefully employed here to guard against the introduction of military Stores that I learn are very deficient among the Rebels here and who are in constant expectation of Supplies by Vessels which have been sent for."[34]

Governor Martin made the same suggestion in a letter to Captain Thornborough on the HMS *Tamar* in Charlestown. Captain Thornborough was the ranking naval officer in the South and thus had the authority to detain the *Cruizer* per Martin's suggestion.

While Governor Martin waited for a decision, he put both the *Scorpion* and *Cruizer* to good use; both ships covered a landing party of forty sailors that finally retrieved the dismounted cannon of Fort Johnston that had been left on the shore all those months ago. The operation took nearly a week and involved cannon fire (grapeshot) from both ships that scoured the woods near the burnt ruins of the fort to drive away any rebel troops who contemplated interfering with the guns' removal.[35]

About a week after the completion of this mission, and unrelated to it, the Continental Congress in Philadelphia agreed to put North Carolina's two provincial regiments onto the "continental establishment" for the next year.[36] Congress had already authorized North Carolina in late June to raise "a body of forces not exceeding one thousand men [that] Congress [would] consider as an American army and provide for their pay."[37] This was the impetus for the two provincial regiments that the provincial congress created in September. The Continental Congress now formally acknowledged the two regiments as part of the Continental Army with its resolution on November 28.

While Congress took responsibility for, and essentially charge of North Carolina's two regiments of regulars, preparations were being made in London and Boston for an expedition against the southern colonies. Governor Martin did not know it yet, but his many appeals and assurances of loyalist support had convinced British leaders that a military expedition in North Carolina might be worthwhile.

SOUTH CAROLINA

Just three days after their successful seizure of Fort Johnson in the early morning hours of September 15, Henry Laurens, president of the South Carolina Council of Safety, penned a long, candid letter to the colony's congressional delegation in Philadelphia. He reported the capture of the fort, now garrisoned with four hundred troops, and added that the council intended to fortify Charlestown Harbor as well as circumstances permitted.[38]

The success of this endeavor should have cheered Laurens, but he revealed that, two days prior to the fort's seizure, Governor Campbell let slip during a confrontation over his letters that "Ships & Troops were to be sent from England to all the Colonies & might be shortly expected."[39] In addition to this worrisome revelation, continued Laurens, were "unfavorable accounts which we have received from the Indians, the danger which we are always exposed to & more especially at this time from domestic Insurrection . . . & you will agree that we have before us a very unpleasant prospect."[40]

Referring to the Continental Congress's support for North Carolina's two provincial regiments, Laurens asked that the same consideration be given to South Carolina and added that two or three thousand stand of arms would be most helpful.[41]

Numerous proposals were considered over the next few weeks to better defend Charlestown. One measure that was agreed upon was to obstruct two channels in the harbor with sunken vessels.[42] Near the end of September the HMS *Tamar* fired two six-pound rounds at thirty armed men in three large canoes that approached too close to it. Neither shot hit anything, and the canoes quickly changed direction and returned to Fort Johnson, but another milestone in South Carolina had occurred, one side had fired upon the other.[43]

A war of words erupted on September 29, when the South Carolina General Committee wrote to Governor Campbell to ask him to return to Charlestown:

> It is with great concern we find that for some days past, your Excellency has been pleased to withdraw yourself from Charlestown, the seat of your Government, and have retired on board the King's ship. The inconveniences which must unavoidably arise to the people, deprived by this step, of that access to your Excellency, which is absolutely necessary for transacting public affairs, is apparent; and we submit to your Excellency's consideration, whether the retirement of our Governor to a King's ship, in this time of general disquietude, when the minds of the people are filled with the greatest apprehensions for their safety, may not increase their alarm, and excite jealousies of some premeditated design against them.[44]

The committee urged the governor to return to his residence (and to his wife, who remained in their home in Charlestown) and assured him that as long as he "Take no active part against the good people of this Colony in the present arduous struggle for the preservation of their civil liberties, we will, to the utmost of our power, secure to your Excellency that safety and respect for your person and character, which the inhabitants of Carolina have ever wished to show to the representative of their Sovereign."[45]

Governor Campbell, no doubt flabbergasted by the audacious proposal of the committee, replied the next day. He charged the committee, which he maintained had no legal authority whatsoever to be in "actual and open rebellion against their Sovereign," and he scoffed at the suggestion that he should "forget my duty to my Sovereign and my country, as to promise I would take no active part in bringing the subverters of our glorious constitution, and the real liberties of the people, to a sense of their duty."[46]

As autumn progressed, Colonel Moultrie of the 2nd Regiment recalled that the South Carolina troops posted on James Island at and around Fort Johnson, some five hundred strong, "began to look, and act like soldiers."[47] They were well supplied, clothed, and even trained, and many served double duty as infantry and artillerists. Artillery batteries were erected on several of Charlestown's wharfs as well as on high ground overlooking the harbor.[48]

On November 4, the Continental Congress agreed to assume the expense of three continental battalions in South Carolina, something that undoubtedly pleased South Carolina's leaders.[49] Efforts to establish a small naval force to defend Charlestown also occurred in early November.

The schooner *Defence*, commanded by Captain Simon Tufts, with two nine-pounder guns, six six-pounder guns, and two four-pounder guns, and a crew of seventy, was the first of South Carolina's military to exchange gunfire with the British on November 11, 1775.[50] Escorting four hulks to be scuttled on the sandbar of Hog Island Creek to obstruct the channel, the *Defence* suddenly found itself under fire from both the HMS *Cherokee* and *Tamar*. Captain Tufts of the *Defence* (who misidentified the *Tamar* as the *Tamer*) reported to the South Carolina Provincial Congress after the engagement, "The *Tamer* fired six shots at him, which he, just coming to an anchor, returned with two; that the *Tamer* continuing the cannonade, he contented himself with returning only one shot more, and then proceeded to sink the hulks."[51]

Captain Tufts was able to scuttle three of the hulks before the tide and nightfall prevented the fourth from being sunk in its proper place. The *Defence* remained on station, ready to complete the task in the morning, but in the darkness the British ships were able to draw closer. Captain Tufts continued his report. "About a quarter to four this morning the *Tamer* and *Cherokee*, having warped nearer to his vessel in the night, discharged their broadsides at him, and continued the cannonade until about seven o'clock."[52]

Captain Tufts reported that, despite the heavy fire from the British ships, he was able to guide the fourth hulk to its proper position and scuttle it, but it sank so slowly that a British party was able to board it, tow it to shallower water, and set it afire. Tufts fired once on the British in a longboat, but finding it ineffectual, he decided not to waste any more ammunition.[53] The twenty-six-pounder cannon of Fort Johnson also fired a few shots at the British ships but without effect.[54]

Surprisingly, despite the heavy fire from the British, the *Defence* suffered little damage. Most of the British shot passed through the rigging and landed on the mainland.[55] Still, although there were apparently no casualties on either side, the Battle of Hog Island Channel was the first engagement in South Carolina in which both sides fired on the other.

William Henry Drayton realized the significance of the engagement and wrote to the Continental Congress on behalf of the provincial congress to inform them of it. "Gentlemen, the actual commencement of hostilities by the British arms in this Colony against the inhabitants is an event of the highest moment to the southern part of the United Colonies."[56] Drayton proceeded to provide the details of battle, the first to occur in South Carolina. Less than a week later a much larger engagement between Tory and Whig colonists erupted at the backcountry settlement of Ninety-Six that resulted in South Carolina's first bloodshed.

In early November an incident occurred in the backcountry that shattered the peace and led to conflict at Ninety-Six. Wagons carrying approximately a thousand pounds of gunpowder and two thousand pounds of lead destined for the Cherokee town of Keowee (as part of South Carolina's treaty arrangements with the nation) were seized about seventeen miles south of Ninety-Six by a party of 150 Tories led by Patrick Cunningham.[57] Moses Cotter, one of the waggoneers hauling the gunpowder and lead, reported that the Tories accosted him on the road to Ninety-Six and surrounded his escort of twenty rangers, who wisely complied with the Tories' demand to surrender their arms.[58] Cunningham justified the seizure of the gunpowder and lead with the claim that it was meant to encourage and enable the Cherokee to attack those settlers in the backcountry (at the behest of the rebels in Charlestown) who refused to sign or abide by the continental association.[59] No doubt a desire to avenge his brother Robert, who had been jailed in Charlestown for his loyalist views, was also a motive for Cunningham's action.

The Tories departed with the powder and lead, leaving Cotter, and the rangers whom they eventually released, to make their way to report the incident. Major Andrew Williamson, a nearby Whig militia commander, assembled the militia, which included a company commanded by Captain Andrew Pickens, and headed for Ninety-Six in hopes of regaining the gunpowder.[60] They were unable to do so, however, and two weeks passed during which Williamson's Whig force of approximately 550 men encamped near Ninety-Six.[61]

On November 18, Major Williamson was informed that a large force of Tories, estimated at between 1,500 to 2,000 strong, had crossed the Saluda River and were only a few miles from Ninety-Six.[62] Williamson reported his reaction to William Henry Drayton, who presided over the provincial congress in Charlestown:

> I immediately ordered the men under arms, and took the resolution of marching to meet them [the loyalists], and demanding their intentions, and if they were determined to come to action . . . and on acquainting the officers and men thereof, found them all cheerful and willing to proceed, but afterwards reflecting on the fatal consequences should we have been defeated, proposed in a Council of War, consisting of Maj. Mayson and all the Captains, to march from the camp near Ninety-Six into the cleared ground of Col. Savage's plantation, where we could use our artillery [swivel guns] with advantage, and there fortify our camp till we should receive more certain information of their strength (being in immediate expectation of being joined by Col. Thomson and the rangers at least, and also some men from the lower part of this regiment and Augusta) which was unanimously approved of, and early next morning we marched to Ninety-Six with all our provision and baggage, and in about three hours erected a kind of fortification of old fence rails joined to a barn and some out houses, which before we had quite completed they had surrounded us with a large body of men with drums and colors.[63]

The Tories were commanded by Major Joseph Robinson, and they approached with drums beating and flags waving, investing the fort and taking possession of the town and jail, just 160 yards from the hastily built Whig fort. A ravine separated the fort and town, making an approach from either position upon the other difficult. Each was in musket range and accurate rifle range of the other, however. The Whigs had an added advantage of several swivel guns, which could reach the town or sweep the field with canister fire if the Tories tried to rush the fort. The Tories, however, had nearly four times more troops than the Whigs and used them to completely surround the fort.

Major Williamson sent an officer out to parlay with the loyalists, but he was sent back; Major Robinson would only talk to the Whig commanders.[64] Major Williamson refused to comply with Robinson's demand and remained in the fort, but he sent Major Mayson and two other officers out who "Met between [the loyalists] and the fort in sight of both, and after about a fifteen minute conference [with the Tory commanders] they returned, and reported that [the Tories] insisted on our immediately delivering up our arms to them and dispersing; which were the only terms they were determined to grant us, and that at parting they told [us] to keep our people within the fort, which was the only place where they could be safe."[65]

Up to this point not a shot had been fired, but as the meeting ended two of Williamson's soldiers who were outside the fort (probably retrieving water) were suddenly taken "before my face," recalled Major Williamson, by the Tories. Williamson ordered his men to rescue their captured comrades, and at that point, "a warm engagement ensued, which continued with very little intermission for three days."[66]

Heavy musket, rifle, and swivel fire erupted from both sides with the Tories using houses, trees, logs, stumps, and fences for protection while the Whigs had the fort. The shooting slackened in the afternoon and nearly stopped at nightfall, except for an occasional shot from the fort to discourage the Tories from attacking in the dark.[67]

Heavy gunfire resumed the next day, but as most of it occurred from long distance and from protected positions, neither side suffered many casualties.[68] At some point during the second day, the Tories ignited a grass fire to create a smokescreen in order to approach the rebel fort behind a mantelet (large shield) of sticks and branches, but a shift in the wind ignited the mantelet and the Tories abandoned their effort.[69]

The gunfire slackened again at nightfall but resumed at the start of the third day and was steady for most of the day. At sunset of the third day Major Robinson, hoping that the Whigs were ready to surrender, displayed a white flag from the jail and sent a messenger to the Whig fort. Major Williamson, whose men were low on gunpowder and famished for both water and bread, had good reason to consider Robinson's message, but when he discovered that all Robinson offered was his original terms, Majors Williamson and Mayson dismissed the messenger with the reply that "they were determined never to resign their arms!"[70]

After another tense night, daylight produced a new parley that resulted in an agreement to end the hostilities. The negotiated treaty allowed the Whigs to march out of the fort with their arms but without their swivel guns. The surrender of the swivel guns was actually for show to appease a number of Tories who insisted that they be surrendered. What most of the Tories did not know was that a secret agreement provided for the swivels to be returned to the Whigs.[71] The Whig fort was to be destroyed, and the loyalists were to march back across the Saluda River.[72]

For the amount of gunfire exchanged between the two sides, the casualties at the first battle of Ninety-Six (sometimes referred to as the Battle of Savage's Field) were relatively light and yet very significant. The Whigs suffered one killed and twelve wounded, and the Tories one killed and fifty-two wounded.[73] These losses were costly to many families and significant for all of South Carolina, for they marked the first bloodshed in battle of the Revolutionary War in South Carolina. Sadly, there would be much more to come.

Georgia

The situation in Georgia in the fall of 1775 was one of uneasy stalemate. Governor Wright remained in Savannah, relatively safe from capture and harm, but he was isolated by an inability to communicate in a secure manner with anyone outside of his immediate reach. In a letter to Lord Dartmouth that Governor Wright had no certainty would ever reach London, he complained about his correspondence woes: "Whatever Letters Your Lordship may have thought Proper to write to me by the July and August Packets, Still remain with Lord Wm. Campbell on board His Majesty's Sloop *Tamer*, and I Can't Say how much longer they may Continue there, for his Lordship Cannot send them to me, nor have I any method of Sending for them with Safety."[74]

Governor Wright's implied message was that he needed naval support to better secure communication and protect royal interests in Georgia. This point was driven home by the governor at the end of his letter: "I Presume His Majesty's *Cruizer* which was ordered to this Providence in February last, has been Employed much more for His Majesty's Service Elsewhere, than She could have been here in Preventing the Gun Powder from being taken away in the manner Your Lordship has been Informed of, and Giving other Assistance which She might Probably have done."[75]

Governor Wright informed Lord Dartmouth a month later (upon the arrival of a letter sent from London four and a half months earlier in July) that the delay in his reception of it was due to there being "no safe opportunity of forwarding it" from Charlestown.[76] Again, the implication was that a British warship stationed in Georgia would relieve this problem. Wright subtly reinforced this point by expressing his gratitude to the king for providing asylum aboard naval vessels for royal officials elsewhere threatened by "the Violence of the People" but noted that in some colonies such protection was too late: "For all the King's officers in Charles Town are Prisoners Already, and nobody knows how soon they may be so here.—and no Ship seen or heard of yet, although ordered last February."[77]

The governor was correct to be concerned for the welfare of royal officials and even royal rule in Georgia, for two weeks prior to his mid-November letter to Dartmouth, the Continental Congress in Philadelphia had approved the formation of one battalion of continental troops, under continental pay and regulation, for Georgia.[78] Although this congressional action depended on Georgia's leaders to implement it by authorizing the formation of such a unit themselves, it was another possible step away from royal authority for Georgia.

EAST FLORIDA

The arrival of the HMS *St. Lawrence* to St. Augustine in early October was welcomed by most colonists in East Florida. The warship provided desperately needed protection to the capital and colony and brought with it many letters from Boston and elsewhere. The turmoil caused by the outbreak of war to the north had disrupted the normal flow of mail, so when the *St. Lawrence* delivered a large packet of letters, the recipients hurriedly composed their replies in hopes of sending them out with the vessel that was about to sail to Virginia with another detachment of 14th Regiment reinforcements. From there, the letters would be forwarded to Boston and England via the security of the British navy.

John Moultrie, the lieutenant governor of East Florida and brother of Colonel William Moultrie of the 2nd South Carolina Regiment, seized his opportunity to write to General James Grant in Boston and described the situation in East Florida: "By our steady attachment to our mother country, we are become an eye-sore to our sister Colonies; particularly so to our foolish young sisters Georgia and Carolina. They threatened, and have done every thing in their power to starve us, which is not in their power to effect."[79]

Moultrie explained that the threats from their sister colonies to embargo their trade and even attack East Florida alarmed the colonists there to action, and as a result, "Almost every planter has made his provision; many a great deal to spare."[80]

One of the letters that arrived in St. Augustine in early October was addressed to John Stuart from General Thomas Gage. Written on September 12, 1775, General Gage ordered the Southern Department Superintendent of Indians to maintain good relations with the Indians, and "when opportunity offers, to make them take arms against His Majesty's enemies and to distress them all in their power, for no terms is now to be kept with them."[81] In other words, when the time was right, Stuart was to encourage the Creek and Cherokee nations to strike all along the Southern frontier.

Stuart received these instructions on October 2 and immediately replied. "I shall pay the strictest attention to your commands . . . nothing in my power shall be neglected to forward the interests of

Government."[82] Stuart reported that he was sending his brother, Henry Stuart, to meet with Creek and Cherokee leaders and added, "I shall immediately take steps to get some Indians here [St. Augustine] which will be an acquisition to this place, in its present weak state."[83]

In a second letter to General Gage written that same day, Stuart introduced Moses Kirkland, the bearer of the letter, and explained that as a former inhabitant of the backcountry of South Carolina, he could confirm that "a great majority of the frontier and back inhabitants of Carolina are attached to and inclined to support Government." In such circumstances, noted Stuart, "I conceive that an indiscriminate attack by Indians would be contrary to your Excellency's idea, and might do much harm."[84] Stuart was likely speaking out of genuine concern for the loyalists, as well as the many women and children of rebels who would also likely suffer by indiscriminate Indian attacks in the backcountry, but another concern weighed on his mind. His wife remained in Charlestown and, according to an acquaintance in St. Augustine, Stuart "thinks she would be massacred should he bring down the red people."[85]

With tension and conflict within the colonies to the north building, the likelihood of an attack by "the Carolina people," as Governor Tonyn referred to them, abated. That did not prevent John Stuart, however, from calling on nearby Indians to come to St. Augustine. "He intends to keep about forty or fifty [Indians] encamped near the town for the winter," noted a resident of the town.[86]

Indians were not the only people the leaders of East Florida hoped to attract to St. Augustine. In early November, Governor Tonyn, per instructions from Lord Dartmouth, issued a proclamation on behalf of the king that offered East Florida as an asylum for any loyalist who fled their colony or residence. He specifically pledged to, "Afford every possible protection to such of His Subjects in the Colonies in Rebellion, as shall be too weak to resist the violence of the times, and too Loyal to concur in the measures of those, who have avowed and supported this unnatural Rebellion, And that this Province may not only prove a secure Asylum to such but induce them to settle here."[87]

"Gratuitous land grants" and a ten-year exemption on quit rents (an annual land tax to the crown that most colonial landowners paid) were included in the proclamation. It was all meant to encourage loyal colonists from throughout British North America to "come and reside in this, His Majesty's Loyal Colony where they may unmolested follow their lawful occupations and enjoy the quiet possession of their Property, and the valuable blessing of that Liberty, which is an enemy to licentiousness, friendly to Government and consistent with the Laws of Great Britain."[88] Governor Tonyn added, "That upon application to me in Council they shall have Grants of Land as a Family Right."[89]

Peter Chester, the royal governor of West Florida (today's Florida Panhandle as well as the coasts of Alabama and Mississippi, all the way to the Mississippi River) presented a nearly identical proclamation less than two weeks later.[90] As there was no printing press to publish the proclamation in.West Florida, however, he sent a copy to Governor William Tryon in New York requesting that he "direct that a number of copies . . . may be printed and published in your Government."[91]

Governor Chester hoped that, once printed and published in New York, word would spread throughout the colonies. One must wonder, however, whether Governor Tryon, as one of the last royal governors still in office, was very eager to publicize the existence of a safe asylum for loyalists under generous conditions for anyone who sought to leave New York.

Four

December

DECEMBER 1775 BEGAN WITH SOME PROMISE FOR THE AMERICAN army in Quebec. Two American forces, albeit rather small, converged on the fortress town of Quebec with hopes of seizing it from the British, an act that would surely disrupt British planning. The situation was not so bright in Boston, where the stalemate continued and the American army suffered from supply shortages and dwindling troop numbers. General Washington and Congress struggled to restructure the army. Fortunately for them, the British in Boston showed no sign of seizing the initiative over the winter, so the stalemate dragged on.

VIRGINIA

Lord Dunmore's victory at Kemp's Landing in mid-November and his proclamation to raise the king's standard and offer freedom to slaves and indentured servants of rebels who fought for him had a tremendous impact in Virginia. Hundreds of colonists in Norfolk and Princess Anne County came forward to pledge their support to the British crown. "The Whole Counties of Norfolk and Princess Ann to a Man has come in to the Standard Which is Now erected in Norfolk and taken the Oaths of Allegiance to his Majesty," reported an inhabitant of Portsmouth.[1] A Norfolk resident noted, "The day after [Dunmore hoisted the King's Standard] the whole Country flocked to it, took the oath of allegiance . . . and declared their readiness to defend his Majesty's Crown & dignity. . . . I can assure you that L. Dunmore is so much admired in this part of the County that he might have 500 Volunteers to march with him to any part of Virginia."[2]

Lord Dunmore confidently informed General Howe, "Immediately on [the victory at Kemp's Landing] I issued the inclosed Proclamation which has had a Wonderful effect as there are not less than three thousand that have already taken and signed the inclosed Oath."[3]

Dunmore was particularly pleased with the impact of the most controversial part of his proclamation, freedom for runaway servants and the enslaved of rebels who agreed to fight under the king's standard. Dunmore reported to General Howe that "The Negroes are flocking in also from all quarters which I hope will oblige the Rebels to disperse to take care of their families, and property, and had I but a few more men here I would March immediately to Williamsburg my former place of residence by which I should soon compel the whole Colony to Submit."[4]

Dunmore emphasized his need for arms and supplies, two items he hoped General Howe might assist him with, and detailed his efforts to organize the large number of runaway slaves and servants and loyal Virginians who had answered his call to arms. "We are in great want of small Arms, and if two or three light field pieces and their Carriages could be Spared they would be of great Service to us, also some Cartridge paper of which not a Sheet is to be got here, and all our Cartridges expended. . . . I have . . . ordered a Regiment (Called the Queens own Loyal Virginia Regiment) of 500 men to be raised immediately consisting . . . Ten Companys each of which is to consist . . . 50 Privates. . . . You may observe by my Proclamation that I offer freedom to the Slaves, (of all Rebels) that join me, in consequence of which there are between two and three hundred already come in and these I form into a Corps as fast as they come in giving them white Officers and Non Commissioned Officers in proportion."[5]

Governor Dunmore's optimism carried into December: "The good effects of this most trifling success [at Kemp's Landing] was manifested strongly by the zeal which the people showed on this occasion to His Majesty's service when unawed by the opposite party. I was immediately determined to run all risks for their support, and on that very day ordered the enclosed proclamation to be published, erected the King's standard (alias a pair of colours as I had no better), and the next day I suppose not less than a hundred of those very men who were forced into the field against me the day before came and took the enclosed oath."[6]

Dunmore added a cautionary note concerning the strength of his forces, citing the inexperience of most of his new volunteers, but concluded by asserting that he was making progress toward building an adequate naval and land force to challenge the rebels: "Your lordship may observe that about three thousand have taken that oath, but of this number not above three or four hundred at most are in any degree capable of bearing arms, and the greatest part of these hardly ever made use of the gun; but I hope a short time (if they are willing) will make them as good if not better than those who are come down to oppose them."[7]

Governor Dunmore's success was grudgingly acknowledged by his opponents. A week after the engagement at Kemp's Landing, John Page described its impact to his friend, Thomas Jefferson, who was still in Philadelphia: "Our late Governor . . . has made a compleat Conquest of Princess Ann and Norfolk and Numbers of Negroes, and Cowardly Scoundrels flock to his Standard."[8]

Page was not completely discouraged by the turn of events, however. He remained hopeful that Colonel Woodford and his combined force of regulars and minutemen would soon turn the situation around for the rebels. Woodford reached Suffolk, fifteen miles southwest of Portsmouth, on November 25.[9] A day earlier, he sent Lieutenant Colonel Charles Scott ahead to the Great Bridge with over two hundred troops to observe the enemy there.[10]

The Great Bridge was actually a long, narrow, manmade causeway with multiple wooden bridges spanning the southern branch of the Elizabeth River and its tributaries and marshland. Norfolk lay eleven miles north of the main bridge span, and since most of the terrain south of Norfolk was marsh and swamp, the Great Bridge Road was the primary southern land route between Norfolk and North Carolina.

Lieutenant Colonel Scott was eager to confront Dunmore's small force of "Tories and Blacks" (who had removed the planks from the main bridge and were posted in a small wooden stockade fort on the north bank of the river adjacent to the dismantled bridge), but Colonel Woodford cautioned against being too aggressive.[11] Woodford informed Scott that a severe shortage of ammunition and arms made it impossible for him to march to the Great Bridge until "a number of Ball is run, cartridges made, arms Repair'd &ct. &ct." [12]

In Norfolk, Lord Dunmore and his force of British regulars, runaway slaves, and Tory volunteers braced for the arrival of Woodford's troops and busily constructed earthworks to protect the city, but to best protect Norfolk he had to prevent the rebels from gaining control of the Great Bridge.[13]

While Colonel Woodford hurried to make cartridges and equip his troops in Suffolk with functioning firearms, Lieutenant Colonel Scott's advance guard entrenched near the Great Bridge and skirmished with Dunmore's forces. A few days after their first clash, Scott reported, "We have been well informed that we killed 16 negroes and 5 white men the first day we got to this place."[14] Although Dunmore's losses were likely much lighter (he claimed that after a week of skirmishes he had only suffered one or two slightly wounded soldiers while the "rebels" had fifteen to twenty soldiers killed), the number of casualties that both sides claimed to have inflicted on the other suggest that the skirmish was heated.[15]

The bulk of Lieutenant Colonel Scott's force of nearly two hundred men was posted behind hastily built breastworks on the southern edge of the causeway. Sentries were posted forward of the breastworks at night, on what was essentially an island, with the Elizabeth River to the north, a small creek to the south (fifty yards in front of the "rebel" breastworks), and marsh on either side of the causeway. Hidden amongst a few buildings and piles of debris close to the dismantled bridge and Dunmore's fort, Scott's sentries were positioned to alarm the "rebels" if the enemy approached at night. For their own safety, the sentinels were withdrawn back to the breastworks at dawn each day.

Scott also detached a party of about forty men five miles downriver to guard a crossing point and prevent a surprise from the enemy.[16] The day after they arrived, this detachment was attacked by Dunmore's troops but held their ground and inflicted losses on the attackers.[17]

Colonel Woodford, with the main body of troops, reached the Great Bridge soon after this skirmish, on December 2. Woodford described the situation he found to Edmund Pendleton, president of the Committee of Safety: "I . . . found the Enemy Posted on the opposite side of the Bridge, in a Stockade Fort, with two four pounders, some swivels & wall pieces, with which they keep up a constant Fire, have done no other damage than kill'd Corpl Davis with a cannon ball."[18]

Woodford estimated that Dunmore's fort was defended by 250 men, most of whom were escaped slaves commanded by sergeants of the 14th Regiment.[19] A handful of Tories also manned the fort. Woodford speculated that it might be possible to capture it, but the presence of cannon meant that its conquest would come at a very high cost in lives. "The Enemys Fort, I think, might have been taken, but not without the loss of many of our Men, their Situation is very advantageous, & no way to attack them, but by exposing most of the Troops to their Fire upon a large open Marsh."[20]

As for his own fortifications, Colonel Woodford reported, "We have raised a strong Breastwork upon the lower part of the street joining the Causeway, from which Centries are posted at some old Rubbish not far from the Bridge (which is mostly destroy'd)."[21]

Although he believed that he held a strong position, Woodford was concerned about his limited supply of gunpowder and the lack of blankets and shoes for his men.[22]

One officer, who likely found shelter in one of the "safe" houses out of range (but not earshot) of Dunmore's guns, was Lieutenant Colonel Scott. It had been over a week since he had led his detachment ahead of Woodford's main body to the Great Bridge, and now that reinforcements had arrived Scott took a moment to relax. He wrote to a friend, "Last night was the first of my pulling off my clothes for 12 nights successively. Believe me, my good friend, I never was so fatigued with duty in my whole life."[23]

Despite the large number of reinforcements, it is likely that Lieutenant Colonel Scott still found it difficult to rest. "We still keep up a pretty heavy fire between us, from light to light. We have only lost two men, and about half an hour ago one of our people was shot through the arm, which broke the bone near his hand."[24]

The skirmishing continued downriver as well. Within days of his arrival, Colonel Woodford sent a large detachment of troops under Colonel Edward Stevens of the Culpeper Minutemen across the river to encircle and surprise Dunmore's guard at the crossing. Woodford reported:

> They crossed about midnight, & got to the Enemy's centinals without being discover'd, one of them challenged & not being answer'd, Fired at our party, the fire was returned by our men, & an over Eagerness at first, & rather a backwardness afterwards, occasion'd some confusion, & prevented the Colo's plan from being so well executed as he intended, however, he [burned] their Fortification & House, in which one negro perished, killed one dead upon the spott, & took two others prisoners . . . this party (consisting of 26 Blacks & 9 Whites) escaped under the cover of night, he also took four new Muskets.[25]

Although the bulk of the enemy guard escaped, their guard post was destroyed. Two nights later, the "rebels" struck again, attacking the same post—reoccupied and reinforced by Dunmore with seventy men—with the same result.[26]

On December 4, Lieutenant Colonel Scott noted the arrival of a company of men from North Carolina and reported that hundreds more (with artillery) were reportedly marching behind them: "The Carolina forces are joining us. One company came in yesterday, and we expect 8 or 900 of them by to-morrow, or next day at farthest, with several pieces of artillery, and plenty of ammunition and other warlike stores."[27]

Rebel cannon would surely alter the situation, and Colonel Woodford reported that his men were preparing artillery positions on "the most advantageous ground" in anticipation of the arrival of guns.[28]

Lord Dunmore was aware that cannon and reinforcements were marching to join Woodford, and he knew he had to act. He explained his thinking to Lord Dartmouth. "The Rebels had procured some Cannon from North Carolina, [which were expected to arrive any day] and that they were also to be reinforced from Williamsburg, and knowing that our little Fort was not in a Condition to withstand anything heavier than Musquet Shot, I thought it advisable to risque Something to save the Fort."[29]

A significant factor behind Dunmore's decision to attack Colonel Woodford's breastworks on December 9 was inaccurate information he reportedly received from a deserter from the rebel camp. Colonel Woodford reported after the battle that "A servant belonging to major [Thomas] Marshal, who deserted the other night from col. [Charles] Scott's party, has completely taken his lordship in. Lieutenant [John] Batut . . . informs, that this fellow told them not more than 300 shirtmen were here; and that imprudent man [Dunmore] catched at the bait, dispatching capt. Leslie with all the regulars (about 200) who arrived at the bridge about 3 o' clock in the morning."[30]

It is uncertain whether the deserter purposefully or accidently misled Dunmore about Woodford's troop strength, but it appears that Dunmore viewed the report of such a small number of rebels across the causeway as an opportunity that would soon disappear when the expected reinforcements arrived. As a result, on the evening of December 8, Dunmore rushed his own reinforcements, including most of the regulars of the 14th Regiment (approximately 120 under Captain Leslie) as well as a detachment of sailors (to help man the fort's cannon) and about sixty Tory volunteers, from Norfolk to the fort at the Great Bridge.[31] These reinforcements joined the garrison of Tories, runaway slaves, and handful of regulars already at the fort early in the morning of December 9.

Worried that his small wooden fort would not hold against an assault by the soon-to-be-reinforced rebels, Lord Dunmore chose to

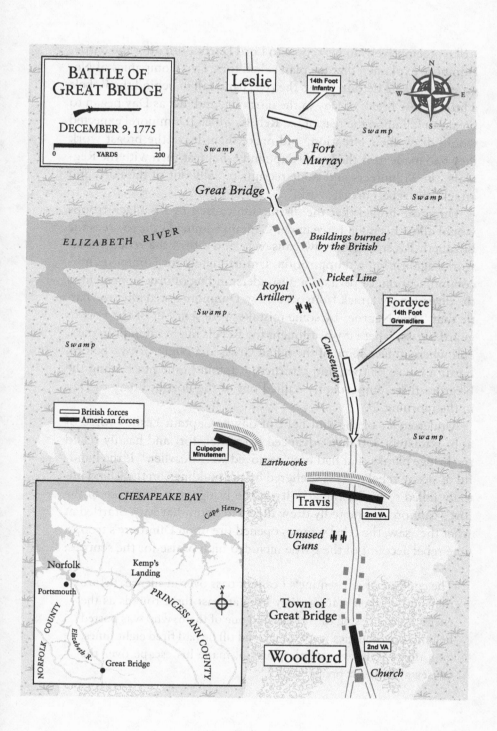

BATTLE OF
GREAT BRIDGE

DECEMBER 9, 1775

0   YARDS   200

Leslie

14th Foot
Infantry

Swamp

Fort
Murray

Swamp

Great Bridge

ELIZABETH RIVER

Swamp

Buildings burned
by the British

Picket Line

Royal
Artillery

Fordyce
14th Foot
Grenadiers

Swamp

Causeway

British forces
American forces

Culpeper
Minutemen

Swamp

Earthworks

Travis

2nd VA

Unused
Guns

CHESAPEAKE BAY

Cape Henry

Norfolk

Kemp's
Landing

Portsmouth

PRINCESS ANN COUNTY

NORFOLK COUNTY

Elizabeth R.

Great Bridge

Town of
Great Bridge

Woodford

2nd VA

Church

strike preemptively. In his report to Lord Dartmouth after the battle, Dunmore explained that his plan called for "Two Companies of Negroes to make a detour, [cross the river] and fall in behind the Rebels a little before break of Day in the morning, and just as Day began to break, to fall upon the rear of the Rebels, which [Dummore] expected would draw their attention, and make them leave the breast work they had made near the Fort, [Captain Leslie] was then with the Regulars, the Volunteers and some recruits to sally out of the Fort, and attack [the rebel] breast work."[32]

Dunmore hoped that the distraction caused by his Black troops would allow his main force under Captain Samuel Leslie to cross the Elizabeth River and narrow causeway and storm the rebel breastworks against limited opposition. Unfortunately for Dunmore, miscommunication, or perhaps a misunderstanding of orders, prevented the diversionary attack from occurring. Dunmore noted after the battle that "The Negroes by some mistake were sent out of the Fort to guard a pass, where it was thought the Rebels might attempt to pass, and where in fact some of them had Crossed a Night or two before, burnt a house or two, and returned; Captain Leslie not finding the Negroes there, imprudently Sallied out of the Fort at break of Day in the morning."[33]

Under cover of the dim light of dawn, Captain Leslie's force of approximately 350 men advanced from their fort and hastily relaid the bridge planks that had been removed weeks earlier.[34] If the handful of sleepy rebel pickets sheltered by the buildings on the island initially failed to notice the activity at the bridge, the discharge of the fort's cannon undoubtedly drew their attention that way. Startled at what they saw, the rebel sentries opened fire upon Dunmore's troops. One rebel account of the battle included high praise for the sentries:

The conduct of our sentinels I cannot pass over in silence. Before they quitted their stations they fired at least three rounds as the enemy were crossing the bridge, and one of them, who was posted behind some shingles, kept his ground till he had fired eight times, and after receiving a whole platoon, made his escape over the causeway into our breast works.[35]

The brave sentinel who stood his ground for so long and fired eight shots was twenty-year-old Billy Flora, a free-born Black volunteer from Norfolk.

As the sentinels scurried back to the earthworks 150 yards to the rear, their comrades behind the breastwork began to stir, realizing that the gunfire they heard was not the usual morning salute of the past few days.

Four hundred yards south of the earthworks at the main rebel encampment, however, few of Colonel Woodford's troops, who had just been awakened by reveille, took much notice of the distant gunfire. Major Thomas Spotswood recalled, "We were alarmed this morning by the firing of some guns after reveille beating, which, as the enemy had paid us this compliment several times before, we at first concluded to be nothing but a morning salute."[36]

Colonel Woodford had a similar reaction: "After reveille beating, two or three great guns, and some musquetry were discharged from the enemy's fort, which, as it was not an unusual thing, was but little regarded."[37]

The situation was much different at the rebel breastworks. Realizing that they were under attack, the commander of the guard, Lieutenant Edward Travis, ordered his small detachment of approximately sixty men "to reserve their fire till the enemy came within the distance of fifty yards."[38] A small stream lay about fifty yards in front of the rebel breastworks and served as an excellent range marker for the rebels. To their front across the narrow, 150-yard causeway were more than five times their number of enemy troops with two cannon that one rebel recalled were "planted on the edge of the island, facing the left of our breast-work, [and] played briskly . . . upon us."[39]

Joining the cannon at the edge of the island were the Tory and Black soldiers of Dunmore, over two hundred strong. Behind them rose the smoke of several buildings—formerly the outposts of the rebel sentries but now torched by Dunmore's troops. Captain Leslie remained on the island with the Tory and Black troops while Captain Charles Fordyce led the British regulars of the 14th Regiment, 120 strong in a column six abreast, across the narrow causeway to storm the rebel earthworks.[40]

Back in the main "rebel" camp, the gravity of the situation had finally become apparent. Major Spotswood recalled,

I heard Adjutant Blackburn call out, Boys! stand to your arms! Colonel Woodford and myself immediately got equipped, and ran out; the Colonel pressed down to the breastwork in our front, and my alarm-post being two hundred and fifty yards in another quarter, I ran to it as fast as I could, and by the time I had made all ready for engaging, a very heavy fire ensued at the breastwork, in which were not more than sixty men.[41]

The heavy fire that Major Spotswood heard came from Lieutenant Travis's guard detail and a few brave reinforcements who had rushed forward at the first alarm. Lieutenant John Marshall of the Culpeper Minutemen (and future chief justice of the Supreme Court) was at Great Bridge and remembered, "As is the practice with raw troops, the bravest rushed to the works, where, regardless of order, they kept up a heavy fire on the front of the British column."[42]

The valor of some of the rebels was also acknowledged by Major Spotswood, who proudly noted in a letter immediately after the engagement that, as the redcoats approached the breastworks with fixed bayonets, "Our young troops received them with firmness, and behaved as well as it was possible for soldiers to do."[43] In his own letter after the battle, Colonel Woodford also commented on the rebel fire from the breastwork, writing that "perhaps a hotter fire never happened, or a greater carnage, for the number of troops."[44]

The hot fire delivered upon the British originated not only from the breastworks directly in front of them but also from breastworks on a small island west of the causeway. Riflemen from the Culpeper Minute Battalion manned this position and poured deadly enfilade fire into the British column's right flank.[45] According to one American account, the intense rebel small arms fire from both positions

Threw [the advancing British regulars] into some confusion, but they were instantly rallied by a Captain Fordyce, and advanced along the causeway with great resolution, keeping up a constant and heavy fire as they approached. The brave Fordyce exerted himself to keep up their spirits, reminded them of their ancient glory, and waving his hat over his head, encouragingly told them the day was their own. Thus pressing forward, he fell within fifteen steps to the breast-work. His wounds were many, and his death would have been that of a hero, had he met it in a better cause.[46]

A British participant in the battle noted,

[The rebel] fire was so heavy, that, had we not retreated as we did, we should every one have been cut off. Figure to yourself a strong breast-work built across a causeway, on which six men only could advance a-breast; a large swamp almost surrounding them, at the back of which were two small breast-works to flank us in our attack on their intrenchments. Under these disadvantages it was impossible to succeed; yet our men were so enraged, that all the intreaties, and scarcely the threats of their Officers, could prevail on them to retreat; which at last they did.[47]

Captain Fordyce, riddled with buck and ball, was one of many redcoats to fall before the rebel earthworks. Strewn about the ground just a few paces from the Virginians were over thirty British dead and wounded. One rebel officer described a scene of bloody carnage. "The scene, when the dead and wounded were bro't off, was too much; I then saw the horrors of war in perfection, worse than can be imagin'd; 10 and 12 bullets thro' many; limbs broke in 2 or 3 places; brains turning out. Good God, what a sight!"[48]
Captain Fordyce and twelve British privates lay dead in front of the breastworks, and nearly a score of wounded redcoats, including Lieutenant John Batut, who led the British advance guard, were taken prisoner. A rebel observer noted,

The progress of the enemy was now at an end; [the survivors] retreated over the causeway with precipitation, and were dreadfully galled in their rear. Hitherto, on our side only the guard, consisting of twenty five, and some others, upon the whole, amounting to not more than ninety, had been engaged. Only the regulars of the

14th regiment, in number one hundred and twenty, had advanced
upon the causeway, and about two hundred and thirty tories and
negroes had, after crossing the bridge, continued upon the island.[49]

Although the British assault had been repulsed, the battle was not
yet over, for Captain Leslie rallied his men on the island. "The regulars, after retreating along the causeway, were again rallied by captain
Leslie, and the two field pieces continued to play upon our men."[50]

While Dunmore's troops regrouped around their cannon, Colonel
Woodford led troops from the main camp through heavy artillery
fire to reinforce the breastworks: "It was at this time that colonel
Woodford was advancing down the street to the breast-work with
the main body, and against him was now directed the whole fire of
the enemy. Never were cannon better served, but yet in the face of
them and the musquetry, which kept up a continual blaze, our men
marched on with the utmost intrepidity."[51]

Major Spotswood also noted the severity of the enemy cannon
fire. "The [enemy] field pieces raked the whole length of the street,
and absolutely threw double-headed shot as far as the church, and
afterwords, as our troops approached, cannonaded them heavily
with grapeshot."[52]

Spotswood credited divine providence for protecting all but one
man, who was wounded in the hand, from the intense artillery barrage.[53]

With Dunmore's battered troops stubbornly remaining on the island, Colonel Woodford sent Colonel Edward Stevens with the
Culpeper Minutemen to reinforce the riflemen on the left flank. The
rebel militia poured deadly rifle fire upon Captain Leslie's troops,
which prompted Leslie, who was dismayed at his losses (especially
that of his nephew, Lieutenant Peter Leslie) to withdraw to the fort.
One "rebel" noted that

The enemy fled into their fort, leaving behind them the two field
pieces, which, however, they took care to spike up with nails.
Many were killed and wounded in the flight, but colonel Woodford very prudently restrained his troops from urging their pursuit
too far. From the beginning of the attack till the repulse from the

breast work might be about fourteen or fifteen minutes; till the total defeat upwards of half an hour. It is said that some of the enemy preferred death to captivity, from fear of being scalped, which lord Dunmore inhumanly told them would be their fate should they be taken alive. Thirty one, killed and wounded, fell into our hands, and the number borne off was much greater.[54]

The Battle of Great Bridge was a decisive victory for the Virginians. Colonel Woodford proudly described it as "a second Bunker's Hill affair, in miniature; with this difference, that we kept our post, and had only one man wounded in the hand."[55] More than one observer attributed the lack of rebel casualties to "providence." The British 14th Regiment of Foot, on the other hand, was shattered in the attack. Their brave, bold assault on the rebel breastworks cost them half their men. Colonel Woodford initially estimated Dunmore's losses at fifty men, noting that some of their dead and wounded were taken back to the fort. He reported, "We buried 12, besides . . . [Captain Fordyce] (him with all the military honors due to his rank) and have prisoners lieutenant Batut, and 16 privates; all wounded; 35 stands of arms and accoutrements, 3 officers [fusils], powder, ball, and cartridges, with sundry other things, have likewise fallen into our hands."[56]

Dunmore's report on the 14th Regiment's losses (which was presumably more accurate) claimed three officers and seventeen men killed and one officer and forty-three men wounded.[57] The number of casualties among Dunmore's Tory and Black soldiers is unknown.

With both sides secure behind their fortifications, shooting ceased. Captain Leslie abandoned the fort shortly after sunset and marched the entire garrison to Norfolk. Lord Dunmore explained Leslie's decision in a letter a few days later:

This loss having so much weakened our before but very weak Corps, and Captain Leslie being much depressed by the loss of Lieutenant Leslie, his Nephew, and thinking that the Enemy elated with this little advantage they had gained over us, might force their way across the branch, either above, or below, and by that means, Cut off the Communication between us, determined to evacuate the Fort, and accordingly left it soon after it was dark, and returned with the whole to this place [Norfolk]; The Rebels however remained at the Bridge for a day or two.[58]

Colonel Woodford's troops took possession of the abandoned fort in the morning and found it in disarray. Woodford reported,

> We have taken possession of [the fort] this morning, and found therein the stores mentioned in the enclosed list, to wit, 7 guns, 4 of them sorry, 1 bayonet, 29 spades, 2 shovels, 6 cannon, a few shot, some bedding, a part of a hogshead of rum, two or more barrels, the contents unknown, but supposed to be rum, 2 barrels of bread, about 20 quarters of beef, half a box of candles, 4 or 5 dozen of quart bottles, 4 or 5 iron pots, a few axes and old lumber; the spikes, I find, cannot be got out of the cannon without drilling.[59]

Woodford made another observation that led him to believe the enemy had suffered much greater than he realized: "From the vast effusion of blood on the bridge, and in the fort, from the accounts of the sentries, who saw many bodies carried out of the fort to be interred and other circumstances, I conceive their loss to be much greater than I thought it yesterday, and the victory to be complete."[60]

The 14th Regiment's heavy losses at Great Bridge apparently had a strong impact on its ranking officer, Captain Samuel Leslie. The Virginia Committee of Safety in Williamsburg reported a few days after the battle that

> The Regulars, disgusted, refused to fight in junction with Blacks; and Captain Leslie, we are told, declared no more of his troops should be sacrificed to whims, and put them on board the ships, in consequence of which Norfolk is abandoned, and we expect is now occupied by our troops, who were on their march there when our last account was dispatched. Many Tories are come to us, and their cases now under consideration. More notorious ones are gone on board the vessels, which have in them very valuable cargoes.[61]

Whether Captain Leslie refused to cooperate further with Lord Dunmore (as the committee's account suggests) is unclear, but it does appear that Leslie had had enough of the land campaign. Upon his midnight arrival in Norfolk, he immediately placed his troops onboard two ships anchored off of the city.[62] The condition of his force, combined with the accounts of the battle, greatly unsettled the Tory and Black troops who had worked so diligently constructing entrenchments on the edge of town. One Tory, who sought refuge aboard the HMS *Kingfisher* (16 guns, 100 crew) noted,

> This unfortunate attack [at the Great Bridge] which was made in the morning about sunrise dispirited most people. . . . All thoughts of defending the Town were given up. The Soldiers are gone on board two Transports and those who have dared to be active in supporting Government are under the necessity also of taking refuge in vessels. Such as had not that in their power are left to the mercy of the Rebels who have taken possession of the Town— a single regiment a few weeks ago would have reduced this colony to a sense of its duty. God only knows when it will be done, now.[63]

Dunmore lamented the panic of his supporters and their abandonment of the trenches protecting the city but speculated to Lord Dartmouth that they might be convinced to return if only reinforcements were sent to him:

> This Town standing on a Neck of Land and by that means pretty easily made defensible against an undisciplined Army [prompted] the few remaining Inhabitants (most of whom are Natives of Great Britain) to throw up a breast work and to defend themselves, for which I had supplied them with the few Arms I had, but this work not being quite finished the News of this little advantage the Enemy had gained, [at the Great Bridge] threw them all into despair, and they at present give themselves up as lost, but their transitions from hope to despair are very quick, should any assistance (which God grant) they possibly may be induced to return to their Trenches, when they may soon put themselves in such a Situation as will make it very difficult for the Enemy to force them.[64]

Dunmore's speculation proved to be wishful thinking, for no assistance was coming, at least for him. Instead, Colonel Woodford's force was reinforced by approximately 450 North Carolina continentals under Colonel Robert Howe.[65] Three companies from the 1st Virginia Regiment as well as roughly 150 North Carolina militia also joined Woodford's forces.

NORTH CAROLINA

The waning months of 1775 were rather uneventful in North Carolina, compared to its neighbors to the north and south. The provincial congress was not in session and Governor Martin, aboard the *Cruizer* in the Cape Fear River, which was joined by the *Scorpion* early in November, remained largely inactive.

Governor Martin did write a long report to Lord Dartmouth in mid-November lamenting the unsecure nature of his correspondence and sharing reports that "The spirit of opposition begins to droop and decline here and . . . some of the foremost promoters of sedition waver."[66] Martin was skeptical of the accuracy of such reports, however, and advocated nothing less than unconditional submission of the rebels as a condition for Britain to reconcile with the colonies.

In Philadelphia, the congressional delegates from North Carolina successfully proposed that the Continental Congress formally raise the two battalions of provincial troops that the colony had formed in September (and Congress had already agreed to pay for) to the continental establishment. On November 28, Congress did so, directing that the two North Carolina battalions in question "be increased to the continental establishment, and kept in pay at the expense of the United Colonies for one year."[67] North Carolina's delegates were authorized to spend up to $300 to purchase drums, fifes, and colors (flags) suitable for the battalions.[68]

All of the southern colonies at this time held a great deal of anxiety about the intentions of the various Native American groups on their borders. Although the British hoped to convince the Indians to ally with them, the colonists just hoped that they would stay neutral in the dispute. Commissioners met in Salisbury in mid-November and sent a message to leaders of the Creek nation to assure them of the colonists' desire for peace and trade, the latter being paramount to the Indians who depended on annual supplies of gunpowder and shot. A much larger congress was planned for May 1 in Augusta, Georgia, to discuss matters. In the meantime, the commissioners urged the Indians to "Give credit to no other Talks but such as you from time to time get from . . . us."[69] With winter approaching, there would be plenty of time for the Indians to consider what was best for them.

In late November, the *Scorpion* sailed to Charlestown with Governor Martin aboard, arriving on November 29.[70] Captain Thornbrough on the *Tamar* in Charlestown had, as the ranking British naval officer in the South, ordered the *Scorpion* to Charlestown at the behest of Governor Campbell, who desired a stronger naval presence in the harbor.[71] Governor Martin sailed with the *Scorpion* to consult with Governor Campbell but, perhaps more importantly, to also convince Captain Thornbrough to send the *Scorpion* back to North Carolina where only the unfit *Cruizer* remained. Captain Thornbrough relented to Martin's appeals, displeasing Governor Campbell, and the *Scorpion* and Governor Martin were back in the Cape Fear River before Christmas.[72]

At about the same time the two governors met in Charlestown, North Carolina's Whig leaders offered military assistance to Virginia, and the Virginia Committee of Safety in Williamsburg instructed Colonel Woodford to accept the offer.[73] The assistance came in the form of approximately 150 militia and 450 continental troops from the 2nd North Carolina Regiment under Colonel Robert Howe.[74] They joined the Virginians at Great Bridge on December 12, and as Colonel Howe's continental commission superseded Woodford's provincial commission, the North Carolina colonel assumed command of the combined forces.

Together they led their troops northward from Great Bridge to Norfolk, occupying the abandoned city on December 14. Offshore aboard a variety of vessels, the harbor was filled with desperate families fearful of retribution for their support of Dunmore. The governor described the bleak scene to Lord Dartmouth:

> All who were friends of Government took refuge on board of the
> Ships, with their whole families, and their most valuable Effects,

some in the Men of War, some in their own Vessels, others have chartered such as were here, so that our Fleet is at present Numerous tho' not very powerful. I do assure your Lordship it is a most melancholy sight to see the Numbers of Gentlemen of very large property with their Ladies and whole families obliged to betake themselves on board of Ships, at the Season of the year, hardly with the common necessarys of Life, and great numbers of poor people without even these, who must have perished had I not been able to supply them with some flour, which I purchased from His Majesty's service some time ago.[75]

Onshore, the streets of Norfolk were full of "rebel" troops. With the arrival of Colonel Howe and his North Carolina troops, the "rebel" force swelled to approximately 1,275 men.[76] While most encamped out of range of the British guns, guard detachments were posted along the shore to observe Dunmore's activities and warn of a possible attack. Some of the sentries succumbed to the temptation to take potshots at Dunmore's ships, especially the ever-unpopular *Otter*, commanded by Captain Matthew Squire, and frequent flags of truce went back and forth between the two sides concerning the issue of whether the sporadic gunfire from shore was authorized.[77]

Oddly enough, despite all of the bloodshed and confrontation over the past month, both sides remained civil, to the point that Lord Dunmore had the audacity to inquire (through Captain Squire) whether the navy and army would be allowed to obtain fresh provisions and water from shore.[78] Colonel Howe politely refused the request. "Col. Howe and col. Woodford's compliments to capt. Squire, and return him for answer to his message, that as his majesty's troops and ships of war have long since committed hostilities upon the persons and property of the good people of this colony, and have actually taken and imprisoned several private gentlemen, and others, who did not bear arms at the time, our express orders are, to prevent, to the utmost of our power, any communication whatever between the said troops and ships of war and this town, or any part of this Colony."[79]

Interestingly, when Captain Henry Bellew of the *Liverpool* (28 guns, 130 crew) arrived in Norfolk in mid-December and posed a similar request for fresh provisions, Colonel Howe referred the request to Edmund Pendleton and the Committee of Safety:

> Yesterday, by a flag of truce, I received a letter from capt. Bellew. . . . Though col. Woodford and myself were sensible it was our duty to withhold from him . . . those supplies he wishes to obtain, yet the moderate conduct he has pursued, and the sentiments of humanity by which he seems to be actuated, induced us to delay an answer till to-day, and to couch it in terms which cannot but show him, that occasion, not inclination, had influence upon our conduct. Capt. Bellew's letter was brought to us by one of his lieutenants; he expressed for himself, and every officer on board, the reluctance they should feel, if compelled by necessity, they should be obliged by marauding parties to snatch from the indigent farmers of this colony those provisions they were so willing to purchase.[80]

Colonel Howe's decision to refer the matter to the Committee of Safety was based on the thinking that Captain Bellew and his crew had done nothing offensive to warrant a denial of provisions and water the way Lord Dunmore and the captains for the other British warships at Norfolk had. In other words, Howe's implication was that the dispute in Virginia was really between the colonists and a few "bad apples" in the British navy and government, not the entire British navy or military. Had Colonel Howe known what the British ministry had in store for North Carolina and its sister colonies, he likely would never have considered Captain Bellew's request.

The day before Colonel Howe received Captain Bellew's request for permission to purchase provisions for his crew, Lord George Germain, who had replaced Lord Dartmouth as secretary of state for the colonies, penned a letter to Governor Martin informing him that the long-planned British expedition to the southern colonies was ready to proceed. Germain reported that seven regiments under General Charles Cornwallis were sailing from Ireland, and nine warships under Commodore Peter Parker were assigned to the expedition.[81] He added, "You will exert every Effort to carry into Execution the

orders [of November 7] and will take every necessary preparatory
step for collecting a Corps of Provincials to serve with the King's
Troops and to join them upon their landing."[82]

The orders Lord Germain referred to called for only a portion of
the British troops in the expedition to land in North Carolina under
the right conditions, namely, they had to be able to land in the Cape
Fear River unopposed and "be joined by any considerable number
of well disposed persons, so as to accomplish the restoration of Government."[83]

In other words, Governor Martin's many claims of strong Tory
support had achieved his goal of attracting British support. These
loyalists were to be the primary force, supported by British regulars,
to suppress the rebels in North Carolina and restore royal authority
in the colony. Lord Dartmouth had written the November instructions and added that if such sufficient Tory support failed to materi-
alize or the landing of British regulars was opposed (because the
Tories had not secured the landing area) "no possible advantage
could attend any Effort in North Carolina," and the expedition
would continue on to Charlestown, which was its primary objective.[84]

Thus, the pressure was now on Governor Martin to rouse the loyalist support he claimed existed in the colony.

SOUTH CAROLINA

In the days following the fighting at Ninety-Six in mid-November,
the Whig forces in the interior of South Carolina grew considerably
while the Tory forces largely dispersed. The meeting agreed to at
Ninety-Six, which was to occur twenty days after the fighting ended,
never occurred. Instead, Colonel Richard Richardson, with the con-
currence of his officers, decided that the treaty was not binding on
him. He collected a large force of militia, over a thousand strong by
the end of the month, and prepared to end Tory opposition in the
backcountry once and for all.[85]

On December 8, Colonel Richardson, bolstered by the steady
growth of his force that now approached three thousand men, issued
a declaration to the Tories (he called them insurgents) under Colonel
Patrick Cunningham.[86] He demanded that they surrender immedi-

ately for their disturbance of the peace, theft of gunpowder, and attacks upon "a number of good people of this Colony" at Ninety-Six, which violated the agreement of September signed between William Henry Drayton and Colonel Thomas Fletchall (who was already a prisoner of Richardson).[87]

Colonel Richardson reported just a few days after the declaration that many Tories had responded positively to it and had turned in their weapons. He noted that since they "have not been capital offenders, I dismiss [them] with soft words and cheerful countenances, and admonish them to use their interest with their friends and neighbors, which seems to have a good effect."[88] Richardson then bragged that "Our army which is now formidable strikes terror, and the opposite party have hitherto fled before us, keeping fifteen or twenty miles distant."[89]

Ten days after this report, Colonel Richardson sent an update to Henry Laurens and the Committee of Safety. Five hundred militia from North Carolina had joined him as well as several other South Carolina units, and he informed the committee that his force numbered somewhere between four to five thousand men, which struck terror among the loyalists in the backcountry. He added that the "principal aggressors" had fled to Cherokee territory, but he sent Colonel Thomson with 1,300 mounted rangers and infantry after them.[90] With it being so late in the season, Richardson expressed concern for the hardships the troops faced: "The men, from their precipitate collecting and marching, [poorly] provided, no tents, shoes wore out, and badly clothed, make it very difficult to keep them here."[91]

As he finished his letter, a messenger arrived from Colonel Thomas with good news: "P.S. This minute, since, or while I was writing my name, a messenger from Colonel Thomson and the detachments arrived with the agreeable account, that they had surprised and taken the camp of Cunningham, and taken the greatest part prisoners."[92]

The Battle of Canes Brake near the Reedy River was a decisive Whig victory. The forces of Colonel Thomson caught up with Colonel Cunningham's small force of Tories before sunrise and lay on their arms until dawn.[93] Catching the Tories by surprise, the Whigs easily routed them and captured about 130 prisoners, but not Colonel Cunningham. A somewhat-amused Colonel Richardson noted that "Patrick Cunningham escaped on a horse bare backed (and they say without breeches) telling every man to shift for himself."[94] Richardson added that he only suffered one man wounded while the Tories had five or six men killed.[95]

The next day, as they prepared to march the prisoners to Charlestown, it started to snow and it did not stop for thirty hours. Nearly two feet of snow fell upon Richardson's men, creating miserable conditions which, noted Richardson, "with the hardship and fatigue the men had suffered before made them very uneasy."[96] With no way to relieve their suffering, Colonel Richardson dismissed all of the North Carolina troops and many of the South Carolina troops on Christmas Day. He then began the march back to Charlestown with the remainder of his force and the captured prisoners. He informed the Committee of Safety that for "Eight days we never set foot on the earth or had a place to lie down, till we had spaded or grabbed away the snow, from which circumstance many are frost bitten, some very badly; and on the third day a heavy cold rain fell, together with sleet, and melted the snow and filled every creek and river with a deluge of water."[97]

The ordeal, which ended on January 2 with their arrival at an encampment on the Congaree River, would be remembered as the Snow Campaign.

In Charlestown, much of the attention of South Carolina's political leaders in December was focused upon the British warships in the harbor. The arrival of the HMS *Scorpion* with Governor Martin of North Carolina on it at the end of November likely alarmed the South Carolina Council of Safety, but nothing came of its presence and it departed by mid-December.

GEORGIA

Two weeks after the Continental Congress authorized the formation of one continental battalion for Georgia, the colony's provincial congress convened in Savannah. Unaware of the decision in Philadelphia, the delegates passed resolutions on the militia and courts and then adjourned, leaving the Council of Safety (which the provincial congress created) to assume the reins of government. The council learned of the continental battalion on December 19 but postponed action on it until the start of the new year.[98]

A more urgent matter for the council arose at almost the same time Georgia's delegates from the Continental Congress had returned from Philadelphia. A few days earlier the South Carolina Council of Safety had written to the Georgia council concerning reports of ships loading produce for shipment to Britain: "Gentlemen, The Council of Safety have heard, with astonishment and concern, that several vessels are loading at Savannah for Great Britain; some with rice, and others . . . with indigo."[99]

The concerned South Carolinians sought clarity on the matter, hoping the report was untrue, but if it was accurate, they urged the Georgians to "take the most effectual measures for preventing so flagrant a breach of the Continental Association."[100]

The Georgia council responded quickly to the letter, sending two representatives to Charlestown to assure the council that they had "put a stop to such proceedings by obliging those concerned to unload one ship, and deterring our enemies from taking such pernicious steps in the future."[101]

While this drama unfolded between the two Councils of Safety, Governor Wright wrote a revealing letter to Lord Dartmouth, lamenting the caliber of Georgia's new leaders:

> In this Province my Lord we are more unhappily Circumstanced, than in any other, for there are very few, Men of real Abilities, Gentlemen or Men of Property in their Tribunals. The Parochial Committees are a Parcel of the Lowest People Chiefly Carpenters, Shoemakers, Blacksmiths etc. with a Few at their Head in the General Committee and Council of Safety, there are some better Sort of Men and Some Merchants and Planters, but many of the Inferior Class and it is really Terrible my Lord that Such People Should be Suffered to Overturn the Civil Government . . . and Sport with Other Men's Lives, Liberty and Property.[102]

In just a matter of weeks, Governor Wright would learn first hand just how terrible the experience was.

EAST FLORIDA

Governor Patrick Tonyn of East Florida turned his attention to negotiations with the Creek and Seminole Indians in late November, sailing up the Florida coast approximately thirty-five miles to the St. John River.[103] Meeting near what is now the city of Jacksonville, Tonyn sought to assure the Indians that, despite Britain's dispute with her colonists, trade and good relations would continue between the loyal colonists of East Florida and their Indian neighbors.

News from Georgia and South Carolina in early December alarmed Governor Tonyn, and he sent word to Lieutenant John Graves of the HMS *Saint Lawrence* that an armed rebel cruiser was seen near the mouth of the St. John River that threatened to disrupt the meeting with the Indians. Expecting Lieutenant Graves to confront the cruiser, the governor offered to place the few troops of the 14th Regiment that were still in East Florida aboard the *Saint Lawrence* and a smaller provincial vessel "in order to attend you and render such Service as may be within her power."[104] The show of force apparently worked, as two days later the meeting successfully concluded and Governor Tonyn boarded the *Saint Lawrence* for the quick trip back to St. Augustine.[105]

A welcome surprise awaited the governor at St. Augustine; the missing troops of the 16th Regiment had arrived during his absence. Relieved that they were finally accounted for, but disappointed in their numbers, Governor Tonyn dashed off a quick note to London. "I have the honour to enclose a Return of [the 16th Regiment]; your Lordship will by it, see the very weak State of this Province, of the 68 Present, there is eleven sick, when the 14th Regiment, or rather the remains of it that are here, shall leave this Province."[106]

A handful of additional troops from Pensacola were expected to follow (there was not enough room for them on the vessels that brought the sixty-eight men), but Governor Tonyn was uneasy and hoped that Lord Dartmouth would allow the remnants of the 14th Regiment (approximately one hundred and twenty officers and men) to remain at St. Augustine with the 16th Regiment.[107]

Events in Boston and Philadelphia in December made Tonyn's need for the remaining troops of the 14th Regiment in St. Augustine all the more critical, for the ship carrying Moses Kirkwood, along with the letters of John Stuart and Governor Tonyn, to Boston, was seized by an American ship and delivered first to General Washington and then to the Continental Congress. Describing Kirkland as "a dangerous fellow," Washington seemed more interested in the opportunity presented by the weak condition of St. Augustine (and particularly the large amount of gunpowder stored in the fort) than General Gage's plan to turn loose their Native American allies on the frontier.[108]

Congress took up the matter of St. Augustine on January 1, 1776, and "earnestly recommended to the colonies of South Carolina, North Carolina, and Georgia to undertake the reduction of St. Augustine, if it be thought practicable."[109] They, of course, had other pressing matters to contend with in the winter of 1776.

Part II
1776

Five

Winter

AT THE START OF 1776, BOTH GENERAL WASHINGTON AND THE Continental Congress waited anxiously for word on the American efforts in Canada. When it finally arrived in late January, the news was not good. The bold American attempt to capture Quebec had failed and cost a promising officer, General Richard Montgomery. A loose siege of the city continued under Colonel Benedict Arnold, who himself was recovering from a leg wound, but the best chance to seize Quebec from the British had failed, and soon the American army in Canada would be in retreat.

The situation in Massachusetts remained relatively stagnant until the end of winter when Colonel Henry Knox arrived from Fort Ticonderoga with heavy cannon that his detachment had dragged across the Berkshire Mountains to be used in Boston. General Washington placed the cannon upon the heights of Dorchester in early March, and within days the British negotiated an agreement with Washington for them to evacuate the city. General Howe decided to withdraw to Halifax, Nova Scotia, to regroup and await reinforcements coming from across the ocean rather than engage in a bloody assault upon Dorchester Heights.

On the political front, no progress whatsoever had been made toward reconciliation. In fact, British policies hardened against all of the colonies. It was clear by the start of 1776 that the dispute between Great Britain and her colonies was to be settled on the battlefield, not the negotiating table.

VIRGINIA

The situation in Virginia in December had swung dramatically in the Virginians' favor thanks to their decisive victory at Great Bridge and Dunmore's evacuation of Norfolk. The good news continued two weeks after the battle when Captain James Barron of Hampton scored a small naval victory over one of Dunmore's tenders off of Hampton (capturing its crew of seventeen) and also seized two vessels loaded with salt, a commodity that was in desperately short supply in Virginia.[1] The Committee of Safety in Williamsburg was so impressed with Captain Barron that it authorized him to fit out three armed vessels.[2]

Fostering a fledgling navy was not the only thing Virginia's leaders in Williamsburg had done to strengthen their military capabilities. In mid-December, the Fourth Virginia Convention, meeting in Williamsburg, expanded the colony's infantry forces from two regiments of regulars to nine and increased the length of service for the seven hundred men of each regiment to two years.[3] By the spring, all nine of these regiments were taken into continental service.

The convention also issued a stinging reply to Dunmore's November proclamation of martial law, asserting that he had assumed powers, "which the king himself cannot exercise," had no real interest in reconciling with the colonies, and was "one of the principal causes of the misfortunes under which we now labour."[4] The convention indicted Dunmore as a "rigid executioner" of "that system of tyranny adopted by the ministry and parliament" and proclaimed that Dunmore "ever zealous in support of tyranny . . . hath broken the bonds of society, and trampled justice under his feet."[5]

In addition to the long-standing charges against Dunmore of pillaging, plundering, and illegal seizure of property and slaves was a new accusation. The convention accused Dunmore of devising a scheme with his aide, Dr. John Connolly, to encourage the Native Americans in the west to enter the conflict as Dunmore's allies and sweep down upon northern Virginia in April to unite with Dunmore in Alexandria.[6] Connolly's capture by Maryland authorities in the fall of 1775 ended this scheme, but the fact that Dunmore was willing to employ indigenous people (in addition to runaway slaves) against the colonists was one more reason many Virginians wished the governor harm.

Even General Washington, stuck in the siege lines outside of Boston, recognized the danger of allowing Dunmore to continue to operate in Virginia. In a letter to Richard Henry Lee written the day after Christmas, Washington candidly shared his views on what should happen to Lord Dunmore:

> If, my Dear Sir, that Man [Dunmore] is not crushed before Spring, he will become the most formidable Enemy America has—his strength will Increase as a Snow ball by Rolling; and faster, if some expedient cannot be hit upon to convince the Slaves and Servants of the Impotency of His designs . . . I do not think that forcing his Lordship on Ship board is sufficient; nothing less than depriving him of life or liberty will secure peace to Virginia.[7]

For the time being, Lord Dunmore was safe, protected in Norfolk Harbor by the guns of the British navy, specifically, the thirty-six-gun *Liverpool*, eighteen-gun *King Fisher*, sixteen-gun *Otter*, the *Dunmore* (formerly *Eilbeck*, number of guns unknown), a sloop with eight guns, and six or seven tenders armed with a few three- and four-pounder cannon and swivel guns. Scores of other vessels were also anchored in the harbor, sheltering Tory refugees who had nowhere else to go.[8]

Like Lord Dunmore and the miserable inhabitants of the floating Tory town in the Elizabeth River, Captain Bellew of the *Liverpool* and Captain Squire of the *Otter* were increasingly annoyed by the daily harassment of the rebels onshore in the form of random small arms fire at the ships and daily formations and sentinels in full view of the harbor. Numerous warnings to curtail the provocations were sent ashore under flags of truce, but the conduct continued. Finally, in late December, Captain Bellew issued an ultimatum: "As I hold it incompatible with the Honor of my Commission to suffer Men in Arms against their Sovereign and the Laws, to appear before His Majesty's Ships I desire you will cause your Centinels in the Town of Norfolk to avoid being seen, that Women and Children may not feel the effects of their Audacity, and it would not be imprudent if both were to leave the Town."[9]

Captain Bellew's request, and his threat, were clear. Rebel sentinels onshore had chided, insulted, and fired upon the ships in the harbor long enough. Either the harassment stopped, or Norfolk would be bombarded.

Colonel Howe replied immediately to Captain Bellew's ultimatum with an assurance that the sentinels had been instructed to avoid any insulting behavior, and if any were guilty of such conduct, he agreed that they should be punished for it. But, continued Colonel Howe, "if . . . you feel it your duty to make your resentment extend farther than merely as to them, we should wish that the Inhabitants of this Town, who have nothing to do in this matter, may have time to remove with their Effects which to Night they have not."[10]

The next day—the last of 1775—passed incident free, but on New Year's Day, rebel sentinels paraded before the harbor with their hats on their bayonets, taunting the British.[11] Captain Bellew, aboard the *Liverpool*, responded:

On the 1st Janry at 3 o'Clock in the Afternoon . . . their Centinels, came to the Wharf very near me, from their Guard House, which was close to it, and used every mark of insult; I then ordered three Guns to be fired into the House, it had its effect by setting them running; my Lord Dunmore sent (under those Guns) his Boats Arm'd to fetch off a Long boat they had taken from him, whose People set fire to some Store houses, which burnt a good number of Houses, the Rebels have since destroyed the greatest part of the Town.[12]

Colonel Howe's account of the bombardment was similar, except he placed the blame for the destruction of the city upon the British:

> The cannonade of the town began about a quarter after three yesterday, from upwards of one hundred pieces of cannon, and continued till near ten at night, without intermission; it then abated a little, and continued till two this morning. Under cover of their guns they landed and set fire to the town in several places near the water, though our men strove to prevent them all in their power; but the houses near the water being chiefly of wood, they took fire immediately, and the fire spread with amazing rapidity. It is now become general, and the whole town will, I doubt not, be consumed in a day or two . . . . The burning of the town has made several avenues, which yesterday they had [not], so that they now may fire with greater effect. The tide is now rising and we expect at high water another cannonade. I have only to wish it may be as ineffectual as the last; for we have not one man killed, and but a few wounded. I cannot enter into the melancholy consideration of the women and children running through a crowd of shot to get out of the town, some of them with children at their breasts, a few have, I hear, been killed.[13]

In Colonel Howe's account, the fire that destroyed Norfolk was set in several places near the water and spread rapidly because of all of the wooden structures. A number of other accounts from both sides of the engagement suggest that the fires set by Dunmore's men quickly spread throughout the city, but Lord Dunmore claimed that the offshore wind (which blew toward the water) prevented the fires set along the shore from spreading to the rest of the city and placed the blame for the destruction of Norfolk upon the rebels:

> The Vessels from the Fleet to shew their Zeal for His Majesty's Service, sent great Numbers of Boats on Shore, by which means the fire soon became general on the Wharfs, the wind rather blowing off Shore would have prevented the fire from reaching any farther than the Wharfs, but the Rebels so soon as the Men of War ceased firing, and our People came off, put the finishing Stroke to

it, by Setting fire to every House, which has given them employ-
ment for these two days past, they have also burnt many houses
on both sides of the River, the property of individuals who have
never taken any part in this contest, in Short from every transac-
tion they appear to me to have nothing more at heart, than the
utter destruction of this once most flourishing Country, Conscious
I suppose that they cannot long enjoy it themselves, they wish to
make it of as little use as possible to others.[14]

Dunmore's claim that the "rebels" actually burned the bulk of
Norfolk was dismissed by most Virginians as a lie, but an official inquiry of the incident in 1777 (which was not made public for over
sixty years) concluded that Dunmore's claim was correct.[15]

Months of anger at the residents of Norfolk for their cooperation
with, and in many cases outright support for, Dunmore erupted into
a combustible fury, and although no one admitted it publicly, Norfolk was looted and burned to the ground by the soldiers under
Colonel Howe and Woodford, some of whom shouted, "Keep up the
Jigg! Keep up the Jigg!" as they torched building after building.[16]
Nearly nine hundred structures were destroyed over three days, and
the destruction spread across the river to the shipyard and ware-
houses in Gosport.[17] Colonel Woodford confirmed the extent of damage, reporting that nine tenths of Norfolk was destroyed.[18]

Unfortunately for Lord Dunmore, the accounts of the devastation
that appeared in the gazettes laid the blame upon the governor and
his naval lackeys:

> It was a shocking scene to see the poor women and children, run-
> ning about through the fire, and exposed to the guns from the
> ships, and some of them with children at their breasts. Let our
> countrymen view and contemplate the scene! . . . The cannonade
> had lasted twenty five hours when the express came away, and the
> flames were raging (it being impossible to extinguish them on ac-
> count of the heavy fire from the ships) and had consumed two
> thirds of the town. . . . It is affirmed that one hundred cannon
> played on the town almost incessantly for twenty five hours.[19]

The destruction of Norfolk did not mean an end to the fighting. The combatants remained where they were, Lord Dunmore's force onboard ships just offshore from the smoldering ruins of Norfolk and Colonel Howe's troops on the outskirts and amongst the ruins of the city. Heated skirmishes occasionally erupted whenever Dunmore sent landing parties ashore and both sides suffered casualties, but for most of January the two sides shared the common misery of a winter encampment—wet, cold weather, and limited provisions and supplies.

It was no secret that Colonel Howe and Colonel Woodford wanted to abandon Norfolk and, in doing so, burn what was left of the city to deny its use to Dunmore. Both officers stressed to the Committee of Safety—before and after Norfolk was burned—that it was dangerous for their force to remain at Norfolk; they ran the risk of being cut off by British reinforcements.[20] Colonel Howe went to Williamsburg in mid-January to report to the convention and gain their approval to withdraw from Norfolk. On January 15, the Virginia convention relented, recommending that Norfolk be evacuated.[21] The rebels departed on February 6, the bulk heading to Suffolk with detachments posted at Kemp's Landing and Great Bridge to block access and provisions from reaching Dunmore.[22] Before the troops left, they torched the remaining buildings of Norfolk, over four hundred of them.[23]

Within a week, Lord Dunmore, covered by the frigate HMS *Roebuck* (44 guns, 280 crew), which sailed into Norfolk Harbor three days after Howe and Woodford marched to Suffolk, landed troops onto Tucker's Point (adjacent to Portsmouth and across the river from Norfolk). They immediately began digging wells to replenish their critically low supply of fresh water. A windmill and a few buildings stood on the point, damaged but not destroyed in all of the conflict, and Dunmore converted some of them to barracks to house his growing number of smallpox cases.[24] Earthworks were erected and ovens were built to supply bread.[25] It was clear that Lord Dunmore, the most despised man in Virginia, had no intention of leaving the colony.

NORTH CAROLINA

While the situation in Virginia settled into an uneasy stalemate, the arrival of the HMS *Syren* (28 guns, 160 crew) in the Cape Fear River on January 3 signaled the beginning of Governor Martin's long-hoped-for operation to restore royal authority in North Carolina.[26] Martin had actually begun the process prior to the *Syren*'s arrival by encouraging his loyalist supporters to secretly organize themselves in December.[27] Concerned at the start of 1776 that his communication with loyalist leaders had been compromised and his plans revealed, the arrival of the *Syren*, with confirmation of a planned British expedition in the South from Lord Germain, convinced Governor Martin that it was time to proceed openly.

The *Syren* was the lead element of a powerful British fleet and army heading to North Carolina, and word of the frigate's arrival surely alarmed the Whigs in North Carolina. Determined to inspire all loyalists and many fence sitters to act, Governor Martin issued a proclamation on January 10 that instructed all loyal subjects to rally to the king's standard and put down the traitorous rebellion that had gone on for too long:

> Whereas a most daring, horrid, and unnatural Rebellion has been
> exerted in the Province against His Majesty's Government, by the
> base and insidious artifices of certain traitorous, wicked, and de-
> signing men, and the same is now openly avowed and declared,
> and actually threatens the sole subversion of the laws and Consti-
> tution of the said Province, and the liberties and privileges of His
> Majesty's subjects, inhabitants thereof, I have thought fit to issue
> this Proclamation, hereby to signify to all His Majesty's liege sub-
> jects within this Province, that I find it necessary, for the safety and
> preservation of the rights, civil and religious, and for the mainte-
> nance of His Majesty's government against the said desperate un-
> natural Rebellion, to erect His Majesty's Royal standard, and to
> collect and unite the forces of His Majesty's people under the same,
> for the purpose of resisting and subduing, with the assistance of
> the Almighty, the said impious and unnatural Rebellion, and to re-
> store the just rights of His Majesty's Crown and Government and

the liberties of his people; and I do, hereby, exhort, require, and command, in the King's name, all His Majesty's faithful subjects, on their duty and allegiance, forthwith to repair to the Royal standard, hereby promising and assuring every aid, encouragement, and support to all such as shall come to vindicate and support the violated laws and Constitution of their country; and at the same time pronouncing all such Rebels as will not join the Royal banner, Rebels and Traitors; their lives and properties to be forfeited. All such as will join shall be forgiven any past offenses.[28]

Governor Martin issued commissions to a long list of Tory leaders after the proclamation, instructing them to "Erect the King's standard, and to raise, levy, muster, and array in arms, all His Majesty's loyal and faithful subjects."[29] Tory leaders were authorized to select company officers and seize whatever arms, ammunition, provisions, and horses they needed (with the intention of reimbursing only loyal subjects for the seized items).[30] Their instructions from the governor were simple: "Resist and oppose all Rebels and Traitors against His Majesty and his Government by force of arms, and . . . apprehend, seize, and detain them, their accomplices and abetters."[31]

Governor Martin desired that the Tory leaders select a convenient rendezvous site and then march as one body to the Cape Fear River, timing their movement to arrive on February 15.[32]

Martin chose Donald McDonald to command the Tory forces with the rank of brigadier general. McDonald was actually a major in the British army who had arrived in North Carolina in July 1775 with Captain Donald McLeod to recruit Highlanders for a new loyalist regiment. McDonald and McLeod had convinced the Committee of Safety in New Bern upon their arrival that they had left the British army after being wounded at Bunker Hill and wished only to seek out friends and relatives in North Carolina to settle among them.[33] They were apparently very convincing, for the committee released them with just a warning, and their loyalist activities during the rest of 1775 went undetected.

Generous offers of land grants (two hundred acres), quitrent exemptions, pay and compensation for personal items such as horses and wagons, and weapons were offered as inducements to join the Tory ranks.[34] The last item offered, weapons, went largely unfulfilled for many, however. By mid-February approximately 1,400 Tories had gathered at Cross Creek, but nearly two thirds of them lacked a firearm—musket or rifle.[35]

North Carolina's Whig forces, on the other hand, were generally equipped with firearms but lacked an adequate supply of gunpowder and lead. Both Virginia and South Carolina responded to appeals from North Carolina for gunpowder in early February.[36]

Colonel James Moore, the commander of the 1st North Carolina Continental Regiment, commanded the Whig forces that assembled in February in response to the growing Tory threat. While the Tories gathered at Cross Creek, Colonel Moore posted his force of several hundred men, with five cannon, at Rockfish Creek, just seven miles away, hoping to block their movement south. Moore also sent word for several militia units to join him at Rock Creek, and by February 19 he had 1,100 men under his direct command.[37]

McDonald had marched his Tory force from Cross Creek to within four miles of Colonel Moore the day before and on February 19 sent a message to Moore giving him until noon the next day to rally to the king's standard as Governor Martin's proclamation demanded.[38]

Colonel Moore, of course, had no intention of doing so, but he delayed his response in hopes that reinforcements, which he knew were marching, would soon arrive. At noon on February 20 Colonel Moore rejected McDonald's demand and waited for the Tory commander to attack.

McDonald, who was aware that rebel reinforcements were moving toward him from all directions, decided to avoid a battle and marched eastward, unnoticed by Moore until the next day. Colonel Moore scrambled to cut the Tories off. He ordered Colonel Richard Caswell, who was marching from New Bern to join Moore with eight hundred men, to go instead to Corbett's Ferry on the Black River to guard that likely crossing point. Colonel James Martin and Colonel James Thackston were ordered to occupy Cross Creek with their militia troops. Colonel Alexander Lillington with 150 Wilmington minutemen and Colonel James Ashe with 100 volunteer riflemen were sent on a forced march to reinforce Caswell, but if they were unable to do so in time, they were ordered to secure Moores Creek Bridge. Colonel Moore marched his force to Elizabeth Town, hoping to intercept the Tories on the march to Corbett's Ferry.[39]

For a moment it looked like the long-anticipated battle was to be at Corbett's Ferry on the Black River where Colonel Caswell waited with eight hundred entrenched militia on the east bank to oppose a Tory crossing. When the Tories got within a few miles of the ferry crossing they learned what awaited them, and McDonald ordered his troops to prepare for battle. He then learned of the location of a sunken flat (a raft used to cross the river) and ordered it retrieved so he could cross his force above the rebel militia and attack them from the rear and flank. While the bulk of McDonald's force slowly crossed the river, a party of troops, accompanied by several men with drums and bagpipes, marched to Corbett's Ferry, careful to remain hidden in the woods and brush, and commenced to "amuse Caswell as if the Army meant to cross the River and force his entrenchments. They kept firing [and presumably playing their instruments] most of the day which kept Caswell and his men in Camp."[40]

The crossing took most of the night to complete, during which Colonel Caswell became aware of the danger and withdrew from his now vulnerable position, marching southeast to Moores Creek Bridge. General McDonald settled for sending a party through the abandoned rebel camp in the morning where they found some horses and provisions left behind from the precipitate rebel withdrawal.[41]

Colonel Caswell reached Moores Creek Bridge in the afternoon of February 26, bringing the Whig troops posted there to over a thousand men.[42] Colonel Lillington and his 150 men were encamped behind hastily built breastworks on the east side of the creek and bridge, which was partially dismantled with the removal of a number of planks. Colonel Caswell initially encamped to the west of the creek but changed his mind in the evening and joined Colonel Lillington on the east side of the creek.[43] It was a wise decision; Moores Creek was a very effective obstacle. The creek was approximately fifty feet wide at the site of the dismantled bridge, with approximately five feet of water covering a slick, muddy bottom. Swampy ground north-west of the creek funneled travelers toward the bridge, which the Tories would have to use to get across Moores Creek.

McDonald led his men toward Moores Creek Bridge on February 27, encamping about six miles northwest of it. He repeated his ploy of sending a messenger to the rebel camp to demand their surrender knowing full well that they would not. Intelligence is what McDonald desired, so he sent his secretary, James Hepburn, with his message. Colonel Caswell had not yet moved across the creek when Hepburn arrived, so when Hepburn returned to the Tory camp, he informed General McDonald that the rebels were deployed on the same side of the creek as the Tories with the bridge and creek to their back. It was thus "very Practicable to attack them." [44]

The news was too good to be true, and of course it was, for while Hepburn reported his observations, Colonel Caswell moved his men to the other side of the creek, leaving his campfires burning. The entire Whig force of over a thousand men, along with a cannon and swivel gun nicknamed "Old Mother Covington and her daughter," now waited behind breastworks on the east bank of Moores Creek for the Tories to arrive. [45]

General McDonald and the other Tory officers agreed that the rebels should be attacked directly, but the Tory commander was too ill to participate, so command of the attack devolved to Captain Donald McLeod. The Tories stepped off from their encampment, six miles from the dismantled bridge, at 1 a.m. with eight hundred men. [46] They reached the outskirts of the abandoned Whig breastworks an hour before dawn and separated into two wings to attack. [47] Captain McLeod led the right wing of the Tory force and observed campfires burning to his front. An unidentified Tory officer recalled, "Upon our entering the Ground of their Encampment, we found their fires beginning to turn weak and Concluded that the Enemy were marched." [48] McLeod and the officers with him decided to pull back and inform General McDonald of the Whig's withdrawal. The rallying cry "King George and Broad Swords" was whispered among them as they waited.

While Captain McLeod and the Tory right wing halted, the left wing looped around the abandoned Whig camp, passed through it, and sent an advance party toward the bridge, unaware of the right wing's withdrawal.[49] A Tory officer explained what occurred next:

Mr. McLean with a party of about 40 men came Accidently to the Bridge, he being a Stranger and it being still dark. He was challenged by the Enemies' Centinels [typically with a shouted question, 'Who goes there?'] they observing him sooner than he observed them. He answered that he was a friend; they asked to whom? He being a stranger, he replied to the King. Upon his making this reply they squatted down upon their faces to the Ground. Mr. McLean, uncertain but they might be some of our own people that had crossed the Bridge, challenged them in [Gaelic] to which they made no Answer. Upon which he fired his own piece and ordered his party to fire.[50]

Captain McLeod rushed forward with the right wing and immediately ordered an advance across the dismantled bridge. Three cheers rang out from the Tories, and drummers and bagpipers started up, encouraging the troops forward.[51] A picked detachment of Scotsmen, armed with only broadswords, was sent forward and carefully made their way in the dark onto the beams of the bridge, which were coated with soap and tallow by the Whigs to make them slick.[52] As the troops arrived on the other side, they charged forward believing they had the Whigs on the run. They were met instead by a devastating barrage of small arms and cannon fire.

Captain McLeod had joined the lead element across the bridge and was pummeled by the rebel fire, which was point blank in his face. The carnage was shocking and described by Colonel James Moore, who arrived a few hours after the battle:

The tory army, with Cap. McLeod at their head, made their attack on Col. Caswell and Col. Lillington . . . in the most furious manner [and] advanced within thirty paces of our breastwork and artillery, where they met a very proper reception. Captain McLeod and Captain Campbell fell within a few paces of the breast-work, the former of whom received upwards of twenty balls through his body, and in a very few minutes their whole army was put to flight.[53]

The brevity of the fight and the panic it produced among the Tories was confirmed in another account shared in a letter two weeks after the battle. "The Insurgents retreated with the greatest precipitation, leaving behind them some wagons etc. They cut the horses out of the wagons, and mounted three upon a horse. Many of them fell into the creek, and were drowned. . . . The battle lasted only three minutes."[54]

Ignoring their officers commands to stand their ground, many Tories fled into the swampy ground northwest of the creek, desperate to return to their camp six miles away. Realizing that the battle was lost, the surviving officers and men followed them, and when they arrived at their camp they found it in disarray. Most of the provisions and many of the men were missing, and those still in camp refused to listen to the officers.[55] A hasty officer's council was held where it was determined that "It [was] needless to persist any longer in endeavouring to keep the Army together, therefore [the council] thought it adviseable to destroy the Ammunition to prevent its falling to the Enemys hand."[56]

Although the Tory officers ended their march to the Cape Fear River, they hoped to get the men that were still with them back to the interior of the colony where they could disperse to perhaps fight another day.[57] General McDonald, too ill to move, remained behind and was captured by Whig forces soon after his men departed. Most of his men met the same fate several days later when they encountered mounted Whig militia north of Cross Creek along the Black River who demanded their surrender.[58] Defeated and dispirited, they complied.

Colonel Moore with the main body of Whig troops arrived at Moores Creek Bridge a few hours after the battle and reported that the enemy lost thirty men killed and wounded but added that a number had fallen into the creek and others were carried off, so the enemy losses were likely closer to seventy.[59] Whig losses were two, one wounded and one who died of his wounds the following day.[60] More

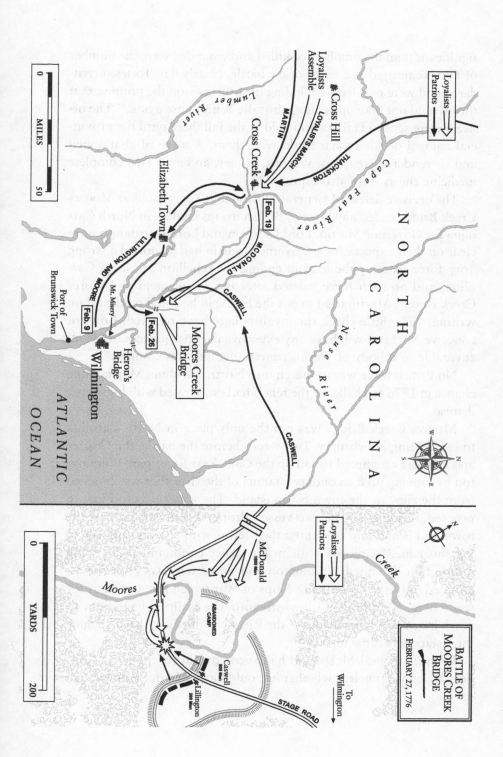

significant than the numbers of killed and wounded were the number of Tories captured as a result of the battle. Nearly 850 Tories surrendered and were paroled—excluding the officers—on the promise that they would not take up arms against the Whig cause again.[61] The officers were sent to Halifax and held in the jail there until the provincial council decided what to do with them. A trove of abandoned and surrendered weapons, wagons, money, and even two complete medicine chests were also captured.[62]

The decisive defeat of General McDonald's Tory troops at Moores Creek Bridge ended any hope of British troops landing in North Carolina for Governor Martin. Lord Germain and Lord Dartmouth were clear on their expectations; Governor Martin had promised a strong Tory force to carry the load in ending the rebellion in North Carolina, and no such force existed after the engagement at Moores Creek Bridge. Martin tried to put the best spin he could on the affair, writing, "The little check the loyalists here have received, I do not conceive My Lord will have any extensive ill consequences. All is recoverable by a body of Troops penetrating into this country."[63]

No British force was to march into North Carolina. Martin's one chance in 1776 to challenge the rebels had evaporated with his army's demise.

Moores Creek Bridge was not the only place in North Carolina to see fighting in February. Two weeks before the battle, the *Cruizer* and a tender attempted to sail up the Cape Fear River past Wilmington by moving up a secondary channel of the river that was blocked from the view of the town by an island. The water was too low to proceed, however, so the two vessels dropped downstream past the town and island and contented themselves with several raids along the shoreline.[64] Colonel William Purviance commanded the Whig militia that defended Wilmington and noted ten days after the attempted movement that "The Ships of War which threatened us for some time, are all fallen [downstream]. The [sailors] have been so much harassed on both sides of the River by Riflemen, that I imagine their station became uneasy."[65]

Even if General McDonald had succeeded in reaching the Cape Fear River, it is unclear whether he could have held out long enough for the British expedition to arrive. The main force was months behind schedule. Delayed by contrary winds, General Cornwallis and most of the British troops did not arrive off the coast of North Carolina until early May, seven weeks after General Clinton arrived from Boston with just two companies of British light infantry and over ten weeks after Governor Martin had expected him. By May, General Clinton's focus had turned squarely to Charlestown, South Carolina, in part because of what happened at Moores Creek Bridge.

SOUTH CAROLINA

Through much of the winter of 1776 it appeared that the conflict with Great Britain had all but ended in South Carolina. To the north, Tory troops marched to their defeat at Moores Creek, and to the south, British ships gathered in the Savannah River, but in Charlestown and throughout South Carolina, there was little activity of significance. The outcome of the Canes Brake fight in late December appeared to have extinguished loyalist sentiment and activity in South Carolina.

Three weeks before that skirmish, the South Carolina Council of Safety ordered the establishment of an artillery battery on Haddrell's Point, north of Charlestown overlooking the harbor and the British vessels within.[66] It took nearly three weeks to prepare the material (not to mention haul the four eighteen-pounder cannon that were to make up the battery into place), but on the evening of December 20, a detachment of South Carolina continentals marched to Haddrell's Point and within hours constructed an artillery battery.[67] The night before, a party of South Carolina rangers landed on Sullivan's Island where, according to Governor Campbell, they "burned the only house upon [the island], consumed the little [provisions] of three poor families who had taken refuge there, carried off the people with two men belonging to the *Cherokee* who were ashore watering & destroyed their Casks."[68] Not surprisingly, the Whig account of the raid was significantly different:

> Lord William Campbell had gone to great lengths in harbouring and protecting negroes on Sullivan's Island, from whence those villains made nightly sallies, and committed robberies and depre-

dations on the sea-coast of Christ-Church. This alarming evil received such a check yesterday morning, as will serve to humble
our negroes in general. . . . The company of foot rangers, or fifty-
four of them . . . made a descent on that island, burnt the house
in which the banditti were often lodged, brought off four negroes,
killed three or four, and also took white prisoners, four men, three
women, and three children, destroyed many things which had
been useful to those wretches in the houses, men of war's water
casks, a great loss to them, exchanged a few shot with some of
the men of war's men, and came off unhurt.[69]

The activities on Sullivan's Island had become a significant point
of contention for the Council of Safety, so much so that just prior to
the raid on the island, the council informed Captain Thornbrough
of the *Tamar* that, since the British navy was harboring runaway
slaves and allowing robberies and depredations to be committed
upon the inhabitants of the coastline by both White and Black assailants operating from Sullivan's Island, they were determined to cut
off all communication and provisions between the shore and the
ships.[70] Amazingly, up until this point, the British navy had continued
to receive fresh water and foodstuffs and other provisions purchased
through an agent on shore. South Carolina's leaders put a stop to
this and enhanced their ability to enforce the ban by building the artillery battery on Haddrell's Point.

The embargo on provisions implemented by the Whigs had a
strong impact on the British in Charlestown Harbor, and by the end
of the year the small British squadron decided to sail from
Charlestown to Savannah to reprovision there. Georgia's leaders
were warned by the South Carolina Council of Safety to expect the
British ships:

The *Tamar*, *Cherokee*, *Sandwich* packet, and an armed schooner
made sail this morning in Rebellion Road, and attempted to go
over the bar, but the wind failing, they all came to an anchor
again. From undoubted intelligence, we learn they are intended
for your river, in order to obtain provisions (of bread particularly)

which since the practice of harbouring and protecting our negroes on board the *Cherokee*, we have refused to supply them with.[71]

The weather delayed their departure to sea until January 6, but on that date they crossed the sandbar outside of Charlestown and were on their way.[72]

In the absence of the governor and British navy, the South Carolina Council of Safety ordered troops to take possession of Sullivan's Island and construct a fort upon it to better guard the shipping channel and harbor of Charlestown.[73] The eighteen-pounder cannon at Haddrell's Point were moved to Sullivan's Island and twelve-pounder guns took their place.[74] The move, and the construction of the fort, would prove very fortuitous in the months to come.

GEORGIA

Savannah was a wise choice for Captain Thornbrough and his small British naval force to seek provisions. It was a short sail from Charlestown, likely well stocked with foodstuffs, and there was every expectation that the Georgians, some of whom tried to ship produce to England and the West Indies just a few weeks earlier, would eagerly sell their provisions to the British navy.

Word of the British ships sailing for Savannah reached Georgia's capital before the ships did, and the Council of Safety reacted by calling out one third of the militia.[75] The council had to rely on the militia because very little progress had been made recruiting the continental battalion authorized by the Continental Congress the previous fall. In at least one case, however, the willingness of the militia to serve proved no better when an entire company from St. Matthew's Parish refused to comply with the council's order to muster.[76] Whether it was because of loyalist sentiment, fear of the British, or disgruntlement with the Council of Safety is unclear, but such blatant noncompliance had to concern Georgia's Whig leaders.

They had little time to address this problem, however, because the first British warship, the *Tamar*, appeared off the Georgia coast on January 13.[77] The other ships from Charlestown soon joined the *Tamar*, and two days later the *Syren* out of North Carolina and the *Raven* (14 guns, 110 crew) out of Boston as well as a prize ship the

Raven had captured and a transport ship unexpectedly appeared.[78] Governor Wright, who was one of the few royal governors who still resided in his colonial capital, must have been relieved when he heard the news. His counterparts on the Council of Safety were obviously not.

Governor Wright summoned two town representatives and offered to act as an intermediary between the town and the British navy. He explained, "He was certain their orders were to treat any of the Colonies who were in arms, had raised fortifications, seized any of the Crown officers, or King's stores, as in a state of rebellion, and would, if in their power, destroy their towns and property, wherever they would come at them; and, he apprehended, they would look on us as in that state, and, as far as in their power treat us accordingly."[79]

Governor Wright speculated (correctly) that the lack of provisions was what drove the ships to Savannah:

> The *Raven*, man-of-war, was stationed here. That [the ships] were all in want of provisions, particularly the *Tamar*, the *Cherokee*, and the packet, which vessels, as well as the *Syren*, he believed, would depart the Province as soon as they were supplied with provisions. That if he, the Governour, could be assured from the inhabitants of the town that they would supply them with provisions, and permit their boats to come to town unmolested, and purchase such provisions as they can get, that he would go down on board these ships and endeavor to settle every thing with the officers in such a manner as to prevent their doing any injury to this town, or the inhabitants of the Province, or their property.[80]

The governor added,

> That if they could not be supplied with provisions they certainly would take it by force, where they can find it, and will, if in their power, attack this town and destroy it, which, as several of the vessels were of an easy draft of water, he presumed they could get up to town and effect.[81]

Wright's last observation was not an idle threat. The British navy had already burned two colonial towns to the ground, Falmouth in Massachusetts (modern-day Portland, Maine) and Norfolk in Virginia (although they were really not responsible for the destruction of Norfolk). There was also Charlestown in Massachusetts, which was burned during the Battle of Bunker Hill.

The Georgia Council of Safety did not see the situation the same way as the governor. To the council, there was little doubt about what the citizens of Savannah and all of Georgia had to do—deny the British navy any assistance whatsoever. The council in fact, issued an arrest order for Governor Wright and several of his councilors to prevent them from communicating or coordinating with the British commanders. Governor Wright was to be, "Arrested and secured and . . . all non-associates [those who did not publicly or privately support the Whig cause] be forthwith disarmed, except those, who will give their parole [promise] assuring that they will not aid, assist, or comfort any persons on board his Majesty's ships of war or take up arms against America in the present unhappy dispute."[82]

It appears that Governor Wright and his councilors were brought before the Council of Safety in the evening of January 18, but they were released to their homes before midnight, pledging to meet at Wright's residence in the morning. Governor Wright also gave assurance that "the peace of the town shall not be disturbed by any persons from the ships of war," suggesting that the council was concerned that Wright might collaborate with the British naval officers to attack Savannah.[83] To ensure that didn't happen, the council made Governor Wright give his parole of honor "not to go out of Town, or hold any correspondence with [the naval officers] without permission of the Council."[84] A violation of the agreement meant rearrest and confinement under guard. Furthermore, if the British ships appeared before Savannah, Governor Wright and his councilors would be removed to and confined in the country.[85] Governor Wright had essentially become a hostage instead of an intermediary.

Despite such disagreeable treatment from the council, Governor Wright remained determined to prevent a confrontation between the Georgians and the British navy. He sent an envoy to meet with the

British commanders and learned that his assumptions were true, only the *Raven* intended to stay. The other vessels were in need of provisions and repair and would depart as soon as they addressed their needs.[86] Governor Wright informed two of Savannah's leaders (whom he apparently trusted not to report him for violating his parole) of this intelligence, asserting that the inhabitants of Savannah had nothing to fear from the British navy. In fact, it was likely they would not even set eyes on the ships, as they intended to obtain all of the water, provisions, and material to repair their ships from along the coast.

The arrival of the HMS *Scarborough* (20 guns, 150 crew) and HMS *Hinchinbrook* (6 guns, 30 crew) on February 4, followed a week later by two transport ships carrying 175 marines and soldiers from Boston under Major James Grant of the 40th Regiment, changed the situation.[87] The mission of the new arrivals was to load the two transport ships with rice and other provisions for the relief of the British army in Boston, which was in great need of such supplies. It was hoped that Governor Wright could arrange for the purchase of the provisions; Major Grant carried cash and bills of exchange for that purpose. If this proved unsuccessful, however, the navy, with the assistance of Major Grant's marines and soldiers, was to secure the provisions by force.[88]

Approximately twenty private vessels were moored off Savannah a few miles upriver from the British ships. Some were already loaded with rice, and all were detained by the Council of Safety to comply with the directives of the Continental Congress, which forbade the export of any rice until March 1.

Governor Wright's efforts to mediate a peaceful resolution to this new situation were ignored by the Council of Safety, who focused most of their attention on preparing to resist an attempt by the British to seize the ships off of Savannah and destroy the city. Several weeks passed during which a number of enslaved persons along Georgia's coast fled to the British, and landing parties scoured the islands and shore for food, water, and material to repair their ships.

Early in the morning of February 12, Governor Wright fled his residence with his family and, along with several members of his privy council, took refuge aboard the *Scarborough*.[89] The day after his flight, he tried one last time to convince the Council of Safety to conduct "a friendly intercourse [for] a supply of fresh provision" with the navy.[90] He added for emphasis that "As (probably) the best friend the people in Georgia have, [I] advise them, without the least hesitation, to comply with, or it may not be in my power to insure them the continuance of the peace and quietude they now have, if it may be called so."[91]

The council ignored Wright's pleas and refused to allow any commerce with the British navy. Colonel Lachlan McIntosh, the commander of Georgia's lone, incomplete, continental regiment, was given responsibility for the defense of Savannah. Few of his troops were in town (or had been recruited for that matter) so he relied on several hundred militia as well as volunteers from South Carolina to defend the town. He described the challenge to General Washington. "Between 3 & 400 of our Militia & 100 from So. Carolina were all that could be got to defend an open, Straggling, defenseless & deserted Town, with Numberless Avenues Leading to it, and those Men under no Controul or Command whatsoever."[92]

Colonel McIntosh placed guards at all of the likely landing spots and detachments to ambush the British along several roads, and waited. Near the end of February several of the British warships and the two transports crept to "within 2 1/2 Miles of Town, near where we Sunk a Hulk in the Channel of the River," reported McIntosh.[93] They remained in place for several days and occasional shots were exchanged, but no harm resulted from it.

On the evening of March 2, the British made their move. Colonel McIntosh reported,

One of the Transport ships, the Schooner *Hinchinbrook* & Sloop *St. John* of 8 or 10 Guns each, with some boats, Sailed in our Sight, up the North River, back of Hutchinson's Island Lying opposite to the Town."[94] Expecting that the British would circle around the island and approach Savannah from upriver by sailing down the south channel, McIntosh redeployed some cannon and men. To his surprise, the British never appeared. Instead, they landed on the island itself and, "with the assistance & contrivance of all our own Sea faring people [complained McIntosh, crossed the island and] . . . hid themselves aboard of our Merchant Ships, which were previously Hauled close to the Island," until daylight.[95]

Early the next morning the *St. John* circled around the island and drifted back toward Savannah down the south channel of the river with the outgoing tide (the *Hinchinbrook* had grounded and was temporarily stuck on the opposite side of the island). At about the same time, the Georgians were informed that the merchant ships were occupied by British troops. They sent two men in a boat across the river to investigate and watched them get taken by British troops, at which point the Georgians started firing upon the merchant ships and then the *St. John* when it drifted into range.[96] The British soldiers, who had brought small cannon and swivel guns with them, and the sailors on the *St. John* returned fire. Colonel McIntosh recalled, "Our Men were inflamed, particularly at our own People who had treacherously Joined the Enemy against us, & were eager to board [the ships] but we had neither Boats, Sailors or Arms proper for the Attempt. . . . The general cry then was, to Sett all the shipping on fire."[97]

Several ships were set on fire below town and set adrift when the tide shifted; one grounded and did no damage other than to itself, but another ignited two merchant ships and spread panic among the crew and soldiers onboard the remaining ships. Most of the merchant ships used the rising tide to maneuver upriver away from the burning ships and out of range of the militia in Savannah, which momentarily ended the gunfire.

Dispatches were sent between the commanders of each side and an understanding was reached that if the British peacefully sailed back downriver, the Georgians would not fire upon them.[98] The understanding, however, soon proved to be anything but. First there was disagreement about the release of several individuals the British had seized, then disagreement about the merchant ships the British captured and moved to the north channel of the river. As these ships were now in the possession of the British navy, Captain Barkley and

Major Grant (the British commanders of the naval and land forces involved in this operation) naturally assumed that the captured merchant ships would leave with them. William Ewen, the president of the Council of Safety, insisted, however, "that the troops and armed vessels only were meant . . . none others were intended."[99]

The British ignored Ewen's protests and made their way down-river on March 8, shielded part of the way by Hutchinson's Island. Governor Wright reported that "14 or 15 Merchant Ships and Vessels of one sort or another," along with 1,600 barrels of rice, were captured at very little loss (a handful of wounded sailors).[100] Still, Governor Wright thought the whole expedition was conducted improperly and noted that "The Rebels are Skulking & increasing every day, Since they found the Troops did not Land, and are now said to be 700 Strong, and . . . have been reinforced by 600 Foot & 60 Horse from South Carolina and have Seized on a great Many Negroes who are Employed in throwing up Works & Fortifying the Town . . . and I am perswaded will oppose any Troops, Which may be Sent against [them]."[101] He added, "Thus Sir you See what a difference a few days have made in the State of affairs here, and I must beg Leave to Observe that not one barrel of Rice more, can ever be got, in the way this Quantity has been . . . and unless Troops come, Sufficient to Reduce this Province, no Provisions can be had from here, nor any from So. Carolina."[102]

Part of the cause for what appeared to be a newfound determination among the Georgians to resist the British may have been a widely spread description of the action that ridiculed the conduct of the British troops. Colonel McIntosh was likely the source of the story, writing to General Washington (and no doubt others) that, once the shooting commenced between the Georgians and the British troops in the merchant ships, "many of the [British] soldiers hastily Landed [back] on the Island in great confusion, running in the Marsh in a Laughable Manner, for fear of our Riflers tho' far past their reach."[103] Henry Laurens in South Carolina heard a similar account, writing in mid-March that "The King's Troops were certainly panic Struck, they not only ran away, when our people fired on them, but cried out for Mercy & left two field pieces behind."[104] Whatever the truth was, such stories emboldened Whig supporters, which was important because the fighting and bloodshed off of Savannah signified that the war had reached Georgia.

EAST FLORIDA

The situation in East Florida at the start of 1776 was much calmer than in the colonies to the north. A successful meeting with indigenous leaders in mid-December eased some of Governor Tonyn's concern, and he spent much of January gathering provisions for the British naval ships posted in Charlestown. On January 15, the lone British warship at St. Augustine, the *St. Lawrence*, departed with a packet ship to deliver much-needed supplies to the *Tamar* and the armed ship *Cherokee* at Charlestown. The *St. Lawrence* carried gunpowder, cartridge paper, and slow match as well as barrels of pork, peas, flour, and beef along with butter and biscuit and that absolute necessity of the British navy, rum.[105] The vessels eventually located the *Tamar* and *Cherokee* off of Georgia in mid-February and remained to assist in operations there.

Governor Tonyn, who was always anxious when there was no British naval presence in Florida, received a disturbing report from one of his privy councilors who had traveled to Georgia to attend to personal affairs. Martin Jollie reported that there was much talk in Savannah of attacking East Florida.[106]

Jollie likely observed the reaction of Georgians to the resolution from the Continental Congress passed in December encouraging the southern colonies to strike at St. Augustine. Upon Jollie's report, an alarmed Governor Tonyn immediately sent for assistance from the Seminole Indians with the intention to post them at key points from St. Augustine to the St. Marys River (the border with Georgia).[107] He also alerted the small contingent of British regulars of the 14th and 16th Regiments at St Augustine and ordered them to prepare to march.

Tension diminished considerably in East Florida near the end of February, however, when Governor Tonyn learned of the British naval operation in Georgia to gather provisions for the army in Boston. Surely the Georgians would be unable to meddle in Florida when their hands were full dealing with the British navy.

The governor's respite from worry was short lived because on March 7 the *St. John* sailed into St. Augustine from New Providence, Bahamas, with shocking news. A squadron of rebel ships had attacked New Providence and seized gunpowder and arms, as well as Governor Montfort Browne. Tonyn instantly worried that St. Augustine was next, a worry that actually had some validity, as Lieutenant Grant of the *St. John* believed the rebel ships were in pursuit.[108] Governor Tonyn wrote directly to Captain Barkley of the *Scarborough*, the ranking naval officer off Georgia, inquiring whether he might undertake "proper measures to destroy this rebel Squadron?"[109] Barkley held an officer's council, but it was agreed that they continue with their mission in Georgia and not go "in quest of the . . . Rebel Vessels and Forces."[110]

To Governor Tonyn's relief the rebel vessels never appeared, and his anxiety diminished considerably in April when three companies of the 60th Regiment arrived from Jamaica to reinforce St. Augustine.[111]

Six

Spring

R ELATIVE PEACE RETURNED TO MASSACHUSETTS IN THE SPRING
of 1776. Boston was liberated from its occupation by British
troops who sailed to Halifax, Nova Scotia, to regroup. Attention
now turned to both New York—the next presumed target of
Britain—and Philadelphia, where the idea of independence now was
mentioned in the Continental Congress more often. Thomas Paine's
pamphlet, *Common Sense*, appeared in early 1776 and created a sen-
sation—and support—for independence. Whether Americans were
ready for such a bold step, however, remained to be seen.

VIRGINIA

When General Henry Clinton sailed into Hampton Roads aboard
the HMS *Mercury* on February 17, he found Governor Dunmore and
his floating town of merchant ships protected by several warships
miserably situated in the Elizabeth River, "driven from the Shore and
the whole Country in arms against him."[1] Clinton confessed, "I could
not see the Use of his Lordship's remaining longer there," but Dunmore was determined to remain, even after he realized that General
Clinton had no assistance to offer.[2] Clinton and his handful of ships

left Virginia less than ten days after they arrived for what the British commander hoped would be a rendezvous with the main body of his expeditionary force at the Cape Fear River in North Carolina.

Lord Dunmore was left with his assorted force of freed slaves now in British military service, bolstered by a handful of Tories, British regulars, and British marines, plus the cannon of a few British warships to maintain royal authority in Virginia from their base at Tucker's Point. To make matters worse, illness swept through Dunmore's ranks, prompting a number of desertions and killing over 150 Black soldiers.[3]

In contrast to Dunmore's struggles, recruitment among Virginia's nine regiments of regular troops went well. By the spring, Virginia had successfully raised an impressive military force of several thousand full-time troops augmented by the militia, and together they looked perfectly capable of subduing Lord Dunmore.

One of the biggest challenges that faced Virginia's military forces in 1776 was not attracting recruits but rather equipping, training, and disciplining them once they enlisted. Linen hunting shirts served as the uniform of Virginia's troops, and they were relatively easy to supply, but firearms were another matter. Authorities scrambled to procure muskets and rifles for the regulars, often at the expense of the militia, who went without weapons. Thirteen-foot-long spears were distributed to two companies of each regiment for a short period of time as the search for more firearms continued.[4]

The arrival of General Charles Lee in Williamsburg in late March offered a solution to the discipline dilemma. Lee, a former British officer with extensive military service in Europe, held the rank of major general in the Continental Army and served with General Washington in Massachusetts in 1775. Although he was a native of Britain and had only arrived in the colonies in 1773, Lee had earned the trust and admiration of many in Congress and held the third-highest rank in the Continental Army. He was the most militarily experienced and knowledgeable officer in the army and was highly esteemed throughout the colonies.

Reports of planned British military operations in the southern colonies prompted Congress to send General Lee southward in

March to oversee the region's defense. He arrived in Williamsburg on March 29 and informed General Washington of the situation in Virginia a week later: "The Regiments in general are very compleat in numbers, the Men (those that I have seen) fine—but a most horrid deficiency of Arms—no entrenching tools, no [effective cannon] (although the Province is pretty well stockd) . . . I have order'd . . . the Artificers to work night and day."[5]

Lee speculated that the unrealistic hope for reconciliation among some and a degree of apathy among others had caused Virginians to procrastinate on important military preparations. He also criticized the scattered deployment of the colony's regiments, something he corrected by ordering several units to march to Williamsburg.[6]

Military affairs were not the only topic to dominate the public's attention; by the spring of 1776, public support for independence in Virginia was widespread. One writer to Purdie's *Virginia Gazette* in March justified his support for independence with the following argument.

> Consider the great preparations England is making for war, the arrival of [warships] . . . that lord Dunmore is actually entrenching on Tucker's Mills, that he is daily recruiting his army of slaves, that there has been a dangerous commotion in North Carolina, and that the English commander in Detroit has instigated some Indians to make an attack on our frontier. . . . I say, whoever knows or considers these things must see that the story of commissioners, repeal, accommodation, was intended but to lull us into security, or to insult and mock us. It is therefore high time to look to ourselves, and if we cannot enjoy the privileges of Englishmen . . . let us instantly break off those [chains] of affection which have hitherto bound us to them; and if England calls in foreign assistance, let us follow the wisdom of her example, and do so likewise.[7]

The assistance of European nations and establishment of foreign trade became important arguments of many pro-independence writers. Influenced no doubt by the writing of Thomas Paine in *Common*

Sense, writers like "An American" argued in the newspapers that, since Britain had sought the assistance of "Russians, Hanoverians, Canadians, Indians, and Negro slaves . . . we should declare ourselves independent of her and call to our assistance the French and Spaniards."[8]

The question of independence from Great Britain was the dominant issue in county elections for delegates to the Fifth Virginia Convention in April. Anxiety over reports of British military plans for the southern colonies created a sense of urgency that pushed many Virginians to support independence.

The Fifth Virginia Convention assembled in the capitol in Williamsburg on May 6 and selected Edmund Pendleton to chair the assembly as president. Although the primary issue on everyone's mind was independence, a week's worth of other business delayed consideration of that issue. Much of what occurred in the first week of the convention was routine: appointments to and reports from committees, petitions from counties and individuals, appeals for payment for items supplied to the troops or losses suffered in the conflict with Dunmore.

General Lee's request to forcibly relocate all of the inhabitants and livestock in Norfolk and Prince Anne Counties within reach of Dunmore at Tucker's Point (estimated to be many thousands of people) generated much debate before it was approved.[9] Time was also spent in the convention discussing a response to an appeal for military assistance from the Carolinas. On May 10, the convention ordered 1,150 minutemen from sixteen counties to accompany the 8th Virginia Regiment and General Lee to North Carolina.[10] It was not until the eighth day of the convention that the issue of independence was considered, and after debating several resolutions, they made their decision, unanimously, on May 15: "Resolved unanimously that the delegates appointed to represent this colony in General Congress be instructed to propose to that respectable body to declare the United Colonies free and independent upon the crown or parliament of Great Britain and that they give the assent of this Colony to such declaration and to whatever measures may be thought proper and necessary by the Congress."[11]

Virginia's leaders had taken an irrevocable step, publically declaring their support for independence from Great Britain. The conflict had evolved from a rebellion against misguided British leaders and their unconstitutional policies to a war for complete separation and independence for Virginians.

NORTH CAROLINA

General Clinton's journey to the Cape Fear River, plagued by bad weather, dragged on for another two weeks, but he finally arrived on March 14.[12] Governor Martin, still smarting from the defeat of his Tory supporters at Moores Creek Bridge, was undoubtedly relieved by Clinton's arrival. Both he and General Clinton must have wondered, however, where Commodore Parker's fleet from Ireland with all its firepower and troops was. Poor weather delayed Commodore Parker's voyage across the Atlantic to such a degree that the fleet's arrival was still seven weeks away.

Governor Martin expected them any day and hoped to convince General Clinton to still use a detachment of the force to march into the interior of North Carolina to rally the Tories.[13] Clinton would have none of it, however; his instructions were clear and Charlestown was now his focus.

While General Clinton and Governor Martin waited for Commodore Parker to arrive, North Carolina's provincial congress assembled in the town of Halifax in early April. They spent several days bolstering the colony's military, increasing the number of provincial regiments from two to six and appointing officers for them.[14] The Congress in Philadelphia had promoted both James Moore and Robert Howe to brigadier general, so their regiments needed new commanders too.

On April 12, the provincial congress, reciting a long list of abuses committed on the colonists by parliament *and* the king, was the first colony to formally support independence for the colonies. The resolution that passed unanimously that day in Halifax declared, "That the delegates for this Colony in the Continental Congress be empowered to concur with the delegates of the other Colonies in declaring Independency."[15]

While it was not an outright declaration of independence for North Carolina, it was a clear expression of the provincial congress's support for such a measure should it be introduced in the Continental Congress in Philadelphia.

The provincial congress remained in session for another month, forming, regulating, and paying for the growing military establishment in the colony. It appeared that every bit of this new force was needed, because in mid-April the first of Commodore Parker's ships, a troop transport, reached North Carolina.[16] Commodore Parker, aboard the HMS *Bristol* (50 guns, 365 crew) arrived on May 3 with General Cornwallis and was pleased to find that most of the fleet was there to meet him.[17]

Although he had no intention of marching against North Carolina, General Clinton did hope that the impressive show of force building upon the coast might convince the colonists there to reconsider their disloyalty to the king. On May 5, Clinton issued a proclamation, "Offering in his Majesty's Name free Pardon to all such as shall lay down their Arms and submit to the Laws."[18]

Only two people were exempted from the pardon, Cornelius Harnett and Robert Howe, both probably identified by Governor Martin for their rebellious leadership in the colony. General Clinton also ordered that the provincial congress, which had already met for nearly a month, end its proceedings and disband along with the various committees of safety.

The proclamation fell largely on deaf ears in North Carolina. The resolution of April 12 calling for independence spoke for the majority of North Carolinians and best represented their answer to Clinton's demands.

Commodore Parker's fleet remained anchored off North Carolina until mid-May, recovering from its grueling journey and preparing for its expedition against Charlestown. Few North Carolinians knew yet with certainty that Charlestown was their objective, and they scrambled to defend themselves. Virginia also reacted, sending a regiment across the border with General Charles Lee in mid-May. By the time they reached Halifax, in eastern North Carolina, the British fleet had departed. When General Lee learned that their destination was Charlestown, he hurried there and ordered the 8th Virginia Regiment to continue south to join him.

SOUTH CAROLINA

The Whig leaders of South Carolina had remained busy over the spring of 1776 on two fronts, improving the defense of Charlestown and addressing the political vacuum that existed with the departure of Governor Campbell. On the political front, the provincial congress approved of both the conduct and resolutions of the Continental Congress in Philadelphia as well as their own delegates in attendance.[19]

One of the resolutions from Philadelphia recommended that the colonies reform their governments to adjust to the absence of so many royal governors and officials. It was during discussion of this issue in mid-February that Christopher Gadsden, one of the colony's congressional delegates who had recently returned from Philadelphia, stunned the provincial congress by declaring "himself not only in favor of the form of government [recommended by a committee]; but for the absolute Independence of America."[20] Colonel William Moultrie reported that "This last sentiment, came like an explosion of thunder upon the members of Congress; as the resolution of the Continental Congress, upon which the [committee's] report for a form of government was grounded, had by no means led them to anticipate so decisive a step."[21]

Gadsden's sentiment was criticized by a majority in attendance, who found talk of independence in February 1776 rash, but the need to restructure the government remained, and the congress voted to proceed to do so.[22]

A committee was formed to draft what essentially became a new constitution for South Carolina. The provincial congress also restructured the colony's military establishment. Two new rifle regiments were authorized, and in the absence of British warships in the harbor, a fort was begun on Sullivan's Island.

Through most of March the provincial congress debated the details of a new constitution and kept watch for the British ships anchored on either side of South Carolina in the Savannah and Cape Fear Rivers. The debate was helped along by news of Britain's Prohibitory Act, which banned all American trade and commerce and authorized the seizure of Americans and their property. This draconian measure amounted to a declaration of war on the colonists, alarming the moderates in the provincial congress who had questioned the need for a new constitution (still hoping for reconciliation).[23] They now swung their support for the new constitution, and although the vote was not unanimous, South Carolina's provincial congress adopted a new plan for government on March 26, 1776.[24]

On that same day, Governor Campbell of South Carolina replied to an inquiry by General Clinton about the situation in South Carolina. Campbell stated that the capture of Charlestown would have a very good effect on the "friends of government," who would likely join the king's troops. The same event would also demoralize the rebels, many of whom would likely desert their cause.[25]

In early April a letter printed in Alexander Purdie's *Virginia Gazette* purportedly from Charlestown reported that "upwards of 130 pieces of cannon, from 26 to 9 pounders, mounted on 13 forts, batteries, and bastions, at the entrance into the harbor, and round the bay; with five continental battalions and 13 complete uniformed minute companies [protected Charlestown]."[26] In addition to all of the cannon and artillery, South Carolina had fitted out three armed ships that were now available to defend Charlestown, the *Prosper* (24 guns), the *Comet* (16 guns), and the *Defence* (12 guns).[27]

On paper at least, it appeared that South Carolina could mount a strong defense of Charlestown. It remained to be seen if it could.

GEORGIA

The confusion and fear that gripped Savannah upon the approach of British warships in early March and the seizure of over ten merchant ships, many loaded with rice, did not chasten the Whigs in Georgia as much as one might expect. In fact, although the colony's leaders had withdrawn to Augusta, there was still plenty of fight among the troops that remained behind. With the British navy still anchored in the mouth of the Savannah River weeks after their raid on Savannah gathering supplies, repairing their ships, and resting on several of the coastal islands, it was decided by the Whigs to pay them a visit. Georgia's Council of Safety sent an account of this "visit" to the Council of Safety of South Carolina:

Finding that the Houses on Great Tybee Island afforded comfortable Shelter for the King's Officers and Tory Refugees, we resolved to send a Detachment of Men there, to destroy them, and to rout the Tories and others who were there . . . despite the imminent Danger [of the British warships and infantry]. Accordingly, Colonel Bullock, with a Party of Men composed of Detachments from Capt. Baker's Riflemen, Capt. Bryan's Light Infantry, Capt. Martin's Volunteers, Capt. Cuthbert's Fusileers, and a Company of Creek Indians, went down upon the island, killed two Marines, one Tory who would not surrender, and took one Marine and several Tories Prisoners; burnt all of the Houses except one, in which was a sick Woman and several Children, and returned safe. In doing this they were exceedingly exposed on the Beach to the Fire of the *Cherokee* and an armed Sloop, which incessantly fired Ball and Grape Shot during the whole Time of the Attack.[28]

The British account of this raid was quite different and filled with accusations of cruelty and torture, claiming that one marine "who having received a wound, was left behind and seized by the Provincials, who immediately tied him to a tree, afterwards cut his legs, thighs, and arms, into several pieces, and then left him in this tortured condition."[29] Whatever the truth concerning the conduct of the Whigs in this raid, it demonstrated their determination to engage against a foe who, just three weeks earlier, caused panic in the capital of Georgia.

The determination to resist Great Britain was also evident in Augusta, where the provincial congress justified the use of force, proclaiming on April 15 that "The unwise . . . system of administration by the British Parliament and Ministry against the good people of America hath . . . driven the latter to take up arms as their last recourse for the preservation of their rights and liberties."[30]

Additionally, the collapse of royal rule in the colony, sparked by the flight of Governor Wright and many of his appointees, required action by the provincial congress to fill the political vacuum.

The representatives decided therefore to empower a president and commander-in-chief to exercise the executive duties of government for a term of six months. Archibald Bulloch, a former delegate to the Continental Congress and respected Whig leader, was appointed to the post. The Council of Safety would serve as a privy council to the president, and the provincial congress would exercise all legislative power.[31]

The provincial congress did not address the issue of independence directly in its proclamation, leaving that issue to the Continental Congress, but by forming a new plan of governance for Georgia, its representatives behaved as if independence from Great Britain was a foregone conclusion.

Governor Wright, formally deposed from a position he had held for over twenty years, was spared the news of Georgia's proclamation for several weeks. He and his family had sailed north aboard the *Scarborough* at the end of March, first to Rhode Island, then Halifax, Nova Scotia, and ultimately England.[32]

EAST FLORIDA

The arrival of three companies of the 60th Regiment in mid-April provided some degree of relief to Governor Tonyn, yet the rebel raid on New Providence in the Bahamas still weighed heavily on his mind. The ship that delivered the reinforcements to St. Augustine, the HMS *Hind* (24 guns, 160 crew), joined the *Hinchinbrook* in a raid along the Georgia coast near Sunbury. The *Hinchinbrook*, with its lower draft, sailed upriver near St. Catherine Island and burned a brig and a ship in the stock that "was intended for a Twenty Gun Privateer."[33] On its way downriver, the *Hinchinbrook* had to contend with hundreds of "crackers," which Captain Bryne of the *Hind* explained were the rebels in Georgia.[34] Following the brief but successful raid, the *Hind* sailed for Antigua while the *Hinchinbrook* sailed for Cape Fear in North Carolina.

That left the schooner *St. John* to once again guard Florida against a growing (in both size and aggressiveness) rebel navy. Governor Tonyn complained of the departure of the *Hinchinbrook*, informing Lord Germain, "I intended my Lord to have stationed the *Hinchinbroook* schooner . . . at St. Marys River [the border between East Florida and Georgia] and to have had another vessel with her, and a detachment of His Majesty's troops of fifty men to have been on board of them. This measure I apprehend would have secured this Province from any depredations of the rebels."[35]

Instead, despite nearly doubling the number of British regulars in East Florida, Governor Tonyn remained anxious about a possible visit from rebels to the north and about rebel ships to the east. The *St. John* remained steadfastly on station in East Florida, patrolling the coast between St. Augustine and the St. Marys River.

If any rebels did pay East Florida a visit, it was likely to be in the form of a raid, not an invasion. As summer approached, most everyone's attention turned northward to Charlestown, where a large British fleet had arrived offshore, and to Philadelphia, where the Continental Congress considered the issue of independence.

Seven

Summer

O N JUNE 7, RICHARD HENRY LEE OF VIRGINIA MOVED TO consider Virginia's resolution on independence in the Continental Congress. Three weeks of debate and consideration followed before Lee's motion was brought to a vote. As the delegates contemplated Virginia's measure, the advance portion of an enormous British invasion force began to appear off of New York and land on Staten Island. To the south, a smaller British invasion force moved in position to strike Charlestown, South Carolina. It appeared that a new phase of the conflict was about to commence.

VIRGINIA

Although Virginians were keenly aware of the large British expeditionary force anchored and encamped in neighboring North Carolina in May, another event within their own border turned their attention away from the south as well as from the activities of the Fifth Virginia Convention in Williamsburg.

Governor Dunmore surprised nearly everyone in late May when he suddenly abandoned Tucker's Point and the Elizabeth River and sailed his flotilla into Hampton Roads. Conditions on Tucker's Point and among the floating town in the river had become intolerably foul and unhealthy. In addition, reports that the rebels were about to deploy cannon in Norfolk and send fire rafts among his ships convinced the governor that it was time to leave.[1] The hope among most Virginians was that Dunmore and his flotilla of nearly a hundred vessels would sail to New York or Nova Scotia, but his destination proved to be much closer, only thirty miles up Chesapeake Bay at Gwynn's Island.

Gwynn's Island was a sparsely populated body of land just a few hundred yards off the coast of Gloucester County. A narrow, two-hundred-yard-wide channel separated the island from the mainland at its closest point, and the flat, roughly four-square-mile island rose just a few feet above sea level.

Although it certainly was not an ideal location to establish a new base of operations, the island offered safe ground, free from rebel attack (or so Dunmore thought), on which his supporters and troops could recover from their long stay aboard overcrowded, unhealthy ships. Gwynn's Island also possessed an abundant supply of livestock and plenty of fresh water (again, so Dunmore thought). Finally, the island allowed Lord Dunmore to maintain the royal standard (and the illusion of royal authority in Virginia) while he awaited reinforcements and assistance from Britain.

Dunmore's fleet arrived off Gwynn's Island on May 26 and anchored in Hills Bay at the mouth of the Piankatank River. A detachment from the 7th Virginia Regiment posted at Burton's Point, overlooking Hills Bay, observed the ships and sent word to Williamsburg. The next day, while Virginia regulars and local militia converged on Gwynn's Island, Governor Dunmore secured the island by landing troops on its northern shore. British marines from the *Roebuck*, *Fowey*, and *Otter* spearheaded the landing.[2]

Dunmore's small force spread quickly across the island. Finding no opposition, the troops converged on the narrow strip of land closest to the mainland. Separated by a deep channel of water, Lord Dunmore believed that this spot was most vulnerable to rebel attack, so he ordered the construction of earthworks and established his main camp behind them. The redoubt that protected the camp was dubbed Fort Hamond, after the captain of the *Roebuck*.

While Dunmore's troops searched the island and established a fort and camp on the narrow strip of land, Captain John Posey and his company of 7th Virginians arrived on the scene, ahead of the rest of their regiment. They joined detachments of local militia who were perplexed on what they should do. Posey recorded in his diary, "I found a number of the militia assembled, which appear'd to be in the utmost consternation, some running one way, and some another, under no kind of control or regularity."[3]

Colonel William Daingerfield, the commander of the 7th Virginia, soon arrived with four more companies of his regiment and assumed command. (The other five companies were in Williamsburg and would arrive a few days later.) He ordered the troops closer to shore to prevent Dunmore's troops from landing on the mainland. Captain Posey observed, "The whole were put in motion, (though I must confess the militia were in very great motion before the orders were given). However, these orders served to put them in something grator; for as soon as we came neare enough for the grape[shot], and cannon shot to whistle over our heads, numbers of the militia put themselves in much quicker motion, and never stopped . . . to look behind them until they had made the best of their way home."[4]

Captain Posey candidly admitted that it was not just the militia that was spooked by the enemy gun fire. "I cant say that our regulars deserved any great degree of credit for after two or three getting a little blood drawn, they began to skulk and fall flat upon there faces."[5]

Despite their apprehension, Colonel Daingerfield's troops and most of the militia held their ground and endured enemy cannon fire and heavy rain into the evening. As the hours passed, they grew more determined to face the enemy. Posey recalled, "We began to grow very firm and only wish them to come into the bushes, where we are certain of beating them."[6]

Rather than attack the mainland, however, Lord Dunmore was content to stay on the island and harass the Virginians with his naval guns. Captain Hamond seemed to agree with this strategy, noting,

"We have taken possession of this Island which is about three or four Miles in length and one in breadth. Separated from the Main 1/2 a mile, except on one place (which is that where Lord Dunmore has his Camp) this is not above the reach of [enemy] Musquet Shot, However this part is defended by the Guns from the Ships."[7]

As the days passed into June and Dunmore's hold on the island strengthened, General Andrew Lewis, in Williamsburg, the commander of Virginia's continental troops during General Charles Lee's absence, ordered artillery positions constructed on the mainland in preparation for several heavy cannon being transported to Gwynn's Island.[8]

This took time, and as the days passed, the Virginians along the shore contented themselves with sniping at Dunmore's camp and at several small vessels that had sailed into Milford Haven (the body of water that separated Gwynn's Island from the mainland). In one incident, they were able to seize a small sloop loaded with liquor that had run aground.[9]

The loss of this sloop did not particularly concern Lord Dunmore; he was confident that his position on Gwynn's Island was secure. Of growing concern to the governor was his fresh water supply, which was inadequate for the hundreds of people who were on the island, and the rampant illness and death (largely to smallpox and fever) that ravaged his troops, particularly his Black soldiers. A report in Dixon's *Virginia Gazette* attributed to a gentleman from Yorktown (who escaped Dunmore's custody) claimed that "there are not above 200 blacks now alive, 75 at least having died within six days after they left Norfolk, and that the number of whites on shore is very inconsiderable."[10]

Lord Dunmore privately acknowledged his losses to sickness to Lord Germain:

I am extreamly sorry to inform your Lordship that the Fever of which I informed you in my Letter No. 1, has proved a very Malignant one and has carried off an incredible Number of our People, especially the Blacks, had it not been for this horrid disorder, I am Satisfied I should have had two thousand Blacks, with whom

I should have no doubt of penetrating into the heart of the Colony.
. . . There was not a ship in the fleet that did not throw one, two,
or three or more dead overboard every night.[11]

The Virginians were well aware of Dunmore's losses. General
Lewis reported daily sightings of bodies washed ashore to General
Lee. "A Great Mortality among the Enemy, some both white and
black, are discovered floating every day."[12] Such daily discoveries
bolstered rebel morale, as it suggested the dire condition of the enemy
on the island.

Despite all the suffering that was endured by Dunmore's troops
and his supporters on Gwynn's Island, they remained secure from attack, protected by the guns of Fort Hamond, several British warships,
and additional land batteries placed along the western shore of the
island.

Lord Dunmore's fortunes suffered a blow on June 19, when the
Oxford, a British transport ship with 217 Scottish Highland troops
aboard, was captured by Captain James Barron in Hampton Roads.
The ship, which was part of a large British reinforcement sent to
America in the spring and meant for the British army in Boston, had
altered its course to Halifax, Nova Scotia, upon word that General
Howe had evacuated Boston. Along the way the *Oxford* and another
transport ship were seized by the continental brig *Andrew Doria,*
which disarmed the *Oxford,* removed most of the crew and officers,
and placed an eight-man prize crew aboard to sail the captured ship
to port. A gale separated the *Oxford* from the *Andrew Doria,* and
the Highland prisoners, led by a carpenter from the *Oxford,* over-
powered the prize crew and retook the ship.[13] They decided to sail
for Virginia and had entered Hampton Road when they unknowingly
encountered two vessels from the fledgling Virginia state navy, the
Liberty and *Patriot.* Lieutenant John Trevett, one of the prize crew
from the *Andrew Doria,* described how the captains of the two Virginia ships, brothers James and Richard Barron, used deception to
capture the *Oxford:*

We got into Hampton roads about sunset, we immediately came
along side 2 small pilot boats, and they informed us that the

Fowey, ship of war, lay 40 miles up James River, and they must immediately get under way, after giving 3 cheers they weighed anchor and stood up the River. . . . After the Capt. of the Pilot boats had found out that we were all officers from on board the *Andrew Doria*, they called on me then having the Command to know how they should retake her. . . . At daylight I informed our new Capt. Canada that he had no more command, and that he must go forward, and all others but the women, and children, they might stay on the quarter deck; which was done, we stood up James River until we arrived at Jamestown, and there we landed 220 highlanders, which was escorted [into Williamsburg] by part of a regiment of riflemen, in their rifle frocks, I think the finest sight I ever saw.[14]

The unarmed Highlanders had no choice but to submit to Captain Barron and the prize crew.

Lord Dunmore took the loss of the Highlanders hard, exclaiming to Lord George Germain in a letter, "of what Service would they not have been to me here!"[15] Captain Hamond confirmed the need for more troops to defend the island, noting,

The Negro Troops, which had been inoculated before they left Norfolk, got thro' the disorder with great success, but the Fever which had been so fatal to them there, followed them also to the Island; so that notwithstanding the Corps was recruited with Six or eight fresh Men every day, yet the mortality among them was so great, that they did not now amount to above 150 effective Men. The detachment of the 14th Regt also became very weak, and the few Men of the New raised Corps [Queen's Own Loyal Virginians] were all down with the small Pox: so that we were still under the necessity of keeping the Marines on Shore to do the Common duty.[16]

Hamond added that it was necessary to strengthen the island's defenses because reports from rebel deserters revealed that General Lewis planned to attack as soon as several artillery batteries were completed.

NORTH CAROLINA

In North Carolina, the presence of Commodore Parker's British fleet in the Cape Fear River in May was disconcerting, yet the relative inactivity of the British force baffled North Carolina's Whig leaders. Fifteen hundred militia were ordered to take the field and reinforce Colonel Moore in Wilmington, and the colony's leaders kept General Charles Lee in Virginia apprised of developments, but they withheld an appeal for assistance until British intentions became clearer.[17] After months aboard ship, General Cornwallis's troops eagerly disembarked and encamped near the ruins of Fort Johnston and along the coast.[18] Provisions were gathered where they could find them, and the small town of Brunswick, a few miles upriver from Fort Johnston, was raided, but for the most part the army seemed more interested in recovering from its long voyage than marching into the countryside to subdue North Carolina.[19]

General Charles Lee needed no invitation to go to North Carolina. That was where the enemy was, so he headed south from Williamsburg on May 11, uniting with the 8th Virginia Regiment (which he had ordered southward from Suffolk several days earlier) in Halifax. Many of the Virginians were unsettled by their march out of Virginia, and General Lee complained of their "disorderly and mutinous disposition."[20] Lee remained uncertain of General Clinton's intentions and warily advanced south from Halifax, concerned that the British might suddenly reembark and sail to Virginia. As it turned out, the British did reembark, but their destination was Charlestown; Commodore Parker's fleet sailed from North Carolina on May 31.

When Virginia's leaders learned of the British movement they rescinded their order for 1,200 minutemen to march to North Carolina.[21] With Governor Dunmore resettled on Gwynn's Island and British troops embarked aboard ships and very mobile, it was too risky to send the minutemen out of Virginia. The 8th Virginia Regiment was thus the only assistance the Old Dominion sent south. North Carolina, on the other hand, seemingly free of enemy occupation or threat, rallied to Charlestown's defense and sent Brigadier General Robert Howe with 1,400 North Carolina continentals to South Carolina.[22]

SOUTH CAROLINA

South Carolina's leaders kept a close eye on Commodore Parker's fleet to the north, not sure whether North Carolina, Virginia, or South Carolina was its objective. As days passed in May with no significant movement, suspicion grew that Commodore Parker and General Clinton were destined for Charlestown. This was confirmed on June 1 when the first ships of the British fleet anchored just a few miles off the coast of Charlestown.[23]

As a combined sea and land operation, several challenges confronted the British upon their arrival, and Commodore Parker and General Clinton would have to work closely and cooperatively. They did neither, and the correspondence between the two commanders highlights their dysfunction.

The first matter of contention between the two revolved around which force would assume primary responsibility for capturing the fort on Sullivan's Island, a long, thin island of sand dunes near the mouth of the harbor that defended the approach to Charlestown. Passage up the narrow shipping channel was uncertain as long as the heavy cannon in the rebel fort on Sullivan's Island were operational. With walls built of spongy palmetto logs stacked ten feet high on the two sides exposed to the harbor and sea and filled with sand that created sixteen-foot-wide walls, it was not a particularly impressive-looking structure, but it proved extremely durable in the heavy fighting to come.[24]

A difficult sandbar at the mouth of Charlestown Harbor extended offshore perpendicularly from Sullivan's Island. The northeast end of the island was outside of the sandbar and thus approachable by sea (although the surf onshore was typically heavy). The fort, which sat on the southwest end of the island, three miles away from the northeast end, was located inside the sandbar. This meant that if the British fleet were to attack the fort directly, it had to cross the sandbar first, a not-so-easy task for Parker's largest and heaviest ships.

Because Clinton declined an offer by Parker to establish his headquarters aboard Parker's flagship, the fifty-gun HMS *Bristol*, much of the discussion on how to attack Sullivan's Island was conducted through letters.[25] On June 2, Parker proposed that Clinton land on the northeast end of Sullivan's Island and then advance on the fort while the navy crossed the sandbar and attacked two small outposts on Morris Island, across from Sullivan's Island, as a distraction.[26] Clinton bristled at the proposal, complaining that Parker's plan placed all of the burden of the fight upon his troops:

> In this Attack I ever understood the Navy were to bear a considerable part, but by your late arrangement you have marked out for them little more than reducing [two] insignificant Batteries. . . . I cannot think of landing on the North side of that Island as you propose without in the first place being assured there is no Surf, that armed Vessels can approach near enough to cover my landing and retreat, and that such Naval force as can be brought into action may be ready at their Stations to co-operate, without which I am free to own any attempt I should make might justly be called rash and absurd.[27]

Stung by Clinton's criticism, Parker replied, "I do now assure You, that His Majesty's Ships under my Command, shall during the Course of the whole Expedition, give every Assistance in Their Power, and that I hope You will find considerable."[28] Soundings of the water depth off of Sullivan's Island and Long Island (which sat just to the north of Sullivan's separated by a narrow cut of water) were conducted over the next few days. The sandbar was also thoroughly sounded in preparation for its crossing. Rough weather and contrary winds slowed the effort, as did the draft of Parker's largest ships, which had to be lightened by removing their cannon and ordnance in order to get across the sandbar.

Informed that at low tide the cut of water that separated Sullivan's Island from Long Island was fordable, Clinton resolved to land his army there. The unoccupied island offered an excellent position from which Clinton could launch an attack upon Sullivan's Island.[29] The northern end of Sullivan's Island (closest to Long Island) was guarded by a body of rebel troops, but Clinton was confident his much larger force could ford the cut between the two islands at low tide and overwhelm the rebels. He would then advance up Sullivan's Island to the fort and storm it from the rear.

Clinton informed Parker that he wished to first send a proclamation to the rebels offering pardons to all who "shall lay down their Arms and submit to the Laws" before they launched an attack.[30] He knew it was unlikely that any rebel would comply but hoped that when the proclamation was delivered to the fort under a flag of truce "an intelligent officer might be able to discover much."[31] Clinton even instructed the route on which the boat carrying the officer ashore should take in order to provide the best "opportunity of squinting at Sullivan's Island":[32] "Point first towards the Angle of the left Bastion, & then finding it difficult to approach the Shore, row up towards the right Bastion, by which he will have discovered Whether they have an Abbatis, & what the state of the Work is."[33]

A rebel sentinel disrupted Clinton's plans by firing on the flag when it approached, causing the boat to return to its ship despite the efforts of a rebel officer to rectify the mistake by waving his own white cloth on the end of a musket from shore.[34] Colonel William Moultrie, the commander of the fort, sent a flag by boat to General Clinton to apologize for the conduct of the sentinel. Later in the day, Clinton sent his proclamation ashore, presumably in the hands of an observant officer, who delivered it and took note of what he saw.[35]

Major General Charles Lee arrived in Charlestown on June 8 and assumed command of the combined rebel forces from South Carolina, North Carolina, and eventually Virginia. He had under his command an impressive force that grew to over 6,500 men and over a hundred cannon by the eve of the battle.[36] Although Lee commanded more than twice as many men as Clinton, the necessity of defending Charlestown meant that they were spread out among several locations that were not within immediate supporting distance of each other. Furthermore, the quality and experience of Lee's troops was suspect compared to the professional troops under Clinton.

That concern did not extend to Lee. Great things were expected from him, and Colonel Moultrie remembered that his arrival "excited the public ardour; and was hoped to presage happy results."[37] Lee threw himself into the task of improving Charlestown's defense, ordering the constructions of earthworks in and around town and in some cases ordering the destruction of buildings to clear fields of fire.

Colonel Charles Pinckney, the commander of Fort Johnson, described the changes to Charlestown to his mother:

> You would scarcely know the environs of the town again, so many lines, bastions, redans, and military mince-pies have been made all around it, that the appearance of it is quite metamorphosed. All of the houses on the wharves are pulled down, so that the town look from the water much handsomer than it ever did. Every person there is obliged to work; and the tories (reluctantly I believe) now work with the rest.[38]

When Lee saw the unfinished fort on Sullivan's Island with its rear walls only seven feet high and with no bastions, he pronounced that it "could not hold out half an hour; and . . . was but a slaughter pen" for whatever troops garrisoned it.[39] Lee made this observation to the fort's commander, Colonel Moultrie, who disagreed with Lee's assessment. Lee believed that once British ships moved into a cove northwest of the fort, deadly enfilade fire from the west would rain down upon the garrison. He predicted that while Commodore Parker's ships maneuvered and pounded the fort with cannon, General Clinton's troops would march to the mainland from Long Island and attack Haddrell's Point, cutting off the one escape route (a rickety pontoon bridge) from Sullivan's Island.[40]

In Lee's view, troops left on Sullivan's Island were doomed, and he wanted to withdraw them to strengthen Haddrell's Point. Lee did ultimately transfer half of Moultrie's garrison and a portion of his ammunition, but he relented to the insistence of South Carolina's leaders to defend the fort and island.[41] Moultrie and approximately 450 men from his 2nd South Carolina Regiment (and a handful of artillerists from the 4th South Carolina Regiment) remained in the fort.[42] They manned a total of thirty-one cannon ranging in size from twenty-six pounds to nine pounds, but not all of them could be brought to bear on the British navy.[43] Some were placed to defend against a land assault on the fort.

About three miles up the island to the northeast, Colonel William Thomson of the 3rd South Carolina defended the most likely spot for a British land attack, the cut of water between Sullivan's and Long Island. Thomson's command, which eventually grew to 780 men, many armed with rifles, was posted behind breastworks and supported by one eighteen-pound cannon and a nine-pound gun.[44]

Rough weather delayed the completion of Clinton's landing upon Long Island until June 18.[45] Most of the British fleet crossed the sandbar into Five Fathom Sound during this time; the heaviest ships had to be lightened by temporarily removing their cannon and ordnance to get across.[46] While the slow process of crossing the bar dragged on, the rebels in and around Charlestown watched and waited and Clinton made a disturbing discovery.

Upon a closer reconnaissance of the southern tip of Long Island, Clinton discovered that there was no fordable spot for his troops to cross over to Sullivan's Island. Seven feet of water remained in the cut at low tide. A frustrated Clinton informed Parker on June 18, "As there is no ford, there is no possibility that the Troops should take the share which we flattered ourselves they would; in this opinion all the Generals concur with me."[47] In other words, the original plan of landing troops on Sullivan's Island from Long Island and attacking the rebels in a coordinated assault with the navy (which would attack the fort at the same time) was not going to work. The British army could not ford the cut and Clinton had no desire to send his troops across the cut piecemeal fashion in the few flat boats he had to attack in detail. He estimated that, with his limited number of boats, he could send at most four to five hundred men across the cut at a time. His outnumbered men would be exposed to a murderous rebel fire from twice that many men in well-entrenched positions and Clinton refused to subject his men to that. The best Clinton could offer Commodore Parker was to transfer two battalions of infantry to the navy if Parker deemed a landing closer to the fort during the naval attack prudent. He also pledged to do his best to distract the rebels by a feigned crossing of the cut.[48]

Parker appeared unfazed by the change of plans and "seemed to imply that he thought himself fully equal to the attempt with the Ships alone, and only expected from the Troops the best Cooperation in their Power when he made it."[49] Nothing was mentioned of Clinton's offer of two battalions, so the idea was dropped.

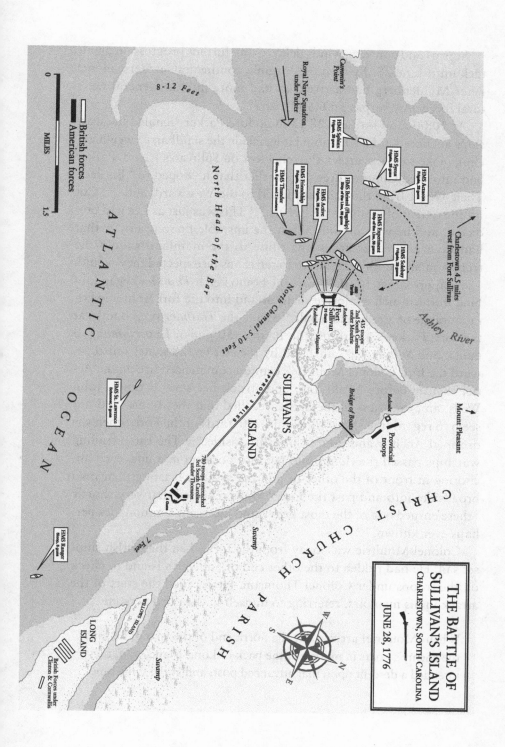

Royal Navy Squadron under Parker

Cummin's Point

8-12 Feet

North Head of the Bar

ATLANTIC OCEAN

HMS Sphinx
Frigate, 20 guns

HMS Syren
Frigate, 28 guns

HMS Actaeon
Frigate, 28 guns

HMS Thunder
Sloop, 8 guns and 2 mortars

HMS Friendship
Frigate, 22 guns

HMS Active
Frigate, 28 guns

HMS Bristol (Flagship)
Ship of the Line, 50 guns

HMS Experiment
Ship of the Line, 50 guns

HMS Solebay
Frigate, 28 guns

Charlestown 4.5 miles west from Fort Sullivan

400 Yards

North Channel 5-10 Feet

2nd South Carolina Redoubt

Fort Sullivan
31 Guns

Redoubt

435 troops under Moultrie

Magazine

Ashley River

HMS St. Lawrence
Schooner, 6 guns

SULLIVAN'S ISLAND

APPROX. 3 MILES

780 troops entrenched 3rd South Carolina under Thomson
6 Guns

Redoubt

Bridge of Boats

Provincial troops

Mount Pleasant

CHRIST CHURCH PARISH

Swamp

HMS Ranger
Sloop, 8 guns

7 Feet

WALTER'S ISLAND

Swamp

LONG ISLAND

British Forces under Clinton & Cornwallis

British forces
American forces

0   MILES   1.5

THE BATTLE OF
SULLIVAN'S ISLAND
CHARLESTOWN, SOUTH CAROLINA
JUNE 28, 1776

Storms and contrary winds delayed any further progress on an attack until June 28. By then the Virginia continentals under Colonel Peter Muhlenberg had arrived, as had more militia: General Lee's total force now surpassed 6,500 men.[50]

At 10:00 a.m. on June 28 Commodore Parker signaled his warships anchored in Five Fathom Hole, inside the sandbar, to weigh anchor, make sail, and attack the rebel fort on Sullivan's Island. Parker had informed Clinton three days earlier that he hoped to "Enfilade Their Works from the Ships stationed to the Westward, and . . . Cut off the retreat of many of the Rebels."[51] This was just as Lee had predicted, and he was anxious about the unstable floating bridge that had been erected as an escape route to the mainland should the troops on Sullivan's Island have to retreat as he expected they would.

At approximately 10:30 a.m. the bomb ketch *Thunder* began lobbing thirteen-inch explosive shells at and into the fort from a maximum range of a mile and a half.[52] While the *Thunder* fired bombs at the fort, Parker's warships, the *Bristol* (50 guns), *Experiment* (50 guns), and *Solbay* (28 guns), led by the *Active* (28 guns) sailed toward the fort. Colonel Moultrie's cannon commenced fire on the *Active* a little before 11:00 a.m. and struck her several times. John Wells, an eyewitness to the battle, recalled that the *Active* "did not seem to regard [the shots] till within 350 Yards of the Fort, when she dropped Anchor and poured in a Broadside."[53] The three trailing warships passed the *Active* and fell into position in a line, each anchoring in front of the other to join the assault, blasting their own broadsides into and past the fort.[54] Wells reported that very shortly "there ensued one of the most heavy and incessant Cannonades perhaps ever known."[55]

Colonel Moultrie was away from the fort when the British ships set sail. He had ridden to the other end of Sullivan's Island to check on the troops under Colonel Thomson. He recalled the start of the attack in his memoirs, referring to himself in the third person:

When [Moultrie] arrived, [at the north end of the island] he saw the enemy's boats in motion at the back of Long-Island, as if, they intended a descent upon that advanced post; and at the same time, he perceived the men of war, loose their top sails. . . . [Moultrie] hurried back to the fort; and on his arrival, immediately ordered the long roll to beat, and the officers and men to their posts.[56]

Moultrie described the British fire upon the fort exactly the same way as John Wells, "heavy and incessant," and added, "While from the fort a return was made, slow, but sure."[57] Moultrie also observed that

This severe trial of metal and skill, was going on between the veteran ships of the British navy, and the newly raised troops of an infant republic, from a low fort of palmetto logs; the *Thunder*, bomb-ship, was throwing thirteen inch shells in quick succession—several of which, fell into the fort; they were however, immediately buried in the loose sand, so that very few of them burst upon the garrison.[58]

While the four British warships and the rebel fort blasted away at each other, three other British ships, the *Actaeon* (28 guns), *Syren* (28 guns), and *Sphynx* (20 guns) sailed past the fight in an attempt to reach a cove to the west of the fort. One by one, each ship grounded upon shoals, the same shoals on which the later Civil War-era fortification, Fort Sumter, was constructed. Each vessel attracted the attention of the fort and received fire. The *Syren* and *Sphynx* managed to free themselves but were unable to reach the cove, so they dropped anchor and commenced long-range fire on the fort.[59] The *Actaeon* stuck fast to the shoals and struggled for the rest of the day to free herself but to no avail.

While the land-sea battle raged at the southern end of Sullivan's Island, General Clinton on Long Island, frustrated at the lack of communication with Commodore Parker, readied his force to act, "as Events should suggest."[60] As Moultrie noted, Clinton's troops appeared to be ready to attack Sullivan's Island, and in fact they were, they just awaited a signal from Parker or a favorable development in the fight. Neither occurred, and as the contest at the southern end of the island raged on into the afternoon, Clinton

Soon grew apprehensive that no serious Impression could be made [against the fort] and even every instant expected to see the Ships draw off. To our great Surprise, however, The Cannonade still continued without any favorable appearances (that we saw) until night, while the Troops remained all the Time on the Sands anxiously looking out for some Signal to let them know what the Squadron was doing but not suspected that the Kings ships could have suffered so materially.[61]

Little of consequence thus occurred at the cut between the two islands; the outcome of the British attack on Charlestown rested on the outcome of the fight at the southern end of Sullivan's Island.

Two particular incidents occurred at the fort during the battle that caught the attention of several witnesses. The details varied a bit with the telling, but an account that appeared in a South Carolina newspaper after the battle captured the essence of the events:

The behavior of two sergeants deserves to be remembered. In the beginning of the action, the flag-staff was shot away, which, being observed by Sergeant Jasper of the Grenadiers, he immediately jumped from one of the embrasures upon the beach, took up the flag, and fixed it on a sponge staff. With it in his hand he mounted the [parapet], and notwithstanding the shot that flew as thick as hail around him, he leisurely fixed it.[62]

Sergeant McDaniels was not nearly so fortunate. "Cruelly shattered by a cannonball" that struck him in the shoulder and stomach, recalled Moultrie, the dying sergeant inspired his comrades by declaring, "Fight on my brave boys; don't let liberty expire with me today!"[63]

As the battle raged on into the afternoon, the supply of gunpowder in the fort became a concern for Moultrie. He recalled that at the beginning of the battle he had 4,600 pounds of gunpowder, enough for approximately twenty-six rounds for each cannon and twenty musket cartridges for each man.[64] His gun crews had to thus be very judicious with their shots. Moultrie noted, "While the British men of war, were pouring their broadsides, in one continued storm of balls and grape shot, the cannon from the fort were slowly discharged after being pointed with precision by the officers commanding; hence almost every shot from the fort took effect."[65]

Whether this last claim by Moultrie was true is unknown, but there is no dispute that the rebel fire from the fort inflicted significant damage upon the two largest British warships and heavy losses among their crew. Commodore Parker's flagship, the *Bristol*, suffered extensive damage and lost forty-six men killed and eighty-six wounded.[66] Captain John Morris of the *Bristol* lost a hand and died soon after from his wound. Parker's other fifty-gun warship, the *Experiment*, was also severely damaged in the fight and lost forty-three men killed and seventy-five wounded, including its captain, who lost his right arm.[67] Parker suffered the indignity of having his breeches torn away in the back as well as a wound to his knee.[68]

Moultrie estimated that the British fired twelve thousand shots of various size at the fort and reported that 1,200 pieces of ordnance were collected in and around the fort after the battle.[69] That was likely more than all of the ordnance Moultrie's men fired at the British. And yet, despite the massed firepower leveled against the fort, the walls held firm and the garrison's losses were surprisingly light with eleven men killed and another twenty-five wounded.[70]

At one point in the afternoon, General Lee sent Colonel Moultrie instructions that, if he ran out of gunpowder, he was to spike his cannon and abandon the fort. Concerned that such a move would leave Colonel Thomson at the cut isolated and prone to encirclement (if the British landed at the fort after it was abandoned) Moultrie significantly slowed down his rate of fire to conserve his remaining powder.[71] Around 5:00 p.m., several hundred pounds of gunpowder, along with General Lee, arrived at the fort. Colonel Muhlenberg's Virginia continentals were also sent to the island to reinforce Colonel Thomson at the cut. Lee finally realized that holding Sullivan's Island was indeed possible. Moultrie and his garrison had thoroughly impressed Lee and had endured what Lee described as "one of the most furious cannonades I ever heard or saw."[72] Lee further admitted,

> The behavior of the Garrison, both men and officers, with Colonel Moultrie at their head, I confess, astonished me; it was brave to

the last degree. I had no idea that so much coolness and intrepidity could be displayed by a collection of raw recruits, as I was witness of in this garrison. Had we been better supplied with ammunition, it is most probably their Squadron would have been utterly destroyed.[73]

To avoid the destruction of his ships, Commodore Parker broke off the engagement at nightfall, drifting with the outgoing tide out of range of the fort. Only the *Actaeon* remained, still stuck on the shoals. Its crew abandoned her in the morning, setting the ship afire. Several boats from the fort rowed out to attempt to extinguish the blaze, but when they failed they grabbed hold of the ship's jack, bell, sails, and some stores before it was engulfed in flame and blew up.[74] The remainder of the day was quiet with no sign that the British intended to resume the fight. The largest battle to date in the South had thus concluded with a decisive American victory.

GEORGIA

Significant political changes occurred in Georgia in the spring of 1776 as the colony transitioned from royal rule to its new government. Archibald Bulloch was appointed to serve as Georgia's first president and commander-in-chief in April. The Council of Safety, which still operated until the new government was fully functioning, approved a brief congratulatory address to Bulloch, reminding Georgians that the formation of the new government "was the only alternative of anarchy and misery, and by consequence the effect of dire necessity."[75]

Georgians near the border with East Florida had endured a number of raids over the spring from loyalist "banditti" in the region. Two of Governor Wright's brothers erected a fort on their plantation on the St. Marys River, reportedly manned by twenty White men and a number of armed slaves.[76] It was assumed that several of the Tory incursions in southern Georgia originated there.

In mid-May President Bulloch ordered Captain William McIntosh to lead his troop (section) of cavalry southward to capture the fort and its inhabitants and ordnance. Upon completion of that mission, McIntosh was to proceed to the St. Marys River and apprehend Martin Jollie, a reputed Tory who reportedly had accumulated a large magazine of gunpowder and arms.[77] McIntosh was ordered to secure all of the military stores and provisions in Jollie's possession as well as "any other persons whose going at large may endanger the liberties of America" (a rather broad directive).[78] A day later, Captain McIntosh received new orders to build log houses or puncheon forts along the Altamaha and St. Marys Rivers and drive a number of Tory-owned cattle near the border with East Florida farther into Georgia.[79] The responsibility to attack Fort Wright, as it became known, would fall to someone else.

The rest of May saw similar directives from President Bulloch. Appointments to militia units were made, fortified positions built, suspected Tories confronted, and private concerns of those harmed by the chaos of revolution addressed.

The arrival of Commodore Parker's powerful British fleet at Charlestown at the start of June sparked an increase in military activity in Georgia. The Council of Safety ordered that "Every man liable to bear arms shall do militia duty in the Parish, or District where he resides, unless he shall be enrolled in some volunteer company."[80]

On June 22, with an attack on Charlestown imminent, President Bulloch ordered Georgia's lone continental battalion, which was scattered in several locations in Georgia, to assemble in Savannah "without loss of time."[81]

Not all of Georgia's movements were defensive in nature that summer. The implementation of Captain William McIntosh's orders from mid-May to attack Fort Wright fell to Captain John Baker of St. John's Parish, and he was unable to carry them out until July. According to historian Hugh McCall, who published the first account of this engagement in 1816 based largely on the recollections of veterans of the Revolution, Captain Baker led approximately seventy mounted militia southward and halted within a short distance of the fort, concealed by a thick wood. Informed that a large party of Indians were encamped nearby and that their number, when added to the fort's garrison, significantly outnumbered his force, Baker resolved to wait for nightfall to attack, hoping that shock and surprise would win the day.[82]

His party was discovered, however, and the alarmed garrison fired their cannon to attract the attention of several boats and the *St. John*, which lay two miles downriver. Anticipating that the warship would send reinforcements, Baker posted some of his men near the boat landing where they waited in ambush. The rest engaged the fort with ineffective musket fire.[83]

Just as Baker predicted, a small cutter approached the landing and was blasted by a volley of militia gunfire, killing two aboard and causing the rest to plead for quarter (surrender).[84] The master and boatswain of the *St. John* and a lieutenant in the 16th British Regiment were captured. Closer to the fort, Baker was able to seize approximately twenty slaves, but the fort held firm.[85]

Realizing that a large number of enemy reinforcements were likely bearing down on him, Baker withdrew with his prisoners. They halted for the evening after proceeding about nine miles. While most of Baker's men slept, brothers Daniel and James McGirth, who were standing guard, gathered up as many of the dismounted horses as they could and deserted to the enemy.[86] They would continue their notorious behavior over the course of the war in the service of the crown and themselves.

EAST FLORIDA

In St. Augustine, Governor Tonyn remained anxious, not only about possible attacks from Georgia rebels but also about a shortage of provisions for the inhabitants of St. Augustine. In mid-June, Captain Andrew Hamond aboard the HMS *Roebuck* in the Chesapeake Bay with Governor Dunmore responded to a report that "The People [at St. Augustine] were in the greatest distress imaginable for want of Provisions."[87] Hamond dispatched his tender with a supply of flour and beef and "everything that could be collected in the Fleet for the relief of the Garrison."[88]

The shortage of food in East Florida was primarily due to the steady influx of Tory refugees who arrived regularly in St. Augustine. Many came with the bare necessities, and their growing number outpaced the supply of food the colony produced and imported. To make matters worse, many of the refugees had abandoned valuable property in their flight, only to be accosted by the British navy who seized what little property they did bring, including the ships they sailed on, per instructions from London to restrict all trade between the colonists. Surely, they pleaded with Governor Tonyn, the British ministry did not mean for the restrictions to apply to loyal British subjects fleeing from the oppression of the rebels.[89]

Tonyn was focused on defending East Florida, a challenge that became a bit easier with the arrival of three companies of the 60th Regiment from Jamaica. With two British schooners, the *Hinchinbrook* and *St. John*, stationed at St. Augustine, Tonyn was able to keep better watch for possible rebel threats. With only six cannon and a crew of thirty on each vessel, however, the governor surely did not have the firepower to stop a large rebel naval force like the one that raided New Providence in the spring.

The *St. John* was given the responsibility of guarding the St. Marys River, the border between East Florida and Georgia. Lieutenant John Graves and his crew spent all of June patrolling the river, skirmishing with parties of Georgian rebels, and supporting an infantry detachment under Captain Graham (probably of the 16th Regiment) posted in the region to also guard the river.[90] The *Hinchinbrook* appears to have been used to patrol the coast of East Florida, all the way down to the Keys.[91]

With two large British forces to the north in South Carolina and New York, Governor Tonyn was no longer overly concerned about a large-scale attack upon St. Augustine. The detachment of troops from the 60th and 16th Regiments, who joined the remnants of the 14th Regiment in the spring, also eased the governor's concern for the safety of the city. Cross-border raids from Georgia, however, remained a strong possibility and became the primary focus of Governor Tonyn in the summer of 1776. Like all of the colonists of British America, he also likely awaited the latest news from both Philadelphia and London in hopes of gaining clearer guidance and direction for his own actions.

Eight

Securing Independence

W HEN INDEPENDENCE WAS FORMALLY DECLARED BY THE Continental Congress on July 4, 1776, the conflict with Great Britain turned into a war for American sovereignty. Although most eyes swung to New York and watched with awe as Britain's enormous invasion force gathered and grew on Staten Island and in New York Harbor, many patriots in the southern states rejoiced in the victory at Charlestown and then at news of American independence. But trouble to the west was brewing, and Britain, with its strong navy, could always return.

VIRGINIA

Although most Virginians rejoiced at the news from South Carolina that the British navy had been repulsed at Charlestown, the threat from Governor Dunmore still existed. The long stalemate at Gwynn's Island in the Chesapeake Bay was shattered on July 9, however, with the crash of American artillery fire from shore. Six weeks had passed since Governor Dunmore's arrival at Gwynn's Island, and he and his supporters believed they were secure from attack, protected by the guns of the British navy, several artillery batteries along the south-western shore of Gwynn's Island, and the narrow body of water that separated the island from the mainland.

The Virginians had erected two artillery batteries during the stalemate, one of two eighteen-pounder cannon, positioned directly across from Dunmore's fortified camp, and within range of Lord Dunmore's ship, the *Dunmore*, and another of four nine-pounder cannon a few hundred yards south of the eighteen-pounders. They were also in range of the *Dunmore* but focused their aim instead on Dunmore's encampment and the three British tenders that were in Milford Haven, the narrow body of water between the island and mainland.

At some point in the morning (reports differ on the start of the bombardment) an eighteen-pounder rebel cannon opened fire on the *Dunmore*, anchored close to the mainland. The first shot reportedly crashed through the stern of the ship, slightly wounding Governor Dunmore, who Purdie's *Virginia Gazette* reported received a splinter in his leg.[1] The other eighteen-pound gun quickly followed and also struck the *Dunmore*. The four nine-pound cannon joined the bombardment, directing their fire upon the camp and earthworks. Captain Hamond on the *Roebuck* reported that it was not long before the *Dunmore* realized it was overmatched: "[The rebels] directed their Fire principally upon Lord Dunmore's Ship . . . . The Dunmore returned the Fire, but seeing that her small Guns had no effect upon either of the Batterys, and that every shot from the Enemy struck the Ship she cut her Cable, and being Calm, [was] towed off out of reach of the Guns."[2]

The *Dunmore* was not the only ship to flee from the rebel cannon fire. Most of the scattered fleet sought safety at a greater distance from shore. While the gun crews of General Andrew Lewis's eighteen-pounders focused their efforts against the *Dunmore*, the gunners of the four nine-pounders concentrated their fire on Dunmore's encampment. Dunmore's troops replied with cannon fire of their own, but the accuracy of the rebel artillery quickly silenced the governor's cannon and raked the encampment, throwing Dunmore's troops into confusion.[3]

The patriot fire briefly halted when the immediate commander of the two eighteen-pounders, Captain Dohickey Arundel, unwisely experimented with a wooden mortar that exploded on its first shot and killed Arundel instantly. This tragic episode was the one sour note to an otherwise immensely successful morning for the rebels. They had little to shoot at by noon, what with Dunmore's fleet drawn off deeper into the bay and many of his troops withdrawn from their camp.

Governor Dunmore and Captain Hamond agreed that the rebel artillery made Gwynn's Island untenable, and they prepared to evacuate the island in the evening. Under cover of darkness, the cannon, tents, and other military stores were loaded onto ships. Guards were posted along the shore to watch for a surprise rebel landing, but a shortage of boats on the mainland prevented any such move by General Lewis.

Lewis's troops gathered a number of canoes and other small boats in the evening in anticipation of crossing Milford Haven the next day. At dawn the patriot batteries resumed their fire on the three British tenders that had remained in Milford Haven. A rebel observer noted, "There were three tenders in the haven, which attempted to prevent our passage. Their works were still manned as if they meant to dispute their ground, but as soon as our soldiers put off in a few canoes, they retreated precipitately to their ships. The tenders fell into our hands, one they set on fire, but our people boarded it and extinguished the flames."[4]

With the tenders eliminated, a detachment of Virginia troops embarked on canoes to cross over to the island. Captain Thomas Posey was one of the first to reach Gwynn's Island and described the landing in his diary:

Crossed into the Island but no fighting ensued except a few shot. By one o'clock the whole of the enemy had evacuated and embarked . . . I cannot help observing, that I never saw more distress in my life, than what I found among some of the poor deluded Negroes which they could not take time, or did not chuse to carry off with them, they being sick. Those that I saw, some were dying, and many calling out for help; and throughout the whole Island we found them strew'd about, many of them torn to pieces by wild beasts—great numbers of the bodies having never been buried.[5]

British losses at Gwynn's Island are difficult to ascertain. Captain Posey estimated "that at least 4 or 500 negroes lost their lives" during the six-week occupation of the island.[6] Posey added that another 150 soldiers were also lost. The vast majority of these deaths occurred prior to the attack as a result of illness. Such losses significantly hampered the effectiveness of Dunmore's force and explained his feeble response to the attack.

The events at Gwynn's Island exasperated Lord Dunmore. His men were weak from disease and demoralized by defeat, and there was little hope of assistance from Britain. Dunmore made preparations to leave Virginia and join General William Howe's large invasion force off of New York. Ships were sent up the Potomac River to obtain badly needed fresh water while Dunmore lingered in the Chesapeake Bay. He abandoned Virginia in mid-August and sailed with half of his force to New York. The other half of Dunmore's flotilla sailed to St. Augustine, Florida.[7]

About three weeks earlier, in late July, news of the Declaration of Independence had reached Virginia. A copy of the declaration appeared on page two of John Dixon and William Hunter's July 20, 1776, edition of their *Virginia Gazette*.[8] Five days later, the declaration was publically read "amidst the acclamations of the people" assembled at the Capitol, the courthouse, and the governor's palace (now occupied by Governor Patrick Henry).[9] Each reading was "accompanied by firing of cannon and musketry," provided by the several continental regiments who paraded in the capital.[10]

Dunmore's departure from Virginia was a significant development, for it ushered in three years of relative peace in eastern and central Virginia and allowed thousands of Virginians to march north to reinforce General Washington's Continental Army in New York. Those Virginians played a crucial role in the battles to come, namely Trenton and Princeton in the winter of 1776-77, as well as those that followed in 1777 and 1778. By the end of July 1776, however, the attention of Virginians was not just on events to the north. Reports of Native American attacks on settlements along the frontier greatly concerned Virginians.

NORTH CAROLINA

News of the Declaration of Independence traveled quickly (relatively speaking) in the colonies, delivered by express riders and disseminated through newspapers. It reached the North Carolina Council of Safety in Halifax on July 22.[11] The council immediately instructed the county committees to summon their people in order to "have the Independency Proclaimed in the most public manner."[12]

North Carolina historian Hugh Rankin notes that the first public reading of the Declaration occurred in Halifax before a large crowd on August 1, 1776. When Cornelius Harnett, the president of the Council of Safety, concluded, a mighty cheer rang out from those assembled. According to Rankin, the jubilant crowd then hoisted Harnett on their shoulders and paraded happily through the town.[13]

As pleased and relieved as many North Carolinians were to have resolved the issue of independence, the state's leaders had little time to dwell on the news. Multiple reports of bloodshed on the frontier at the hands of the Cherokee forced them to concentrate their attention on this new crisis.

SOUTH CAROLINA

The news of the Declaration of Independence reached South Carolina on the heels of the departure of the last British ships in early August. Following the Battle of Sullivan's Island on June 28, the battered and bloodied British fleet sat anchored in Five Fathom Hole repairing the damage and preparing to sail to New York. General Clinton was anxious to get underway to join General William Howe's enormous invasion force at New York, but the navy had to once again navigate across the tricky sandbar, which was finally completed by early August.[14]

As the last British ships disappeared from the South Carolina coast, an express rider arrived in Charlestown with news of the Declaration. Colonel William Moultrie recalled that the express arrived on August 2, and "The account was received, with the greatest joy, and on the 5th of August, Independency was declared by all the officers, civil and military, making a grand procession on the occasion.

. . . all of the troops in town were paraded near the Liberty Tree where the Declaration of Independence was read."[15]

South Carolina's attention now turned west, where reports of Native American unrest had to be addressed, and south, where the British still held East Florida.

GEORGIA

Georgians had been focused on East Florida for several months, sending armed parties to the border along the St. Marys River to confront suspected Tories as well as secure cattle and other useful provisions. For much of July they were also petrified that General Clinton's failed expedition off Charlestown would come next to Savannah, and they pleaded with General Lee for reinforcements.[16] Lee sought approval from South Carolina officials to include some of their militia in the force he planned to march to Savannah. The crisis calmed considerably by the end of July when reports that Clinton and Parker's fleet had not, as reported previously, appeared off the mouth of the Savannah River.[17]

Lee was still determined to march a force into Georgia and then into East Florida to "attempt breaking up the whole Province."[18] He recognized that laying siege to St. Augustine itself was impractical, "having neither boats, horses, waggons, nor any other means of conveying Cannon, Ammunition, or provision for [such a] purpose."[19] He contended, however, that attacking the several Tory outposts along the St. Marys River as well as the plantations outside of St. Augustine would "Be a security to Georgia, occasion infinite distress to the Garrison of St. Augustine, but above all, make a salutary impression on the minds of the Creeks who now are thought to stand wavering."[20]

It took Lee two more weeks to reach Savannah with his combined force of Virginia, North Carolina, and South Carolina troops. Before he arrived, in mid-August, exciting news from Philadelphia electrified Georgia.

When news of the Declaration of Independence reached Savannah on or about August 10, it was met with much revelry. The news arrived in a letter from Congress that was read before President Bulloch and the Council of Safety. Following the reading, they "proceeded to the square before the Assembly House and read it likewise before a great concourse of people, when [the troops] fired a general volley."[21]

The celebration continued with a procession to the Liberty Pole, where the militia and more of the public joined them. The declaration was read again and this time saluted by a discharge of cannon. The procession continued to one more location, the battery near the Trustees Gardens, where the declaration was read a final time and saluted again with musketry. The officers and gentlemen then "dined under the Cedar Trees, and cheerfully drank to the United, Free, and Independent States of America."[22]

In the evening, Savannah was illuminated, and a very solemn mock funeral was held in front of the courthouse for the statue of George III where it was proclaimed,

> For as much as George III, of Great Britain, hath most flagrantly violated his coronation oath and trampled upon the constitution of our country and the sacred rights of mankind, we therefore commit his political existence to the ground, corruption to corruption, tyranny to the grave, and oppression to eternal infamy, in sure and certain hope that he will never obtain a resurrection to rule again over these United States of America. But my friends and fellow-citizens, let us not be sorry as men without hope for tyrants that thus depart; rather let us remember America is free and independent; that she is, and will be, with the blessing of the Almighty, great among the nations of the earth. Let this encourage us in well-doing to fight for our rights and privileges, for our wives and children, for all that is near and dear unto us. May God give us his blessing, and let all the people say Amen![23]

Attention turned to Lee's proposed expedition against East Florida when he arrived in Savannah a few days later. Lee was surprised to learn that the British outposts on the St. Marys River had been abandoned and the whole country between that river and the St. John River was already broken up. He put it to the Georgia Council of Safety whether, given this development, it was still worthwhile to proceed with an expedition into East Florida.[24] The council assured

Lee that it was and outlined their plan to supply Lee's troops with provisions.[25]

Sickness among the troops (particularly malaria), which significantly reduced Lee's troop strength, combined with supply deficiencies, plagued the expedition, and only a portion of Lee's force reached Sunbury, thirty miles south of Savannah.[26] That was as far as the expedition would get. Lee, still stuck in Savannah near the end of August, vented his frustration to General John Armstrong in Charlestown:

> The people here are if possible more harum skarum than their sister Colony. They will propose anything and after they have propos'd it, discover that they are incapable of performing the least. They have propos'd securing their Frontier by constant patroles of horse Rangers, when the scheme is approv'd of they scratch their heads for some days, and at length inform you that there is a small difficulty in the way; that of the impossibility to procure a single horse—Their next project is to keep their inland Navigation clear . . . by a fleet of *Guards Costa* arm'd boats, when this is agreed to, they recollect that they have not a single boat—Upon the whole I shou'd not be surpriz'd of they were to propose mounting a body of Mermaids on Alligators![27]

Lee was soon relieved of his frustration when orders from Congress arrived instructing him to join Washington in New York. With Lee's departure, the expedition against East Florida dissolved and Georgians returned to worrying about British and Tory raiders to their south and Indian raids to their west and north.

EAST FLORIDA

When word of the Declaration of Independence reached St. Augustine and the rest of East Florida, presumably in mid to late August, it was likely received with dismay and disappointment. Governor Tonyn and the loyalists of East Florida had no time to dwell on such sentiment, however. Prior to word of the Declaration of Independence, East Florida's inhabitants were alarmed by a rebel attack upon the lone British warship assigned to the colony, the *St. John*. The vessel was posted, along with a detachment of British troops, on the St. Marys River, and the engagement occurred near the mouth of the river off Amelia Island.

Lieutenant William Grant, the commander of the *St. John*, reported to Governor Tonyn that early in the morning of August 7 a lookout spotted what Lieutenant Grant described as a "large flat (barge) resembling a Vessel cut down and made into a floating Battery, with one Mast and liberty Colours flying, full of . . . a great Number of Men."[28] Grant ordered his crew to prepare for battle, noting in the ship's log, "We . . . loaded all of the Guns with round & Grape Shot . . . [and] loaded the small Arms, Got up the Hand granadoes."[29]

The rebel barge was towed by oarsmen in several smaller boats, and when they came within range of the *St. John*, the barge opened fire with several cannon, prompting return shots from the British warship. Grant noticed several other rebel vessels, also being towed, moving to the barge, so he decided to disengage. As there was little wind to maneuver with, Grant had his own sailors tow the *St. John* across the sandbar and out to sea.[30]

This brief engagement off Amelia Island in early August caused the British to abandon the St. Marys River, but their absence was brief. The cancellation of Lee's expedition to East Florida presented new opportunities in the months that followed for Governor Tonyn and his supporters to strike back at Georgia.

WAR WITH THE CHEROKEE
One other event erupted in the summer of 1776 that impacted most of the southern colonies, a brutal war along the frontier. Although British efforts to convince Creek leaders to declare war against the rebellious colonists in Georgia and South Carolina failed, the Cherokee embraced the idea and were joined by warriors to their north, as well as young Creek warriors who participated against the wishes of their leaders. Cherokee, Shawnee, Mingo, Creek, and other warriors struck throughout the southern frontier in the summer of 1776, not so much to support British interests but to defend their land from the steady encroachment of white settlers.

It was not for a lack of trying that the British failed to convince the Indians to go to war on British terms. In February 1776, Thomas

Brown, the embittered Tory leader had who fled to St. Augustine earlier in the winter, presented a bold plan to Governor Tonyn calling for the recruitment of Indians all along the southern frontier. In conjunction with Tory militia in the backcountry, of which Brown assured Tonyn there were thousands, the Indians and Tories would strike at the rebellious colonists in Georgia and South Carolina (apparently believing that the reported British expedition sailing for the South was destined for Savannah). Brown argued that the attacks on the frontier should be coordinated with the arrival of the British expedition.[31]

He asserted that such a show of force on the coast and backcountry would demoralize rebels throughout the South and invigorate loyalists, who had remained quiet after the disastrous Battle at Long Canes in South Carolina in December and crown force reverses at Moores Creek and Charlestown. The colonies would then fall one at a time as British forces advanced north from Georgia.[32]

Indian Superintendent Henry Stuart had been working for some time to supply the Creeks and Cherokee with ammunition and trade items in the event they were needed to fight. General Gage had requested that Stuart cultivate Indian support in September 1775, and although Stuart likely worried about the bloodshed that would be unleashed on the frontier, bloodshed that would strike rebel and Tory alike as well as Indian, he strove to comply with Gage's instructions, sending his brother Henry Stuart to Pensacola by boat with a supply of gunpowder and lead.[33]

Henry Stuart arrived in Pensacola in early February and was surprised to learn that the renowned Cherokee warrior Tssiyugunsini, son of Attakullakulla (Little Carpenter), was in Mobile with eighty warriors, waiting to talk to Stuart.[34] Tssiyugunsini, who the colonists called Dragging Canoe, was angry about the steady encroachment of White settlers upon Cherokee land that had been, at least in some cases, encouraged by Cherokee leaders including his father, who struck land deals with the colonists.

Dragging Canoe and his warriors accompanied Stuart on an arduous two-month trek by pack horse and canoe into Creek and then Cherokee country.[35] While Stuart and Dragging Canoe slowly trekked northward, American representatives attempted to gain Indian support. The Continental Congress in Philadelphia sent representatives with several thousand pounds sterling to purchase native neutrality. They met at Fort Charlotte in South Carolina with representatives from the Lower Cherokee and left with the impression that they had succeeded.[36] They were mistaken. The delegation was more successful with the Creeks, meeting Creek leaders in Augusta, Georgia.

Henry Stuart joined Alexander Cameron in the Cherokee town of Toquah in late April, and together they met with Cherokee leaders in Chota. Many of the Cherokee wished to drive out the settlers of Watauga and Nolichucky (in what was then western North Carolina and Virginia), but Stuart and Cameron convinced them to wait until they sent letters giving the settlers a chance to leave peacefully.[37] Indiscriminate Indian attacks upon these settlements would do little to further the British cause and cause bloodshed among rebel and Tory settlers alike. They also wished to better coordinate any Indian attack with the British efforts to the east.

The Cherokee agreed to wait, and letters were sent to the settlers warning them that they had to leave immediately. The settlers stalled for more time and sought military aid from the governments of Virginia and North Carolina.[38] While the Cherokee impatiently waited, representatives from several northern Indian groups arrived to advocate for war.[39] They too were aggrieved by White encroachment of their lands and planned to strike back.

The situation was becoming unmanageable for Stuart and Cameron. If there were to be attacks on the frontier, they wished them to be coordinated with the British and targeted against rebel settlers. But the Indians wanted all of the trespassing settlers gone and would thus attack rebel and Tory alike. There was nothing Cameron and Stuart could do to stop them.

Fighting had already erupted on the Georgia and South Carolina frontier in late June; by mid-July the full force of the Indian attacks was felt. Settlements in Kentucky and all along the southern frontier were attacked at significant loss to both sides. As the goal of the Cherokee and their allies was to remove the trespassing settlers from their land, they spared nothing. Cabins were burned, livestock and

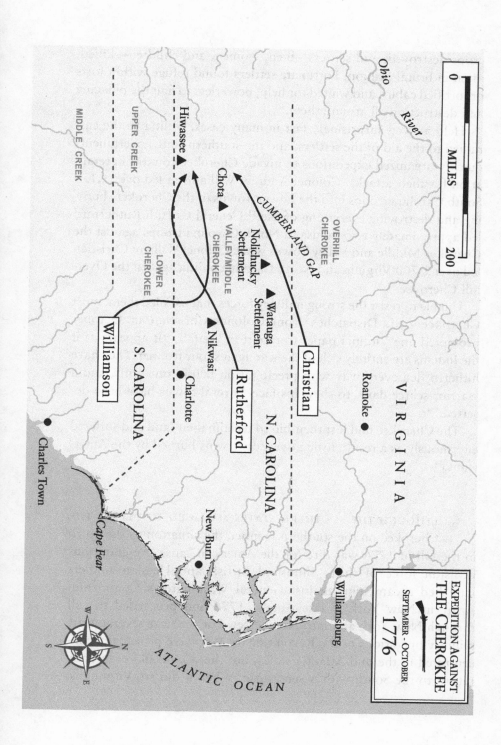

EXPEDITION AGAINST
THE CHEROKEE
SEPTEMBER – OCTOBER
1776

crops destroyed, and settlers—men, women, and children—killed, often in brutal fashion. Fortunate settlers found refuge within forts or fortified cabins and waited for help, powerless to halt the pillaging and destruction all around them.[40]

Help arrived surprisingly fast in many cases. Militia to the east rallied to the aid of the settlers, and the southern state governments quickly organized expeditions to invade Cherokee country in retaliation for their attacks. Colonel Andrew Williamson led over 1,150 South Carolina troops into the Lower Towns of the Cherokee, burning and destroying everything of use.[41] General Griffith Rutherford led approximately two thousand North Carolina troops against the Cherokee Middle and Valley Towns while Colonel William Christian led over 1,700 Virginia and North Carolina militia against the Over-hill Cherokee.[42]

Unable to resist the strong military forces that assailed them, most Cherokee fled. Dispatches from Colonel Christian in October prompted one Virginia paper to report in the fall, "It appears as if the Indians are entirely sick of the war against our frontier. They have hitherto fled every way with precipitation before our army, and a warrior scarce dares to shew his face. Several towns have been deserted."[43]

The Cherokee had lost their bid to reclaim their land and suffered enormously as a result, losing over fifty towns burned by the Americans.[44]

ALTHOUGH THE SOUTHERN STATES MANAGED TO DEFEAT THE Cherokee on the southern frontier, the situation to the north in the fall of 1776 was dire for the American cause. An enormous invasion force of thirty thousand British and Hessian soldiers launched a campaign against General Washington's Continental Army in New York in late August 1776 and proceeded to roll through New York and into New Jersey. For the next several years military operations of the Revolutionary War were principally concentrated in the mid-Atlantic states, but the war would eventually return to the South with a vengeance. When it did so, Virginians,

North Carolinians, South Carolinians, and Georgians, bolstered by their experiences at the start of the war, did their best to meet the challenge. The loyalists of East Florida hoped they would fail.

The sixteen months that passed between the start of the Revolutionary War in Massachusetts in April 1775 through the summer of 1776 were eventful in all of the American colonies. While much of the focus for this time period has traditionally centered on events in New England with an assumption that American independence was inevitable, we see that the reality in the southern colonies during this span of time was much more complex. Each colony had unique circumstances, challenges, and experiences in the first years of the war that, had things gone differently, could have significantly altered the history of each province and perhaps the Revolution itself.

NOTES

INTRODUCTION

1. "Estimated Population of American Colonies: 1610 to 1780," *Historical Statistics of the United States: Colonial Times to 1970*, Part 2 (U.S. Census Bureau), 1168.

2. James H. Soltow, "Table V: Number of Hogsheads of Tobacco Exported from Virginia, 1745-56, 1768-69, and 1773," *The Economic Role of Williamsburg* (Colonial Williamsburg Foundation Library Research Report Series, 1956), 20.

3. "Value and Quantity of Articles Exported from British Continent Colonies, by Destination: 1770," *Historical Statistics of the United States: Colonial Times to 1970*, Part 2 (U.S. Census Bureau), 1184.

4. Lorena Walsh, Ann Smart Martin, and Joanne Bowen, "Table 2.7: Population and Estimated Food Requirements in 1775," *Provisioning Early American Towns, The Chesapeake: A Multidisciplinary Case Study: Final Performance Report*, Colonial Williamsburg Foundation Library Research Report Series, No. 0404, 1997, 62.

5. "Estimated Population of American Colonies: 1610 to 1780," *Historical Statistics of the United States: Colonial Times to 1970*, Part 2 (U.S. Census Bureau), 1168.

6. Ibid.

7. Ibid.

8. Charles C. Jones Jr., *The History of Georgia*, Vol. 2 (Boston: Houghton, Mifflin and Co., 1883), 130.

9. Ibid., 133-134.

10. Carole Watterson Troxler, "Refuge, Resistance, and Reward: The Southern Loyalists' Claim on East Florida," *Journal of Southern History*, Vol. 55, No. 4 (November 1989), 566.

11. William Clark, ed., "Governor Tonyn to Lord Dartmouth, January 23, 1776," *Naval Documents of the American Revolution*, Vol. 1 (Washington, DC, 1964), 70-72.

CHAPTER ONE: SPRING 1775

1. Clark, ed., "Journal of His Majesty's Schooner *Magdalen*, April 20, 1775," *Naval Documents of the American Revolution*, Vol. 1, 204.

2. K. G. Davies, ed., "Governor Earl of Dunmore to Earl of Dartmouth, May 1, 1775," *Documents of the American Revolution*, Vol. 9 (Shannon: Irish University Press), 107-108.

3. Ibid.

4. John P. Kennedy, ed., "John Randolph Testimony," *Journal of the House of Burgesses: 1773-1776* (Richmond, VA, 1905), 233; and Alexander Purdie, "April 21, 1775," *Virginia Gazette Supplement*, 3.

5. Davies, ed., "Dunmore to Dartmouth, May 1, 1775," *Documents of the American Revolution*, Vol. 9, 108.

6. Robert L. Scribner, ed., *Revolutionary Virginia: The Road to Independence*, Vol. 3 (Charlottesville: University Press of Virginia, 1977), 55.

7. Davies, ed., "Dunmore to Dartmouth, May 1, 1775," *Documents of the American Revolution*, Vol. 9, 108.

8. Scribner, ed., *Revolutionary Virginia: The Road to Independence*, Vol. 3, 55.

9. Kennedy, ed., "Testimony of Mayor John Dixon," *Journal of the House of Burgesses: 1773-1776*, 233.

10. Kennedy, ed., "Testimony of Benjamin Waller," *Journal of the House of Burgesses: 1773-1776*, 231-232.

11. Ibid.

12. Kennedy, ed., "Testimony of Mayor John Dixon," *Journal of the House of Burgesses: 1773-1776*, 233.

13. Kennedy, ed., "Testimony of Dr. William Pasteur," *Journal of the House of Burgesses: 1773-1776*, 231.

14. Ibid., 231.

15. Alexander Purdie, "April 21, 1775," *Virginia Gazette Supplement*, 2.

16. Purdie, "April 28, 1775," *Virginia Gazette Supplement*, 3.

17. Davies, ed., "Dunmore to Dartmouth, May 1, 1775," *Documents of the American Revolution*, Vol. 9, 109.

18. Ibid.

19. Ibid.

20. Ibid., 110.

21. Clark, ed., *Naval Documents of the American Revolution*, Vol. 1, 214-215.

22. Scribner, ed., "Peyton Randolph to Mann Page Jr..., April 27, 1775," *Revolutionary Virginia: The Road to Independence*, Vol. 3, 63-64.

23. Scribner, ed., "Fairfax County Committee to Prince William County Committee, April 28, 1775," *Revolutionary Virginia: The Road to Independence*, Vol. 3, 68.

24. John Pinkney, "April 28, 1775," *Virginia Gazette Supplement*, 2.

25. Ibid.

26. Scribner, ed., "Spotsylvania Council, April 29, 1775," *Revolutionary Virginia: The Road to Independence*, Vol. 3, 71.

27. William Wirt, *Sketches in the Life and Character of Patrick Henry* (Philadelphia, 1817), 137.

28. Note: Newcastle was a bustling colonial community and a crossing point over the Pamunkey River in Hanover County that has since completely disappeared.

29. Purdie, "May 5, 1775," *Virginia Gazette Supplement*, 2.

30. Pinkney, "May 4, 1775," *Virginia Gazette*, 3.

31. Scribner, ed., *Revolutionary Virginia: The Road to Independence*, Vol. 3, 9.

32. Wirt, 142.
33. Scribner, ed., *Revolutionary Virginia: The Road to Independence,* Vol. 3, 100-101.
34. John Selby, *The Revolution in Virginia: 1775-1783* (Colonial Williamsburg Foundation, 1988), 41.
35. Pinkney, "June 1, 1775," *Virginia Gazette,* 3.
36. Davies, ed., "Dunmore to Dartmouth, June 25, 1775," *Documents of the American Revolution,* Vol. 9, 200-201.
37. Kennedy, ed., "June 1, 1775," *Journal of the House of Burgesses: 1773-1776,* 174-75.
38. Ibid.
39. Kennedy, ed., "June 5, 1775," *Journal of the House of Burgesses: 1773-1776,* 187-88.
40. Ibid.
41. Ibid., 190.
42. Selby, 42.
43. John Dixon and William Hunter, "June 10, 1775," *Virginia Gazette,* 2.
44. Purdie, "June 9, 1775," *Virginia Gazette Supplement,* 2.
45. Pinkney, "June 8, 1775," *Virginia Gazette,* 3.
46. Kennedy, ed., "June 6, 1775," *Journal of the House of Burgesses: 1773-1776,* 198.
47. Ibid.
48. Ibid.
49. Kennedy, ed., "June 7, 1775," *Journal of the House of Burgesses: 1773-1776,* 199, 201.
50. Pinkney, "June 8, 1775," *Virginia Gazette,* 3.
51. Ibid.
52. William L. Saunders, ed., "Governor Martin to Lord Dartmouth, March 23, 1775," *Colonial Records of North Carolina,* Vol. 9 (Raleigh, 1890), 1174.
53. Ibid.
54. Ibid.
55. Saunders, ed., "Governor Martin's Proclamations of April 2 and April 5 and Proceedings of the 2nd Provincial Congress, April 5, 1775," *Colonial Records of North Carolina,* Vol. 9, 1177, 1187, 1181.
56. Saunders, ed., "Proceedings of the 2nd Provincial Congress, April 5, 1775," *Colonial Records of North Carolina,* Vol. 9, 1181.
57. Saunders, ed., "Governor Martin to Lord Dartmouth, April 7, 1775," *Colonial Records of North Carolina,* Vol. 9, 1214.
58. Ibid.
59. Saunders, ed., "Governor Martin to Lord Dartmouth, April 20, 1775," *Colonial Records of North Carolina,* Vol. 9, 1228.
60. Ibid.
61. Ibid.
62. Alonzo T. Dill Jr., "Eighteenth Century New Bern: A History of the Town and Craven County, 1700-1800," Part 7, *North Carolina Historical Review,*

Vol. 23, No. 3 (July 1946), 331; and Saunders, ed., "Governor Martin to Lord Dartmouth, May 18, 1775," *Colonial Records of North Carolina*, Vol. 9, 1256.

63. *North Carolina Gazette*, May 12, 1775.

64. Saunders, ed., "Governor Martin to Lord Dartmouth, May 18, 1775," *Colonial Records of North Carolina*, Vol. 9, 1256.

65. William L. Saunders, ed., "Governor Martin to Lord Dartmouth, June 30, 1775," *Colonial Records of North Carolina*, Vol. 10 (Raleigh, 1890), 46.

66. Ibid.

67. Ibid.

68. Ibid.

69. Clark, ed., "South Carolina Gazette, June 20, 1775," *Naval Documents of the American Revolution*, Vol. 1, 598.

70. Saunders, ed., "Mecklenburg Resolves, May 31, 1775," *Colonial Records of North Carolina*, Vol. 9, 1282-283. Note: The Mecklenburg Resolves of May 31, 1775, are often confused with another set of resolves that were reportedly passed in Charlotte eleven days earlier on May 20, 1775, which declared Mecklenburg County's independence from Great Britain. "Resolved, That we the citizens of Mecklenburg County do hereby dissolve the political bands which have connected us to the mother country and hereby absolve ourselves from all allegiance to the British Crown." It is unclear whether the May 20th declaration is actually authentic; there is evidence to support both sides of the argument. The resolves were never published during the Revolution, and if an original document existed it has long since disappeared. Yet, in his article entitled "The Mecklenburg Declaration in Revolutionary War Pension Applications," published on March 10, 2015, in the *Journal of the American Revolution*, Scott Syfert argues that although there are four references to the Mecklenburg Declaration of Independence in pension applications that lend credence to the argument that the declaration actually took place, the applications are not definitive proof so "the case continues."

71. Ibid.

72. William Moultrie, *Memoirs of the American Revolution*, Vol. 1 (New York, 1802), 55.

73. Ibid., 57.

74. Ibid., 60.

75. David Chestnut, ed., "Henry Laurens to John Laurens, April 22, 1775," *The Papers of Henry Laurens*, Vol. 10 (Columbia: University of South Carolina Press, 1985), 103-104.

76. Ibid.

77. John Drayton, *Memoirs of the American Revolution from its Commencement to the year 1776*, Vol. 1, 1821, 221

78. Drayton, "Lt. Governor William Bull to the South Carolina Assembly, April 24, 1775," *Memoirs of the American Revolution from its Commencement to the year 1776*, Vol. 1, 224-225.

79. Moultrie, 60.

80. Drayton, *Memoirs of the American Revolution from its Commencement to the year 1776*, Vol. 1, 246.

81. Chesnut, ed., "Henry Laurens to John Laurens, May 9, 1775," *The Papers of Henry Laurens*, Vol. 10, 115.

82. Chesnut, ed., "Henry Laurens to John Laurens, May 15, 1775," *The Papers of Henry Laurens*, Vol. 10, 118-119.

83. Clark, ed., "Alexander Innes to Lord Dartmouth, May 16, 1775," *Naval Documents of the American Revolution*, Vol. 1, 346.

84. Ibid., 347.

85. Ibid., 348.

86. Chesnut, ed., "Henry Laurens to William Manning, May 22, 1775," *The Papers of Henry Laurens*, Vol. 10, 128.

87. Moultrie, 62.

88. Ibid., 63.

89. Ibid.

90. Ibid.

91. Ibid.

92. Ibid.

93. Drayton, *Memoirs of the American Revolution from its Commencement to the year 1776*, Vol. 1, 263.

94. Chesnut ed., "Henry Laurens to John Laurens, June 18, 1775," *The Papers of Henry Laurens*, Vol. 10, 183.

95. Ibid.

96. Moultrie, 67.

97. Clark, ed., "Governor William Campbell to General Thomas Gage, July 1, 1775," *Naval Documents of the American Revolution*, Vol. 1, 800.

98. Clark, ed., "William Henry Drayton to William Drayton, July 4, 1775," *Naval Documents of the American Revolution*, Vol. 1, 816.

99. Clark, ed., "Governor William Campbell to General Thomas Gage, July 29, 1775," *Naval Documents of the American Revolution*, Vol. 1, 1007.

100. Clark, ed., "Captain Edward Thornbrough to Admiral Samuel Graves, July 29, 1775," *Naval Documents of the American Revolution*, Vol. 1, 1008.

101. Jones, *History of Georgia*, Vol. 2, 169.

102. Ibid.

103. Stan Deaton, "James Wright (1716-1781)," *New Georgia Encyclopedia*, September 29, 2020, Web 14, January 2021.

104. Ford, ed., "Georgia Delegates to Peyton Randolph, April 6, 1775," *Journals of the Continental Congress, 1774-1789*, Vol. 1, 326.

105. Ibid.

106. Ibid., 326-327.

107. Ford, ed., "An Address of the Inhabitants of St. John's Parish, Georgia, to the Continental Congress, February 9, 1775," *Journals of the Continental Congress, 1774-1789*, Vol. 2, 45.

108. Ford, ed., "May 17, 1775," *Journals of the Continental Congress, 1774-1789*, Vol. 2, 54.

109. Chesnut, ed., "Henry Laurens to William Manning, May 22, 1775," *The Papers of Henry Laurens*, Vol. 10, 128-129.

110. Ibid.

111. Clark, ed., "Lieutenant William Grant to Admiral Samuel Graves, June 18, 1775," *Naval Documents of the American Revolution*, Vol. 1, 716.

112. Ibid.

113. Ibid.

114. Clark, ed., "Lieutenant William Grant to Admiral Samuel Graves, June 18, 1775," *Naval Documents of the American Revolution*, Vol. 1, 716.

115. Ibid.

116. Clark, ed., "Journal of His Majesty's Schooner *Saint John*, June 18, 1775," *Naval Documents of the American Revolution*, Vol. 1, 715.

117. Clark, ed., "Governor Wright to Admiral Samuel Graves, June 27, 1775," *Naval Documents of the American Revolution*, Vol. 1, 764.

118. Clark, ed. "Copy of the Letter from Governor James Wright to Admiral Samuel Graves as Substituted by the South Carolina Committee of Safety, June 27, 1775," *Naval Documents of the American Revolution*, Vol. 1, 765.

119. Rev. George White, "Proceedings of the Georgia Provisional Congress, July 4–July 17, 1775," *Historical Collections of Georgia* (New York, 1855), 65-80.

120. Ford, ed., "July 20, 1775," *Journals of the Continental Congress, 1774-1789*, Vol. 2, 193.

121. Clark, ed., "Governor Tonyn to Lord Dartmouth, January 23, 1775," *Naval Documents of the American Revolution*, Vol. 1, 70-72.

122. Ford, ed., "May 17, 1775," *Journals of the Continental Congress, 1774-1789*, Vol. 2, 54.

123. Clark, ed., "John Stuart, Superintendent for Indian Affairs in the Southern Department to South Carolina Committee of Intelligence, July 18, 1775," *Naval Documents of the American Revolution*, Vol. 1, 923.

124. Drayton, "John Stuart to the South Carolina Provincial Congress, July 18, 1775," *Memoirs of the American Revolution from its Commencement to the year 1776*, Vol. 1, 292-294.

125. Davies, ed., "Governor Tonyn to Lord Dartmouth, July 1, 1775," *Documents of the American Revolution*, Vol. 11, 31.

126. Peter Force, ed., "Monthly Return of His Majesty's Forces in the Province of East-Florida, August 1, 1775," *American Archives, Fourth Series*, Vol. 4, 322.

127. Davies, ed., "Governor Tonyn to Lord Dartmouth, July 1, 1775," *Documents of the American Revolution*, Vol. 11, 31.

128. Ibid.

129. Ibid.

CHAPTER TWO: SUMMER 1775

1. Kennedy, ed., "June 8, 1775," *Journal of the House of Burgesses: 1773-1776*, 206.

2. Kennedy, ed., "June 10, 1775," *Journal of the House of Burgesses: 1773-1776*, 214-215.

3. Ibid.

4. Kennedy, 215. Note: Lord Dunmore proposed that the following measures take place before he would agree to return to Williamsburg: Reopen the civil courts;

Disarm and dismiss the independent militia companies; Demand the return of the stolen arms and equipment from the public magazine; Stop harassing supporters of the government; Accept Lord North's Olive Branch reconciliation plan.

5. Dixon and Hunter, "June 24, 1775," *Virginia Gazette.*
6. Scribner, ed., *Revolutionary Virginia: The Road to Independence,* Vol. 3, 218.
7. Davies, ed., "Dunmore to Dartmouth, June 27, 1775," *Documents of the American Revolution,* Vol. 9, 206.
8. Ibid., 206-207.
9. Purdie, "July 14, 1775," *Virginia Gazette.*
10. Clark, ed., "Dunmore to Dartmouth, July 12, 1775," *Naval Documents of the American Revolution,* Vol. 1, 873.
11. Ibid.
12. Ibid.
13. Ibid.
14. Ibid.
15. Clark, ed. "A Midshipman on Board the Otter to a Friend in London, July 11, 1775," *Naval Documents of the American Revolution,* Vol. 1, 866.
16. Clark, ed., "Dunmore to Dartmouth, July 12, 1775," *Naval Documents of the American Revolution,* Vol. 1, 873.
17. R.A. Brock, ed., "George Gilmer to Thomas Jefferson in Papers, Military and Political, 1775-1778 of George Gilmer, M.D. of Pen Park, Albemarle Co., VA," *Miscellaneous Papers 1672-1865: First Printed from the Manuscripts in the Virginia Historical Society* (Richmond, VA, 1937), 101.
18. Scribner, ed., "Proceedings of Third Day of VA Convention," *Revolutionary Virginia: The Road to Independence,* Vol. 3, 319
19. Rutland, ed., "George Mason to Martin Cockburn, July 24, 1775," *The Papers of George Mason,* Vol. 1, 241.
20. William W. Henings, *The Statutes at Large: Being a Collection of all the Laws of Virginia,* Vol. 9 (Richmond: J. & G. Cochran, 1821), 9.
21. Ibid., 10.
22. Ibid, 16.
23. Clark, ed., "Journal of His Majesty's Sloop Otter, July 15, 1775," *Naval Documents of the American Revolution,* Vol. 1, 893.
24. Peter Force, ed., "Monthly Return of His Majesty's Forces in the Province of East-Florida, August 1, 1775," *American Archives, Fourth Series,* Vol. 4, 322.
25. Purdie, "August 4, 1775," *Virginia Gazette.*
26. Ibid.
27. Clark, ed., "Lord Dunmore to Lord Dartmouth, Aug. 2, 1775," *Naval Documents of the American Revolution,* Vol. 1, 1045.
28. Saunders, ed., "Governor Martin to Henry White, June 13, 1775," *Colonial Records of North Carolina,* Vol. 10, 6.
29. Saunders, ed., "A Proclamation by Governor Martin, June 16, 1775," *Colonial Records of North Carolina,* Vol. 10, 16-19.
30. Saunders, ed., "Address from the North Carolina Congressional Delegates, June 19, 1775," *Colonial Records of North Carolina,* Vol. 10, 20-22.

31. Saunders, ed., "Letter from the Safety Committee of New Bern to Samuel Johnston, June 8, 1775"; and "New Hanover County Association, June 9, 1775," *Colonial Records of North Carolina*, Vol. 10, 14, 39.

32. Saunders, ed., "Proceedings of the Safety Committees for the District of Wilmington, June 20, 1775," *Colonial Records of North Carolina*, Vol. 10, 24.

33. Saunders, ed., "Address of Governor Martin to his Council, June 25, 1775," *Colonial Records of North Carolina*, Vol. 10, 38-39.

34. Ibid.

35. Saunders, ed., "Governor Martin to Lord Dartmouth, June 30, 1775," *Colonial Records of North Carolina*, Vol. 10, 41.

36. Ibid.

37. Ibid.

38. Saunders, ed., "Proceedings of the Safety Committee of Wilmington, July 7, 1775," *Colonial Records of North Carolina*, Vol. 10, 72.

39. Saunders, ed., "Letter from the Safety Committee of Wilmington to Samuel Johnston, July 13, 1775," *Colonial Records of North Carolina*, Vol. 10, 91.

40. Saunders, ed., "Notice for Calling the Hillsborough Convention, July 10, 1775," *Colonial Records of North Carolina*, Vol. 10, 88.

41. Saunders, ed., "Proceedings of the Safety Committee of Wilmington, July 10, 1775," *Colonial Records of North Carolina*, Vol. 10, 87.

42. Saunders, ed., "Proceedings of the Safety Committee of Wilmington, July 15, 1775," *Colonial Records of North Carolina*, Vol. 10, 93.

43. Clark, ed., "Governor Martin to Lord Dartmouth, July 16, 1775," *Naval Documents of the American Revolution*, Vol. 1, 899.

44. Clark, ed., "Captain John Collet to General Gage, July 8, 1775," *Naval Documents of the American Revolution*, Vol. 1, 844.

45. Clark, ed., "Governor Martin to Lord Dartmouth, July 20, 1775," *Naval Documents of the American Revolution*, Vol. 1, 937.

46. Saunders, ed., "Proceedings of the Safety Committee of Wilmington, July 10, 1775," *Colonial Records of North Carolina*, Vol. 10, 112-115.

47. Clark, ed., "Proceedings of the Wilmington Safety Committee, July 21, 1775," *Naval Documents of the American Revolution*, Vol. 1, 939-940.

48. Clark, ed., "Captain Parry to Admiral Graves, July 26, 1775," *Naval Documents of the American Revolution*, Vol. 1, 981.

49. Saunders, ed., "Letter from Samuel Johnston to Committee of Wilmington, July 21, 1775," *Colonial Records of North Carolina*, Vol. 10, 116.

50. Saunders, ed., "Proceedings of the Safety Committee of Wilmington, July 31, 1775," *Colonial Records of North Carolina*, Vol. 10, 124.

51. Saunders, ed., "Proclamation of Governor Martin, August 8, 1775," *Colonial Records of North Carolina*, Vol. 10, 141-150.

52. Saunders, ed., "Governor Martin to Lord Dartmouth, August 28, 1775," *Colonial Records of North Carolina*, Vol. 10, 236.

53. Saunders, ed., "Prefatory Notes," *Colonial Records of North Carolina*, Vol. 10, iv.

54. Saunders, ed., "Proceedings of the Provincial Congress, August 23, 1775," *Colonial Records of North Carolina*, Vol. 10, 171.

55. Saunders, ed., "Proceedings of the Provincial Congress, August 24, 1775," *Colonial Records of North Carolina*, Vol. 10, 174.

56. Saunders, ed., "Proceedings of the Provincial Congress, August 25, 1775," *Colonial Records of North Carolina*, Vol. 10, 180.

57. Ford, ed., Proceedings of the Continental Congress, June 26, 1775 and Nov. 6, 1775," *Journals of the Continental Congress, 1774-1789*, Vol. 3, 107, 330.

58. Saunders, ed., "Proceedings of the Provincial Congress, September 1, 1775," *Colonial Records of North Carolina*, Vol. 10, 186-187.

59. Saunders, ed., "Proceedings of the Provincial Congress, September 7 and 5, 1775," *Colonial Records of North Carolina*, Vol. 10, 196, 192.

60. Gibbes, ed., "Thomas Fletchall to the President of the Council of Safety, July 24, 1775," *Documentary History of the American Revolution*, Vol. 1, 124.

61. Ibid. and George Kotlik, "Thomas Fletchall's Association: A Loyalist Proclamation in the South Carolina Backcountry," *Journal of the American Revolution*, June 24, 2019.

62. Clark, ed., "Journal of the South Carolina Provincial Congress, November 12, 1775," *Naval Documents of the American Revolution*, Vol. 2, 1002-1003.

63. Davies, ed., "Governor Campbell to Lord Dartmouth, July 19, 1775," *Documents of the American Revolution*, Vol. 10, 50.

64. Drayton, *Memoirs of the American Revolution from its Commencement to the year 1776*, Vol. 1, 318.

65. Ibid., 321-322.

66. Ibid., 331.

67. Moultrie, 77.

68. Gibbes, ed., "Drayton and Tennent to the Council of Safety, August 7, 1775," *Documentary History of the American Revolution*, Vol. 1, 128.

69. Gibbes, ed., "Mr. Tennent to Mr. Laurens, August 20, 1775," *Documentary History of the American Revolution*, Vol. 1, 145.

70. Gibbes, ed., "Mr. Tennent to Mr. Laurens, August 24, 1775," *Documentary History of the American Revolution*, Vol. 1, 156-157.

71. Gibbes, ed., "Mr. Drayton to the Council of Safety, August 30, 1775," *Documentary History of the American Revolution*, Vol. 1, 162-163.

72. Gibbes, ed., "Mr. Drayton to the Council of Safety, September 11, 1775," *Documentary History of the American Revolution*, Vol. 1, 173.

73. Gibbes, ed., "A Declaration of the Honorable William Henry Drayton, September 13, 1775," *Documentary History of the American Revolution*, Vol. 1, 182-183.

74. Robert Gibbes, ed., "Treaty of Ninety-Six, September 16, 1775," *Documentary History of the American Revolution*, Vol. 1 (New York, 1853), 184-186.

75. James H. O'Donnell, "Cameron, Alexander," *Dictionary of North Carolina Biography*, ed. William S. Powell, 6 Volumes (Chapel Hill: University of North Carolina Press, 1979-1996).

76. Moultrie, 76

77. Clark, ed., "Journal of the South Carolina Council of Safety, July 19, 1775," *Naval Documents of the American Revolution*, Vol. 1, 931.

78. Davies, ed., "Governor Wright to Lord Dartmouth, July 10, 1775," *Documents of the American Revolution*, Vol. 1, 44.
79. Clark, ed., "Governor Patrick Tonyn to Lord Dartmouth, July 21, 1775," *Naval Documents of the American Revolution*, Vol. 1, 949.
80. Clark, ed., "Journal of the South Carolina Council of Safety, July 18, 1775," *Naval Documents of the American Revolution*, Vol. 1, 920.
81. Clark, ed., "Admiral Graves to Philip Stephens, Secretary of the British Admiralty, July 29, 1775," *Naval Documents of the American Revolution*, Vol. 1, 1002.
82. Ibid.
83. Ibid.
84. Clark, ed., "Arthur Middleton to William Henry Drayton, August 11, 1775," *Naval Documents of the American Revolution*, Vol. 1, 1122.
85. Clark, ed., "Governor Tonyn to General Gage, September 14, 1775," *Naval Documents of the American Revolution*, Vol. 2, 104.
86. Ibid.
87. Clark, ed., "Peter Timothy to William Henry Drayton, August 13, 1775," *Naval Documents of the American Revolution*, Vol. 1, 1135.
88. Clark, ed., "Governor Campbell to Lord Dartmouth, August 19, 1775," *Naval Documents of the American Revolution*, Vol. 1, 1185.
89. John W. Gordon, *South Carolina and the American Revolution: A Battlefield History* (Columbia: University of South Carolina Press, 2003), 21.
90. Clark, ed., "Governor Campbell to Lord Dartmouth, August 19, 1775," *Naval Documents of the American Revolution*, Vol. 1, 1184-1185.
91. Moultrie, 80.
92. Clark, ed., "Governor Campbell to Lord Dartmouth, August 19, 1775," *Naval Documents of the American Revolution*, Vol. 1, 1185.
93. Clark, ed., "Excerpt from South-Carolina and American General Gazette, September 8, 1775," *Naval Documents of the American Revolution*, Vol. 2, 56.
94. Drayton, *Memoirs of the American Revolution from its Commencement to the year 1776*, Vol. 2, 26.
95. Clark, ed., "Journal of HM Sloop *Tamar*, September 14, 1775," *Naval Documents of the American Revolution*, Vol. 2, 102.
96. Chesnut, ed., "Council of Safety to Colonel Moultrie, September 13, 1775," *The Papers of Henry Laurens*, Vol. 10, 380-381.
97. Clark, ed., "Diary of Captain Barnard Elliott, September 14, 1775," *Naval Documents of the American Revolution*, Vol. 2, 102.
98. Clark, ed., "Diary of Captain Barnard Elliott, September 15, 1775," *Naval Documents of the American Revolution*, Vol. 2, 114.
99. Ibid.
100. Ibid., 115.
101. Drayton, *Memoirs of the American Revolution from its Commencement to the year 1776*, Vol. 2, 40.
102. Davies, ed., "Governor Wright to Lord Dartmouth, July 8, 1775," *Documents of the American Revolution*, Vol. 11, 42-43.

103. Ibid.

104. Davies, ed., "Governor Wright to Lord Dartmouth, July 10, 1775," *Documents of the American Revolution*, Vol. 11, 44.

105. Clark, ed., "Journal of the South Carolina Council of Safety, July 18, 1775," *Naval Documents of the American Revolution*, Vol. 1, 920.

106. Davies, ed., "Governor Wright to Lord Dartmouth, September 23, 1775," *Documents of the American Revolution*, Vol. 11, 130.

107. Ford, ed., "July 20, 1775," *Journals of the Continental Congress, 1774-1789*, Vol. 2, 193.

108. Paul Smith, ed., "Richard Smith's Diary, Sept. 13, 1775," *Letters of Delegates to Congress* (Washington, DC, Library of Congress, 1977), Vol. 2, 9.

109. Smith, ed., "John Adams Diary, Sept. 15, 1775," *Letters of Delegates to Congress*, Vol. 2, 13.

110. Smith, ed., "John Adams Diary, Sept. 27, 1775," *Letters of Delegates to Congress*, Vol. 2, 70.

111. Smith, ed., "John Adams Diary, Sept. 24, 1775," *Letters of Delegates to Congress*, Vol. 2, 51.

112. Ibid.

113. Roger Smith, "The Failure of Great Britain's Southern Expedition of 1776: Revisiting Southern Campaigns in the Early Years of the American Revolution, 1775-1779," *Florida Historical Quarterly*, Vol. 93, No. 3 (Winter 2015) 390

114. Force, ed., "A Proclamation of Governor Patrick Tonyn, August 21, 1775," *American Archives*, 4th Series, Vol. 3, 705-706.

115. Ibid.

116. Force, ed., "General Gage to Admiral Graves, September 8, 1775," *American Archives*, Fourth Series, Vol. 3, 703.

117. Clark, ed., "Governor Tonyn to Admiral Graves, September 14, 1775," *Naval Documents of the American Revolution*, Vol. 2, 105.

118. Ibid.

119. Ibid.

120. Clark, ed., "Governor Tonyn to Admiral Graves, October 3, 1775," *Naval Documents of the American Revolution*, Vol. 2, 287-289.

121. Force, ed., "State of the Fourteenth Regiment of Infantry, in the Province of East Florida, September 30, 1775," *American Archives, Fourth Series*, Vol. 4, 327.

CHAPTER THREE: FALL 1775

1. Clark, ed., "Captain Squire to the Hampton Town Committee, September 10, 1775," *Naval Documents of the American Revolution*, Vol. 2, 74. Note: The king's stores that Captain Squires demanded be returned included: six swivel guns, five muskets, five cutlasses, two powder horns, two cartouch boxes, swivel shot, seine and rope, and an anchor.

2. Robert L. Scribner and Brent Tarter, ed., *Revolutionary Virginia: The Road to Independence*, Vol. 4, 96.

3. Clark, ed., "Hampton Committee to Captain Squire, September 16, 1775," *Naval Documents of the American Revolution*, Vol. 2, 123.

4. Clark, ed., "Captain Leslie to General Howe, November 1, 1775," *Naval Documents of the American Revolution*, Vol. 2, 844-845.

5. Clark, ed., "Captain Leslie to General Howe, November 1, 1775," *Naval Documents of the American Revolution*, Vol. 2, 844-845.

6. Davies, ed., "Lord Dunmore to Lord Dartmouth, October 22, 1775," *Documents of the American Revolution*, Vol. 11, 161.

7. Dixon and Hunter, "October 28, 1775," *Virginia Gazette*, 3.

8. Davies, ed., "Lord Dunmore to Lord Dartmouth, December 6, 1775 through February, 1776," *Documents of the American Revolution*, Vol. 3, 58.

9. Pinkney, "November 2, 1775," *Virginia Gazette*, 2.

10. Clark, ed., "John Page to Thomas Jefferson, November 11, 1775," *Naval Documents of the American Revolution*, Vol. 2, 991-992.

11. Davies, ed., "Lord Dunmore to Lord Dartmouth, December 6, 1775 through February, 1776," *Documents of the American Revolution*, Vol. 3, 58.

12. Pinkney, "November 2, 1775," *Virginia Gazette*, 2.

13. David John Mays, ed., "Edmund Pendleton to Thomas Jefferson, November 16, 1775," *The Letters and Papers of Edmund Pendleton*, Vol. 1 (Charlottesville: University Press of Virginia, 1967), 130

14. Purdie, "November 3, 10, 17, 1775," *Virginia Gazette*, 2, 2, 1.

15. Davies, ed., "Lord Dunmore to Lord Dartmouth, October 5, 1775," *Documents of the American Revolution*, Vol. 11, 137.

16. Davies, ed., "Lord Dunmore to Lord Dartmouth, December 6 through February 18, 1776," *Documents of the American Revolution,* Vol. 12, 58-59.

17. Clark, ed., "Captain Samuel Leslie to General William Howe, November 26, 1775," *Naval Documents of the American Revolution*, Vol. 2, 1148.

18. Davies, ed., "Lord Dunmore to Lord Dartmouth, December 6 through February 18, 1776," *Documents of the American Revolution*, Vol. 12, 59.

19. Clark, ed., "Captain Samuel Leslie to General William Howe, November 26, 1775," *Naval Documents of the American Revolution*, Vol. 2, 1148.

20. Pinkney, "November 16, 1775," *Virginia Gazette*, 3.

21. Boyd, ed., "John Page to Thomas Jefferson, November 24, 1775," *The Papers of Thomas Jefferson*, Vol. 1, 264-265.

22. Clark, ed., "Lord Dunmore's Proclamation, November 7, 1775," *Naval Documents of the American Revolution*, Vol. 2, 920.

23. Saunders, ed., "Governor Martin to Lord Dartmouth, September 12, 1775," *Colonial Records of North Carolina*, Vol. 10, 244.

24. Ibid.

25. Ibid.

26. Clark, ed., "Intelligence from New Bern, September 22, 1775," and "Governor Martin to Lord Dartmouth, October 16, 1775," *Naval Documents of the American Revolution*, Vol. 2, 184, 484.

27. Saunders, ed., "Governor Martin to Lord Dartmouth, October 16, 1775," *Colonial Records of North Carolina*, Vol. 10, 264-278.

28. Ibid.

29. Saunders, ed., "Proceedings of the Provincial Council, October 20, 1775," *Colonial Records of North Carolina*, Vol. 10, 285-289.

30. Saunders, ed., "Proceedings of the Provincial Council, October 21, 1775," *Colonial Records of North Carolina*, Vol. 10, 290-292.
31. Clark, ed., "Governor Martin to Lord Dartmouth, November 12, 1775," *Naval Documents of the American Revolution*, Vol. 2, 1001-1002.
32. Clark, ed., "Disposition of the Fleet upon Admiral Graves quitting the command of it on 27 January, 1776," *Naval Documents of the American Revolution*, Vol. 3 (Washington, DC, 1968), 1008.
33. Clark, ed., "Governor Martin to Lord Dartmouth, November 12, 1775," *Naval Documents of the American Revolution*, Vol. 2, 1002.
34. Ibid.
35. Clark, ed., "Journal of HM Sloop *Cruizer*, November 17-20, 1775," and "Journal of HM Sloop *Scorpion*, November 13-23, 1775," *Naval Documents of the American Revolution*, Vol. 2, 1088, 1148.
36. Ford, ed., "Proceedings of November 28, 1775," *Journals of the Continental Congress*, Vol. 3, 387-388.
37. Ford, ed., "Proceedings of June 26, 1775," *Journals of the Continental Congress*, Vol. 2, 107.
38. Chesnut, ed., "Council of Safety to the South Carolina Delegates in the Continental Congress, September 18, 1775," *The Papers of Henry Laurens*, Vol. 10, 396-397.
39. Ibid.
40. Ibid.
41. Ibid.
42. Chesnut, ed., "Henry Laurens to John Laurens, September 26, 1775," *The Papers of Henry Laurens*, Vol. 10, 426.
43. Clark, ed., "Journal of HM Sloop *Tamar*, September 28, 1775," *Naval Documents of the American Revolution*, Vol. 2, 235.
44. Clark, ed., "South Carolina General Committee to Governor Campbell, September 29, 1775," *Naval Documents of the American Revolution*, Vol. 2, 243.
45. Ibid.
46. Clark, ed., "Governor Campbell to Henry Laurens, September 30, 1775," *Naval Documents of the American Revolution*, Vol. 2, 260.
47. Moultrie, 93-94.
48. Ibid.
49. Ford, "Proceedings of November 4, 1775," *Journals of the Continental Congress*, Vol. 3, 325.
50. Clark, ed., "William Henry Drayton to the Georgia Council of Safety, November 12, 1775," *Naval Documents of the American Revolution*, Vol. 2, 1004.
51. Clark, ed., "Journal of the South Carolina Provincial Congress, November 12, 1775," *Naval Documents of the American Revolution*, Vol. 2, 1002-1003.
52. Ibid.
53. Ibid.
54. Peter Force, ed., "William Henry Drayton to the Continental Congress, November 12, 1775," *American Archives*, Fourth Series, Vol. 4, 51-52.
55. Clark, ed., "Journal of the South Carolina Provincial Congress, November 12, 1775," *Naval Documents of the American Revolution*, Vol. 2, 1002-1003.

56. Force, ed., "William Henry Drayton to the Continental Congress, November 12, 1775," *American Archives*, Fourth Series, Vol. 4, 51

57. Gibbes, ed., "Major Williamson to Edward Wilkinson, November 6, 1775," *Documentary History of the American Revolution*, Vol. 1, 209.

58. Moultrie, 97-98.

59. Ibid.

60. Gibbes, ed., "Major Williamson to Edward Wilkinson, November 6, 1775," *Documentary History of the American Revolution*, Vol. 1, 209-210.

61. Gibbes, ed., "A Report of the Militia and Volunteers on Duty in the Fortified Camp at Ninety-Six on Sunday November 19, 1775," *Documentary History of the American Revolution*, Vol. 1, 221.

62. Gibbes, ed., "Major Williamson to Mr. Drayton, November 25, 1775," *Documentary History of the American Revolution*, Vol. 1, 217.

63. Ibid.

64. Ibid.

65. Ibid.

66. Ibid.

67. Ibid., 119.

68. Jerome Greene, *Historic Resource Study and Historic Structure Reports: Ninety-Six, A Historical Narrative*, 70.

69. Ibid.

70. Drayton, 119.

71. Ibid., 120.

72. Gibbes, ed., "Agreement for a Cessation of Arms . . . at Ninety-Six, November 22, 1775," *Documentary History of the American Revolution*, Vol. 1, 214-215.

73. Greene, *Historic Resource Study and Historic Structure Reports: Ninety-Six, A Historical Narrative*, 72-73.

74. Davies, ed., "Governor Wright to Lord Dartmouth, October 14, 1775," *Documents of the American Revolution*, Vol. 11, 144.

75. Ibid.

76. Davies, ed., "Governor Wright to Lord Dartmouth, November 16, 1775," *Documents of the American Revolution*, Vol. 11, 180.

77. Ibid.

78. Ford, ed., "Proceedings November 4, 1775," *Journals of the Continental Congress, 1774-1789*, Vol. 3, 325.

79. Force, ed., "John Moultrie to General Grant, October 4, 1775," *American Archives*, Fourth Series, Vol. 4, 336.

80. Ibid.

81. Davies, ed., Lieut.-General Thomas Gage to John Stuart, September 12, 1775," *Documents of the American Revolution*, Vol. 11, 105.

82. Force, ed., "John Stuart to General Gage, October 3, 1775," *American Archives*, Fourth Series, Vol. 4, 316-317.

83. Ibid.

84. Force, ed., "John Stuart to General Gage, October 3, 1775," *American Archives*, Fourth Series, Vol. 4, 317.

85. Force, ed., "Frederick George Mulcaster to General Grant, October 3-4," *American Archives*, Fourth Series, Vol. 4, 333.
86. Ibid.
87. Clark, ed., "Proclamation of Governor Tonyn, November 2, 1775," *Naval Documents of the American Revolution*, Vol. 2, 864.
88. Ibid.
89. Ibid., 865.
90. Force, ed., "Proclamation by Governor Peter Chester, November 11, 1775," *American Archives*, Fourth Series, Vol. 4, 341-342.
91. Force, ed., "Governor Peter Chester to Governor William Tryon, November 18, 1775," *American Archives*, Fourth Series, Vol. 4, 340.

CHAPTER FOUR: DECEMBER 1775

1. Scribner and Tarter, ed., "Robert Shedden, Portsmouth, VA to Mr. John Shedden, In Glasgow: An Intercepted Letter, November 20, 1775," *Revolutionary Virginia, The Road to Independence*, Vol. 4, 439.
2. Scribner and Tarter, ed., "John Brown, Virginia, to Mr. William Brown, An Intercepted Letter, November 21, 1775," *Revolutionary Virginia, The Road to Independence*, Vol. 4, 445.
3. Clark, ed., "Lord Dunmore to General William Howe, November 30, 1775," *Naval Documents of the American Revolution*, Vol. 2, 1209-1211.
4. Ibid.
5. Ibid.
6. Davies, ed., "Lord Dunmore to Lord Dartmouth, December 6 through February 18, 1776," *Documents of the American Revolution*, Vol. 12, 59.
7. Ibid.
8. Boyd, ed., "John Page to Thomas Jefferson, November 24, 1775," *The Papers of Thomas Jefferson*, Vol. 1, 264-265.
9. D.R. Anderson, ed., "Colonel Woodford to Edmund Pendleton, November 26, 1775," in "The Letters of Colonel William Woodford, Colonel Robert Howe, and General Charles Lee to Edmund Pendleton," *Richmond College Historical Papers* (June 1915), 104.
10. Ibid.
11. Ibid.
12. Ibid.
13. Clark, ed., "Lord Dunmore to General William Howe, November 30, 1775," *Naval Documents of the American Revolution*, Vol. 2, 1209-1211.
14. Clark, ed., "Lt. Col. Charles Scott to a Williamsburg Correspondent, December 4, 1775," *Naval Documents of the American Revolution*, Vol. 2, 1274-1275.
15. Clark, ed., "Lord Dunmore to Lord Dartmouth, December 6 through February 18, 1776," *Documents of the American Revolution*, Vol. 12, 59.
16. Anderson, ed., "Colonel Woodford to Edmund Pendleton, December 4, 1775," *Richmond College Historical Papers*, 106.
17. Clark, ed., "Lt. Col. Charles Scott to a Williamsburg Correspondent, December 4, 1775," *Naval Documents of the American Revolution*, Vol. 2, 1274-1275.

18. Anderson, ed., "Colonel Woodford to Edmund Pendleton, December 4, 1775," *Richmond College Historical Papers*, 106.
19. Ibid.
20. Ibid, 107.
21. Ibid., 107.
22. Ibid., 108-09.
23. Clark, ed., "Lt. Col. Charles Scott to a Williamsburg Correspondent, December 4, 1775," *Naval Documents of the American Revolution*, Vol. 2, 1274-1275.
24. Ibid.
25. Anderson, ed., "Colonel Woodford to Edmund Pendleton, December 5, 1775," *Richmond College Historical Papers*, 110.
26. Anderson, ed., "Colonel Woodford to Edmund Pendleton, December 7, 1775," *Richmond College Historical Papers*, 114.
27. Clark, ed., "Lt. Col. Charles Scott to a Williamsburg Correspondent, December 4, 1775," *Naval Documents of the American Revolution*, Vol. 2, 1274-1275.
28. Anderson, ed., "Colonel Woodford to Edmund Pendleton, December 4, 1775," *Richmond College Historical Papers*, 108.
29. Clark, ed., "Lord Dunmore to Lord Dartmouth, December 13, 1775," *Naval Documents of the American Revolution*, Vol. 3, 140-141.
30. Clark, ed., "Colonel Woodford to Edmund Pendleton, December 9, 1775," *Naval Documents of the American Revolution*, Vol. 3, 28. Note: Colonel Woodford repeated this account in a second letter to Edmund Pendleton the next day. A similar account was included in the *Annual Register for the Year 1776*, p. 29: "It has been said, that we were led into this unfortunate affair, through the designed false intelligence of a pretended deserter, who was tutored for the purpose."
31. Clark, ed., "Letter from a Midshipman on Board H.M. Sloop Otter, December 9, 1775," *Naval Documents of the American Revolution*, Vol. 3, 29.
32. Clark, ed., "Lord Dunmore to Lord Dartmouth, December 6 through February 18, 1776," *Naval Documents of the American Revolution*, Vol. 3, 141.
33. Ibid. Note: Lord Dunmore claimed in this letter that he left the discretion of whether to actually launch the attack with Captain Leslie.
34. Clark, ed., "Letter to John Pinkney, December 20, 1775," *Naval Documents of the American Revolution*, Vol. 3, 186-189.
35. Ibid.
36. Force, ed., "Major Spotswood to a Friend in Williamsburgh, December 9, 1775," *American Archives*, Vol. 4, 224.
37. Clark, ed., "Col. Woodford to Edmund Pendleton, December 10, 1775," *Naval Documents of the American Revolution*, Vol. 3, 39-40.
38. Force, ed., "Major Spotswood to a Friend in Williamsburgh, December 9, 1775," *American Archives*, Vol. 4, 224; and Clark, "Letter to Pinkney, December 20, 1775," *Naval Documents of the American Revolution*, Vol. 3, 186-89.
39. Clark, "Letter to Pinkney, December 20, 1775," *Naval Documents of the American Revolution*, Vol. 3, 186-189.
40. Clark, "Letter from a Midshipman on Board H.M. Sloop Otter, December 9, 1775" *Naval Documents of the American Revolution*, Vol. 3, 29.

41. Force, ed., "Major Spotswood to a Friend in Williamsburgh, December 9, 1775," *American Archives*, Vol. 4, 224.

42. John Marshall, *The Life of George Washington*, Vol. 2 (Fredericksburg, VA: Citizens Guild of Washington's Boyhood Home, 1926), 132.

43. Force, ed., "Major Spotswood to a Friend in Williamsburgh, December 9, 1775," *American Archives*, Vol. 4, 224.

44. Clark, ed., "Col. Woodford to Edmund Pendleton, December 10, 1775," *Naval Documents of the American Revolution*, Vol. 3, 39-49.

45. *The Annual Register for the Year 1776*, 4th ed., 29.

46. Pinkney, "Letter to Pinkney, December 20, 1775," *Virginia Gazette*, 2-3.

47. Clark, "Letter from a Midshipman on Board *H.M. Sloop Otter*, December 9, 1775," *Naval Documents of the American Revolution*, Vol. 3, 29.

48. Charles Campbell, ed., "Richard Kidder Meade to Theodorick Bland Jr., December 18, 1775." *The Bland Papers*, Vol. 1 (1840), 38-39.

49. Pinkney, "Letter to Pinkney, December 20, 1775," *Virginia Gazette*, 2-3.

50. Ibid.

51. Ibid.

52. Force, ed., "Major Spotswood to a Friend in Williamsburgh, December 9, 1775," *American Archives*, Vol. 4, 224.

53. Ibid.

54. Pinkney, "Letter to Pinkney, December 20, 1775," *Virginia Gazette*, 2-3.

55. Clark, ed., "Colonel Woodford to Edmund Pendleton, December 10, 1775," *Naval Documents of the American Revolution*, Vol. 3, 39-40.

56. Ibid.

57. Clark, ed., "Lord Dunmore to Lord Dartmouth, December 13, 1775," *Naval Documents of the American Revolution*, Vol. 3, 141.

58. Clark, ed., "Lord Dunmore to Lord Dartmouth, December 13, 1775," *Naval Documents of the American Revolution*, Vol. 3, 140-141.

59. Clark, ed., "Colonel Woodford to Edmund Pendleton, December 10, 1775," *Naval Documents of the American Revolution*, Vol. 3, 40-41.

60. Ibid.

61. Clark, ed., "Letter from the Virginia Committee of Safety, December 16, 1775," *Naval Documents of the American Revolution*, Vol. 3, 132.

62. Clark, "Letter from a Midshipman on Board H.M. Sloop Otter, December 9, 1775," *Naval Documents of the American Revolution*, Vol. 3, 29; and "Thomas Macknight to Reverend Macknight, December 26, 1775," *Naval Documents of the American Revolution*, Vol. 3, 260-261.

63. Clark, ed., "Thomas Macknight to Reverend Macknight, December 26, 1775," *Naval Documents of the American Revolution*, Vol. 3, 260-61.

64. Clark, ed., "Lord Dunmore to Lord Dartmouth, December 13, 1775," *Naval Documents of the American Revolution*, Vol. 3, 141-142.

65. Force, ed., "A Morning Return of the Forces under the command of Colonel Howe, December 17, 1775," *American Archives*, Fourth Series, Vol. 4, 294.

66. Saunders, ed., "Governor Martin to Lord Dartmouth, November 12, 1775," *The Colonial Records of North Carolina*, Vol. 10, 326.

67. Ford, ed., "Proceedings of the Continental Congress, November 28, 1775," *Journals of the Continental Congress*, Vol. 3, 387.

68. Ibid., 388.

69. Saunders, ed., "A Talk from the Rebel Commissioners to the Creeks, November 13, 1775," *The Colonial Records of North Carolina*, Vol. 10, 330-331.

70. Clark, ed., "South Carolina American General Gazette, December, 8, 1775," *Naval Documents of the American Revolution*, Vol. 3, 14.

71. Clark, ed., "Governor Martin to Lord Dartmouth, January 12, 1776," *Naval Documents of the American Revolution*, Vol. 3, 757-759.

72. Clark, ed., "Journal of H.M. Sloop Scorpion, December 19, 1775," *Naval Documents of the American Revolution*, Vol. 3, 244.

73. Mays, ed., "The Virginia Committee of Safety to Colonel William Woodford, December 1, 1775," *The Letters and Papers of Edmund Pendleton*, Vol. 1, 134.

74. Force, ed., "A Morning Return of the Forces under the command of Colonel Howe, December 17, 1775," *American Archives*, Fourth Series, Vol. 4, 294.

75. Ibid., 142.

76. Force, ed., "A Morning Return of the Forces under the command of Colonel Howe, December 17, 1775," *American Archives*, Fourth Series, Vol. 4, 294.

77. Clark, ed., "Captain Matthew Squire R.N., to the Officer Commanding at Norfolk, December 15, 1775," *Naval Documents of the American Revolution*, Vol. 3, 119.

78. Clark, ed., "Lord Dunmore to Lord Dartmouth, December 13, 1775," *Naval Documents of the American Revolution*, Vol. 3, 142.

79. Clark, ed., "Colonel Woodford to Edmund Pendleton, December 17, 1775," *Naval Documents of the American Revolution*, Vol. 3, 140.

80. Clark, ed., "Extract of a Letter from Col. Robert Howe to Edmund Pendleton, December 25, 1775," *Naval Documents of the American Revolution*, Vol. 3, 244.

81. Saunders, "Lord George Germain to Governor Martin, December 23, 1775," *The Colonial Records of North Carolina*, Vol. 10, 364.

82. Ibid.

83. Saunders, "Lord Dartmouth to Governor Martin, November 7, 1775," *The Colonial Records of North Carolina*, Vol. 10, 306-307.

84. Ibid.

85. Gibbes, ed., "Colonel Richardson to Mr. Drayton, November 27, 1775," *Documentary History of the American Revolution*, Vol. 1, 219-220.

86. Gibbes, ed., "Colonel Richardson to Henry Laurens, December 12, 1775," *Documentary History of the American Revolution*, Vol. 1, 239-241.

87. Gibbes, ed., "Declaration by Colonel Richardson to Insurgents Under Cunningham, December 8, 1775," *Documentary History of the American Revolution*, Vol. 1, 224-225.

88. Gibbes, ed., "Colonel Richardson to Henry Laurens, December 12, 1775," *Documentary History of the American Revolution*, Vol. 1, 239-241.

89. Ibid.

90. Gibbes, ed., "Colonel Richardson to Henry Laurens, December 23, 1775," *Documentary History of the American Revolution*, Vol. 1, 242.

91. Ibid., 243.
92. Ibid., 244.
93. Gibbes, ed., "Colonel Richardson to Henry Laurens, January 2, 1775," *Documentary History of the American Revolution*, Vol. 1, 246.
94. Ibid., 247.
95. Ibid.
96. Ibid.
97. Ibid.
98. Allan Candler, ed., "Journal of the Council of Safety, December 19, 1775," *The Revolutionary Records of the State of Georgia*, Vol. 1 (1908), 77.
99. Clark, ed., "South Carolina Council of Safety to the Georgia Council of Safety, December 14, 1775," *Naval Documents of the American Revolution*, Vol. 3, 104.
100. Ibid.
101. Clark, ed., "Minutes of the South Carolina Council of Safety, December 20, 1775," *Naval Documents of the American Revolution*, Vol. 3, 191.
102. Candler, ed., "Governor Wright to Lord Dartmouth, December 19, 1775," *Collections of the Georgia Historical Society*, Vol. 3, 228.
103. Clark, ed., "Journal of HM Schooner *St. Lawrence*, November 27, 1775," *Naval Documents of the American Revolution*, Vol. 2, 1168.
104. Clark, ed., "Governor Tonyn to Lieutenant John Graves, December 8, 1775," *Naval Documents of the American Revolution*, Vol. 3, 15-16.
105. Clark, ed., "Journal of HM Schooner *St. Lawrence*, December 10, 1775," *Naval Documents of the American Revolution*, Vol. 3, 43.
106. Clark, ed., "Governor Tonyn to Lord Dartmouth, December 24, 1775," *Naval Documents of the American Revolution*, Vol. 3, 231.
107. Ibid. and Force, ed., "Monthly Return of His Majesty's Forces in the Province of East-Florida, October, 1, 1775," *American Archives*, Fourth Series, Vol. 4, 325-326.
108. Philander D. Chase, ed., "General Washington to John Hancock, December 18, 1775," *The Papers of George Washington*, Vol. 2, 573-574.
109. Ford, ed., "Proceedings of January 1, 1776," *Journals of the Continental Congress*, 1774-1789, Vol. 4, 15.

CHAPTER FIVE: WINTER 1776

1. Pinkney, "December 23, 1775," *Virginia Gazette*, 3.
2. Clark, ed., "Virginia Committee of Safety to Maryland Delegates in Congress, December 29, 1775," *Naval Documents of the American Revolution*, Vol. 3, 296-297.
3. Scribner and Tarter, ed., *Revolutionary Virginia, The Road to Independence*, Vol. 5, 125-128.
4. Ibid.
5. Ibid.
6. Scribner and Tarter, ed., "Major John Connolly to General Thomas Gage: Captured Proposals," *Revolutionary Virginia, The Road to Independence*, Vol. 4, 82-83. Printed in Purdie's *Virginia Gazette* on December 22, 1775.

7. Chase and Runge, "George Washington to Richard Henry Lee, December 26, 1775," *The Papers of George Washington,* Vol. 2, 611.

8. Clark, ed., "Ships in Norfolk and Hampton Roads, December 30, 1775," *Naval Documents of the American Revolution,* Vol. 3, 309-310.

9. Clark, ed., "Captain Henry Bellow to Colonel Robert Howe, December 30, 1775," *Naval Documents of the American Revolution,* Vol. 3, 310.

10. Clark, ed., "Colonel Robert Howe to Captain Henry Bellew, December 30, 1775," *Naval Documents of the American Revolution,* Vol. 3, 315.

11. Clark, ed., "A Letter from a Midshipman aboard the Liverpool, January 4, 1776," *Naval Documents of the American Revolution,* Vol. 3, 621-622.

12. Clark, ed., "Captain Bellew to Philip Stephens, January 11, 1776," *Naval Documents of the American Revolution,* Vol. 3, 737.

13. Clark, ed., "Colonel Howe to the Virginia Convention, January 2, 1776," *Naval Documents of the American Revolution,* Vol. 3, 579-580.

14. Clark, ed., "Lord Dunmore to Lord Dartmouth, Aboard the Dunmore off Norfolk, January 4, 1776," *Naval Documents of the American Revolution,* Vol. 3, 617-618.

15. *Journal of the House of Delegates, 1835-36, Doc. No. 43* (Richmond, 1835), Virginia State Library, 16.

16. Scribner and Tarter, *Revolutionary Virginia: Road to Independence,* Vol. 5, 16.

17. Ibid.

18. Clark, ed., "Colonel William Woodford to Thomas Elliot, January 4, 1776," *Naval Documents of the American Revolution,* Vol. 3, 617.

19. Pinkney, "Account of the Burning of Norfolk, January 6, 1776," *Virginia Gazette,* 2-3.

20. Anderson, ed., "Colonel Robert Howe to Edmund Pendleton, December 22, 1775," January 2, 1776, and "Colonel William Woodford to Edmund Pendleton, December 22, 1775," *Richmond College Historical Papers,* 136-139, 148.

21. Scribner and Tarter, ed., "Proceedings of the 4th Virginia Convention, January 15, 1776," *Revolutionary Virginia, Road to Independence,* Vol. 5, 405.

22. Clark, ed., "Purdie, February 9, 1776," *Virginia Gazette*; and "Letter in London Chronicle," *Naval Documents of the American Revolution,* Vol. 3, 1187 and Vol. 4, 23.

23. *Journal of the House of Delegates, 1835-36, Doc. No. 43* (Richmond, 1835), Virginia State Library, 16.

24. Selby, 86.

25. Clark, ed., "Journal of HMS *Liverpool,* February 13-14, 1776," *Naval Documents of the American Revolution,* Vol. 3, 1293, and Selby, 86.

26. Clark, ed., "Journal of HMS *Syren,* January 3, 1775," *Naval Documents of the American Revolution,* Vol. 3, 622.

27. Saunders, ed., "Governor Martin to Lord Germain, March 21, 1776," *The Colonial Records of North Carolina,* Vol. 10, 486-490.

28. Saunders, ed., "Proclamation of Governor Martin, January 10, 1775," *The Colonial Records of North Carolina,* Vol. 10, 396-397.

29. Force, ed., "Governor Martin to . . . January 10, 1775," *American Archives, Fourth Series,* Vol. 4, 981.

30. Ibid.
31. Ibid.
32. Ibid.
33. Hugh Rankin, "The Moore's Creek Bridge Campaign, 1776," *North Carolina Historical Review*, Vol. 30 (1953), 32.
34. Rankin, 36.
35. Charles E. Hatch, Jr., "Appendix A, A Narrative of the Proceedings of a Body of Loyalists in North Carolina," *The Battle of Moores Creek Bridge* (1969), 65.
36. Rankin, 37.
37. Saunders, ed., "Extract of a letter from Brigadier James Moore to the Provincial Council, March 2, 1776," *The Colonial Records of North Carolina*, Vol. 11, 283-284.
38. Hatch, Jr., "Appendix A, A Narrative of the Proceedings of a Body of Loyalists in North Carolina," *The Battle of Moores Creek Bridge,* 65-66.
39. Saunders, ed., "Extract of a letter from Brigadier James Moore to the Provincial Council, March 2, 1776," *The Colonial Records of North Carolina*, Vol. 11, 284.
40. Hatch, Jr., "Appendix A, A Narrative of the Proceedings of a Body of Loyalists in North Carolina," *The Battle of Moores Creek Bridge*, 68.
41. Ibid., 68-69.
42. Saunders, ed., "Colonel Caswell to President Harnett, February 29, 1776," *The Colonial Records of North Carolina*, Vol. 10, 482.
43. Rankin, 47.
44. Hatch, Jr., "Appendix A, A Narrative of the Proceedings of a Body of Loyalists in North Carolina," *The Battle of Moores Creek Bridge*, 69.
45. Rankin, 50.
46. Hatch, Jr., "Appendix A, A Narrative of the Proceedings of a Body of Loyalists in North Carolina," *The Battle of Moores Creek Bridge*, 69.
47. Robert M. Dunkerly, *Redcoats on the Cape Fear: The Revolutionary War in Southeastern North Carolina,* (Jefferson, NC: McFarland & Co., 2012), 63.
48. Hatch, Jr., "Appendix A, A Narrative of the Proceedings of a Body of Loyalists in North Carolina," *The Battle of Moores Creek Bridge*, 69
49. Dunkerly, 63-64.
50. Hatch, Jr., "Appendix A, A Narrative of the Proceedings of a Body of Loyalists in North Carolina," *The Battle of Moores Creek Bridge*, 70.
51. Rankin, 49.
52. Ibid., 50
53. Saunders, ed., "Extract of a letter from Brigadier James Moore to the Provincial Council, March 2, 1776," *The Colonial Records of North Carolina*, Vol. 11, 285.
54. Force, ed., "Extract of a Letter from a Gentleman in North Carolina to his Friend in Philadelphia, March 10, 1776," *American Archives*, Fourth Series, Vol. 5, 170.
55. Hatch, Jr., "Appendix A, A Narrative of the Proceedings of a Body of Loyalists in North Carolina," *The Battle of Moores Creek Bridge*, 70.

56. Ibid., 71.
57. Rankin, 53.
58. Ibid.
59. Ibid., 52.
60. Saunders, ed., "Extract of a letter from Brigadier James Moore to the Provincial Council, March 2, 1776," *The Colonial Records of North Carolina*, Vol. 11, 285.
61. Force, ed., "Letter from an Unknown Source, March 10, 1776," *American Archive*, Fourth Series, Vol. 4, 485-486.
62. Ibid.
63. Saunders, ed., "Governor Martin to Lord Germain, March 21, 1776," *The Colonial Records of North Carolina*, Vol. 10, 492.
64. Saunders, ed., "Colonel William Purviance to the Provincial Council, February 23, 1776," *The Colonial Records of North Carolina*, Vol. 10, 466-467.
65. Ibid., 468
66. Clark, ed., "Council of Safety Motion, December 2, 1775," *Naval Documents of the American Revolution*, Vol. 2, 1242.
67. Clark, ed., "Journal of *H.M. Sloop Tamar*, December 21, 1775," and "Minutes of the South Carolina Council of Safety, December 17, 1775," *Naval Documents of the American Revolution*, Vol. 3, 202, 143.
68. Clark, ed., "Governor Campbell to Lord Dartmouth, January 1, 1776," *Naval Documents of the American Revolution*, Vol. 3, 568.
69. Clark, ed., "Minutes of the South Carolina Council of Safety, December 19, 1776," *Naval Documents of the American Revolution*, Vol. 3, 191.
70. Clark, ed., "Minutes of the South Carolina Council of Safety, December 18, 1775," *Naval Documents of the American Revolution*, Vol. 3, 164.
71. Clark, ed., "Minutes of the South Carolina Council of Safety, January 2, 1776," *Naval Documents of the American Revolution*, Vol. 3, 582.
72. Clark, ed., "Minutes of the South Carolina Council of Safety, January 6, 1776," *Naval Documents of the American Revolution*, Vol. 3, 665.
73. Clark, ed., "Minutes of the South Carolina Council of Safety, January 9, 1776," *Naval Documents of the American Revolution*, Vol. 3, 705.
74. Clark, ed., "Minutes of the South Carolina Council of Safety, January 18, 1776," *Naval Documents of the American Revolution*, Vol. 3, 851.
75. Clark, ed., "Journal of the Georgia Council of Safety, January 7, 1776," *Naval Documents of the American Revolution*, Vol. 3, 674.
76. Candler, ed., "Meeting of the Georgia Council of Safety, January 12, 1776," *The Revolutionary Records of the State of Georgia*, Vol. 1, 95.
77. Candler, ed., "Meeting of the Georgia Council of Safety, January 13, 1776," *The Revolutionary Records of the State of Georgia*, Vol. 1, 98.
78. Clark, ed., "Journal of the HM Sloop *Tamar*, January 15, 1776," *Naval Documents of the American Revolution*, Vol. 3, 830.
79. Clark, ed., "Information to the Town of Savannah from Governor Sir James Wright, January 18, 1776," *Naval Documents of the American Revolution*, Vol. 3, 852.

80. Ibid.
81. Ibid.
82. Candler, ed., "Journal of the Council of Safety, January 18, 1775," *The Revolutionary Records of the State of Georgia*, Vol. 1, 101.
83. Ibid., 102-103.
84. Candler, ed., "Journal of the Council of Safety, January 19, 1775," *The Revolutionary Records of the State of Georgia*, Vol. 1, 103.
85. Ibid.
86. Clark, ed., "Information to the Town of Savannah from Governor Wright, January 22, 1776," *Naval Documents of the American Revolution*, Vol. 3, 933.
87. Clark, ed., "Vice Admiral Samuel Graves to Philip Stephens, January 26, 1775," *Naval Documents of the American Revolution*, Vol. 3, 992-993.
88. Ibid., 993.
89. Clark, ed., "Journal of the HMS *Scarborough*, February 12, 1775," *Naval Documents of the American Revolution*, 1239.
90. Clark, ed., "Governor James Wright to the Council at Savannah, February 13, 1776," *Naval Documents of the American Revolution*, Vol. 3, 1269.
91. Ibid.
92. Clark, ed., "Colonel Lachlan McIntosh to General Washington, March 8, 1776," *Naval Documents of the American Revolution*, Vol. 4, 247.
93. Ibid.
94. Ibid.
95. Ibid.
96. Ibid., 247-248.
97. Ibid.
98. Clark, ed., "Raymond Demere and Daniel Roberts to Colonel Lachlan McIntosh, March 4, 1776," *Naval Documents of the American Revolution*, Vol. 4, 168-169.
99. Clark, ed., "William Ewen to Captain Barkley and Major Grant, March 7, 1776," *Naval Documents of the American Revolution*, Vol. 4, 223-224.
100. Clark, ed., "Governor Wright to General Clinton, March 10, 1776," *Naval Documents of the American Revolution*, Vol. 4, 293.
101. Ibid.
102. Ibid., 293-294.
103. Clark, ed., "Colonel Lachlan McIntosh to General Washington, March 8, 1776," *Naval Documents of the American Revolution*, Vol. 4, 248.
104. Clark, ed., "Henry Laurens to William Manning, March 16, 1776," *Naval Documents of the American Revolution*, Vol. 4, 370.
105. Clark, ed., "Ordnance Stores . . . for HM Sloop *Tamar* and HM Armed Ship *Cherokee*, January 8, 1776," and "Provisions from St. Augustine . . . January 13, 1776," *Naval Documents of the American Revolution*, Vol. 3, 688, 741.
106. Clark, ed., "Martin Jollie to Governor Tonyn, February 13, 1776," *Naval Documents of the American Revolution*, Vol. 3, 1270-1271.
107. Clark, ed., "Governor Tonyn to Lord Dartmouth, February 16, 1776," *Naval Documents of the American Revolution*, Vol. 3, 1328.

108. Clark, ed., "Lieutenant Grant to Governor Tonyn, March 7, 1776," *Naval Documents of the American Revolution*, Vol. 4, 225.

109. Clark, ed., "Governor Tonyn to Lord Dartmouth, March 8, 1776," *Naval Documents of the American Revolution*, Vol. 4, 250.

110. Clark, ed., "Minutes of a Council Held on Board . . . HMS *Scarborough*, March 14, 1776," *Naval Documents of the American Revolution*, Vol. 4, 344.

111. Clark, ed., "Governor Tonyn to Lord Germain, April 22, 1776," *Naval Documents of the American Revolution*, Vol. 4, 1210.

CHAPTER SIX: SPRING 1776

1. Clark, ed., "Narrative of Sir Henry Clinton, February 17-27, 1776," *Naval Documents of the American Revolution*, Vol. 4, 102.

2. Ibid.

3. Purdie, "March 8, 1776," *Virginia Gazette*, 2-3.

4. Chase, ed., "General Charles Lee to General George Washington, May 10, 1776," *The Papers of George Washington*, Vol. 4, 258.

5. Chase, ed., "General Charles Lee to General George Washington, April 5, 1776," *The Papers of George Washington*, Vol. 4, 43.

6. Ibid.

7. Purdie, "March 8, 1776," *Virginia Gazette*, 3.

8. Purdie, "March 29, 1776," *Virginia Gazette*, 1.

9. Tarter, ed., "Proceedings of the Sixth Day of the Virginia Convention, May 11, 1776," *Revolutionary Virginia: Road to Independence*, Vol. 7, part 1, 96.

10. Tarter, ed., "Proceedings of the Fifth Day of the Virginia Convention, May 10, 1776," *Revolutionary Virginia: Road to Independence*, Vol. 7, part 1, 88.

11. Tarter, ed., "Proceedings of the Fifth Day of the Virginia Convention, May 15, 1776," *Revolutionary Virginia: Road to Independence*, Vol. 7, part 1, 143.

12. Clark, ed., "Journal of HM Sloop *Cruizer*, March 14, 1776," *Naval Documents of the American Revolution*, Vol. 4, 369.

13. Clark, ed., "Governor Martin to General Clinton, March 20, 1776," *Naval Documents of the American Revolution*, Vol. 4, 429-430.

14. Saunders, ed., "Proceedings of the North Carolina Provincial Congress, April 6-10, 1776," *The Colonial Records of North Carolina*, Vol. 10, 503-508.

15. Saunders, ed., "Proceedings of the North Carolina Provincial Congress, April 12, 1776," *The Colonial Records of North Carolina*, Vol. 10, 512.

16. Clark, ed., "Journal of the HMS *Syren*, April 18, 1776," *Naval Documents of the American Revolution*, Vol. 4, 1156.

17. Clark, ed., "Journal of HM Sloop *Cruizer*, May 3, 1776," *Naval Documents of the American Revolution*, Vol. 4, 1411; and William J. Morgan, ed., "General Charles Cornwallis to Lord Germain, May 16, 1776," *Naval Documents of the American Revolution*, Vol. 5, 131.

18. Saunders, ed., "Proclamation by General Henry Clinton, May 5, 1776," *The Colonial Records of North Carolina*, Vol. 10, 591-592.

19. Moultrie, 170.

20. Ibid., 172.

21. Ibid., 172-173.

22. Ibid., 173.
23. Ibid., 178.
24. Ibid., 180.
25. Clark, ed., "Governor Campbell to General Clinton, March 26, 1775," *Naval Documents of the American Revolution*, Vol. 4, 531.
26. Purdie, "April 5, 1776," *Virginia Gazette*, 3.
27. Ibid.
28. Clark, ed., "Extract of a Letter from the Council of Safety of Georgia, to the Council of Safety of . . . South Carolina, April 2, 1776," *Naval Documents of the American Revolution*, Vol. 4, 636.
29. Clark, ed., "Extract of a Letter from Georgia, March 24, 1776," *Naval Documents of the American Revolution*, Vol. 4, 495.
30. Candler, ed., "Proclamation of Georgia Provincial Congress, April 15, 1775," *Revolutionary Records of the State of Georgia*, Vol. 1, 274.
31. Ibid., 276-277.
32. Clark, ed., "General William Howe to Lord Germain, May 7, 1776," *Naval Documents of the American Revolution*, Vol. 4, 1437.
33. Morgan, ed., "Captain Bryne to Vice Admiral Young, May 21, 1776," *Naval Documents of the American Revolution*, Vol. 5, 197.
34. Ibid.
35. Clark, ed., "Governor Tonyn to Lord Germain, April 22, 1776," *Naval Documents of the American Revolution*, Vol. 4, 1210.

CHAPTER SEVEN: SUMMER 1776
1. Morgan, ed. "Narrative of Captain Andrew Snape Hamond," *Naval Documents of the American Revolution*, Vol. 5, 321.
2. Ibid., 322.
3. Thomas Posey, "May 27, 1776," *Revolutionary War Journal*, Thomas Posey Papers, Indiana Historical Society Library, Indianapolis, IN.
4. Ibid.
5. Ibid.
6. Ibid.
7. Morgan, ed. "Captain Hamond to Commodore Parker, June 10, 1781," *Naval Documents of the American Revolution*, Vol. 5, 460.
8. "General Andrew Lewis to General Charles Lee, June 12, 1776," *Lee Papers*, Vol. 2, 63.
9. "General Lewis to General Lee, June 12, 1776," *Lee Papers*, Vol. 2, 64.
10. Dixon and Hunter, "June 15, 1776," *Virginia Gazette*, 3.
11. Morgan, ed., "Lord Dunmore to Lord Germain, June 26, 1776," *Naval Documents of the American Revolution*, Vol. 5, 756.
12. "General Lewis to General Lee, June 12, 1776," *Lee Papers*, Vol. 2, 64.
13. Morgan, ed., "Extract of a Letter from Williamsburg June 22, 1776," *Naval Documents of the American Revolution*, Vol. 5, 687.
14. Morgan, ed., "Trevett's Journal," *Naval Documents of the American Revolution*, Vol. 5, 688.

15. Morgan, ed., "Lord Dunmore to Lord George Germain, June 26, 1776," *Naval Documents of the American Revolution*, Vol. 5, 757.

16. Morgan, ed., "Narrative of Captain Andrew Snape Hamond, June 10, 1781," *Naval Documents of the American Revolution*, Vol. 5, 840.

17. Walter Clark, ed., "Committee of Secrecy, War, and Intelligence of North Carolina to General Lee, May 6, 1776," *Colonial Records of North Carolina*, Vol. 11 (Winston, NC: 1895), 296-297.

18. Ibid., 297.

19. Ibid., 297-298.

20. "General Lee to Edmund Pendleton, May 24, 1775," *Lee Papers*, Vol. 2, 34-35.

21. Brent Tarter, ed., "Proceedings of the 5th Virginia Convention, May 29, 1776," *Revolutionary Virginia: The Road to Independence*, Vol. 7, Part 1 (Charlottesville: University Press of Virginia, 1983), 299.

22. Moultrie, 282.

23. Moultrie, 279.

24. Moultrie, 290.

25. Morgan, ed., "General Clinton to Commodore Parker, June 5, 1776," *Naval Documents of the American Revolution*, Vol. 5, 388.

26. Morgan, ed., "Commodore Parker to General Clinton, June 2, 1776," *Naval Documents of the American Revolution*, Vol. 5, 351.

27. Morgan, ed., "General Clinton to Commodore Parker, June 2, 1776," *Naval Documents of the American Revolution*, Vol. 5, 352.

28. Morgan, ed., "Commodore Parker to General Clinton, June 2, 1776," *Naval Documents of the American Revolution*, Vol. 5, 354.

29. Morgan, ed., "Narrative of General Clinton, June 7-16, 1776," *Naval Documents of the American Revolution*, Vol. 5, 573.

30. Morgan, ed., "A Proclamation by General Clinton, June 6, 1776," *Naval Documents of the American Revolution*, Vol. 5, 406-407.

31. Morgan, ed., "General Clinton to Commodore Parker, June 6, 1776," *Naval Documents of the American Revolution*, Vol. 5, 406.

32. Ibid.

33. Ibid.

34. Morgan, ed., "Colonel Moultrie to General Clinton, June 8, 1776," *Naval Documents of the American Revolution*, Vol. 5, 352.

35. Ibid.

36. Moultrie, 282, 288.

37. Moultrie, 281.

38. Gibbes, ed., "General Charles Pinckney to His Mother, June 15, 1776," *Documentary History of the American Revolution*, Vol. 2, 3-4.

39. Moultrie, 282.

40. Ibid.

41. Ibid., 283.

42. Gibbes, ed., "A Return of the Troops in Fort Moultrie 28th June, 1776," *Documentary History of the American Revolution*, Vol. 2, 5.

43. Moultrie, 290-291.

44. Ibid., 289.

45. Morgan, ed., "A British Journal of the Expedition to Charlestown, June 17-18, 1776," *Naval Documents of the American Revolution*, Vol. 5, 607.

46. Morgan, ed., "Richard Hutson to Isaac Hayne, June 24, 1776," *Naval Documents of the American Revolution*, Vol. 5, 721.

47. Morgan, ed., "General Clinton to General Vaughan, June 18, 1776," *Naval Documents of the American Revolution*, Vol. 5, 609.

48. Morgan, ed., "A British Journal of the Expedition to Charleston, June 18, 1776," *Naval Documents of the American Revolution*, Vol. 5, 607.

49. Morgan, ed., "Narrative of General Clinton, June 16-27, 1776," *Naval Documents of the American Revolution*, Vol. 5, 783.

50. Moultrie, 282.

51. Morgan, ed., "Commodore Parker to General Clinton, June 25, 1776," *Naval Documents of the American Revolution*, Vol. 5, 745.

52. Morgan, ed., "John Wells' Account of the British Attack on Charleston," *Naval Documents of the American Revolution*, Vol. 5, 804-805.

53. Ibid.

54. Morgan, ed., "Journal of HMS *Active*, June 28, 1776," *Naval Documents of the American Revolution*, Vol. 5, 825.

55. Ibid., 805.

56. Moultrie, 295.

57. Ibid., 294.

58. Ibid.

59. Morgan, ed., "Journal of HMS *Active*, June 28, 1776," *Naval Documents of the American Revolution*, Vol. 5, 825.

60. Morgan, ed., "Narrative of General Henry Clinton, June 28, 1776," *Naval Documents of the American Revolution*, Vol. 5, 801.

61. Ibid.

62. Gibbes, ed., "Account of the Attack on Fort Moultrie in the *South Carolina and American General Gazette*, August 2, 1776," *Documentary History of the American Revolution*, Vol. 2, 18.

63. Moultrie, 303.

64. Moultrie, 296.

65. Moultrie, 296-297.

66. Morgan, ed., "Account of the Attack made upon Sullivans Island off CharlesTown by Sir Peter Parker's Squadron . . . June 28, 1776," *Naval Documents of the American Revolution*, Vol. 5, 804.

67. Ibid.

68. Gibbes, ed., "Account of the Attack on Fort Moultrie in the *South Carolina and American General Gazette*, August 2, 1776," *Documentary History of the American Revolution*, Vol. 2, 17.

69. Moultrie, 297.

70. Gibbes, ed., "A Return of the Troops in Fort Moultrie, June 28, 1776," *Documentary History of the American Revolution*, Vol. 2, 5.

71. Moultrie, 297.

72. "General Lee to the President of the Convention of Virginia, June 29, 1776," *Lee Papers*, Vol. 2, 92.

73. Ibid.

74. Gibbes, ed., "Account of the Attack on Fort Moultrie in the *South Carolina and American General Gazette*, August 2, 1776," *Documentary History of the American Revolution*, Vol. 2, 17.

75. Candler, ed., "The Address of the Council of Safety for Georgia, April 30, 1776, *Revolutionary Records of Georgia*, Vol. 1, 115.

76. Candler, ed., "At a Council of Safety, May 14, 1776," *Revolutionary Records of Georgia*, Vol. 1, 122-123.

77. Candler, ed., "President Archibald Bulloch to Captain William McIntosh, May 15, 1776," *Revolutionary Records of Georgia*, Vol. 1, 124.

78. Ibid.

79. Candler, ed., "President Archibald Bulloch to Captain William McIntosh, May 16, 1776," *Revolutionary Records of Georgia*, Vol. 1, 127-128.

80. Candler, ed., "Meeting of the Council of Safety, June 20, 1776," *Revolutionary Records of Georgia*, Vol. 1, 141.

81. Candler, ed., "President Bulloch to Colonel Elbert, June 22, 1776," *Revolutionary Records of Georgia*, Vol. 1, 145.

82. Hugh McCall, *The History of Georgia*, Vol. 2 (Savannah: Seymour & Williams, 1816), 72-74.

83. Ibid.

84. Morgan, ed., "Governor Patrick Tonyn to Lord George Germain, July 18, 1776," *Naval Documents of the American Revolution*, Vol. 5, 1140.

85. Ibid.

86. McCall, 308.

87. Morgan, ed., "Narrative of Captain Andrew Snape Hamond, June 19, 1776," *Naval Documents of the American Revolution*, Vol. 5, 840.

88. Ibid.

89. Morgan, ed., "Petition of Refugees from South Carolina and Georgia to Governor Tonyn, June 20, 1776," *Naval Documents of the American Revolution*, Vol. 5, 654-656.

90. Morgan, ed., "Journal of HMS *St. John*, June 1-30, 1776," *Naval Documents of the American Revolution*, Vol. 5, 327-328, 465-466, 611-612, 761-762, 844.

91. Morgan, ed., "Journal of the HMS *Hinchinbrook*, June 27, 1776," *Naval Documents of the American Revolution*, Vol. 5, 785.

CHAPTER EIGHT: SECURING INDEPENDENCE

1. Purdie, "July 12, 1776," *Virginia Gazette*, 3.

2. Morgan, ed., "Narrative of Captain Snape Hamond, July 9, 1776," *Naval Documents of the American Revolution*, Vol. 5, 1078.

3. Morgan, ed., "Extract of a letter from Williamsburg, July 13, printed in the *Pennsylvania Packet*, July 22, 1776," *Naval Documents of the American Revolution*, Vol. 5, 1068.

4. Ibid.

5. Posey *Journal*, July 10, 1777.

6. Ibid.

7. Selby, 126.

8. Dixon and Hunter, "July 20, 1776," *Virginia Gazette*, 2.

9. Purdie, "July 25, 1776," *Virginia Gazette*, 2.

10. Ibid.

11. Clark, Walter, ed., "North Carolina Council of Safety to Sam Johnston, July 22, 1776," *The State Records of North Carolina*, Vol. 11, 321.

12. Clark, Walter, ed., "North Carolina Council of Safety to Colonel Armstrong, July 29, 1776," *The State Records of North Carolina*, Vol. 11, 335.

13. Hugh F. Rankin, *North Carolina in the American Revolution* (Raleigh, 1959), 22.

14. Edwin C. Bearss, *The Battle of Sullivan's Island and the Capture of Fort Moultrie: A Documented Narrative and Troop Movement Maps* (US Dept. of the Interior, 1968), 107.

15. Moultrie, 315.

16. "General Lee to Archibald Bulloch, July 18, 1776"; "General Lee to President Rutledge, July 23, 1776;" "Colonel McIntosh to General Lee, July 25, 1776," *Lee Papers*, Vol. 2, 146, 157-160, 168-169.

17. "Archibald Bulloch to General Lee, July 26, 1776," *Lee Papers*, Vol. 2, 171.

18. "General Lee to Richard Peters, August 2, 1776," *Lee Papers*, Vol. 2, 187-189.

19. Ibid.

20. Ibid.

21. Peter Force, ed., *American Archives, Fifth Series*, Vol. 1 (Washington, DC, 1848), 882.

22. Ibid.

23. Ibid.

24. "Conference with the Georgia Council of Safety, August 19, 1776," *Lee Papers*, Vol. 2, 233.

25. Ibid., 234-235.

26. "Orders Issued on the Expedition to Georgia, August 21, 1776," *Lee Papers*, Vol. 2, 253.

27. "General Lee to General John Armstrong, August 27, 1776," *Lee Papers*, Vol. 2, 346.

28. William J. Morgan, ed., "Lieutenant William Grant to Governor Tonyn, August 7, 1776," *Naval Documents of the American Revolution*, Vol. 6, 108.

29. Morgan, ed., "Journal of HM Schooner *St. John*, August 7, 1776," *Naval Documents of the American Revolution*, Vol. 6, 109.

30. Ibid.

31. Davies, ed., "Thomas Brown to Governor Tonyn, February 1776," *Documents of the American Revolution*, Vol. 12, 69-73.

32. Ibid.

33. Davies, ed., "John Stuart to Henry Stuart, October 24, 1775," *Documents of the American Revolution*, Vol. 11, 162-163,

34. Nadia Dean, *A Demand for Blood: The Cherokee War of 1776* (Cherokee, NC: Valley River Press, 2012), 62-64.

35. Ibid., 66-68.

36. Ford, ed., "Proceedings of the Continental Congress, July 12, 1775 and August 19, 1776," *Journals of the Continental Congress,* Vol. 2, 175 and Vol. 5, 669; and Dean, 70.

37. Dean, 72-75.

38. Ibid., 86.

39. Ibid., 89.

40. Purdie, "August 16, 1776," *Virginia Gazette,* 3.

41. Drayton, *Memoirs,* 344.

42. Gibbes, ed., "Colonial Williamson to W.H. Drayton, August 22, 1776," *Documentary History of the American Revolution,* Vol. 2 (New York: Appleton & Co., 1857), 32; and Dean, "A General Return of the Troops under Command of Col. William Christian . . . Oct. 6, 1776," *A Demand of Blood,* 228.

43. Dixon and Hunter, "Williamsburg, November 15, 1776," *Virginia Gazette,* 2.

44. Dean, 314.

BIBLIOGRAPHY

PRIMARY SOURCES

Anderson, D.R., ed. "The Letters of Colonel William Woodford, Colonel Robert Howe, and General Charles Lee to Edmund Pendleton." Richmond, VA: Richmond College Historical Papers, 1915.

Annual Register for the Year 1776. 4th ed. London: J. Dodsley, 1777.

Boyd, Julian P., ed. *The Papers of Thomas Jefferson.* Vol. 1. Princeton, NJ: Princeton University Press, 1950.

Brock, R.A, ed. *Miscellaneous Papers 1672-1865: First Printed from the Manuscripts in the Virginia Historical Society.* Richmond, VA: Virginia Historical Society, 1937.

Campbell, Charles, ed. *The Bland Papers: Being a Selection from the Manuscripts of Colonel Theodorick Bland Jr. of Prince George County.* Vol. 1. Petersburg, VA: Edmund & Julian Ruffin, 1840.

Candler, Allan, ed. *The Revolutionary Records of the State of Georgia.* Vol. 1. Atlanta, GA: Franklin Turner Co., 1908.

Chase, Philander D., ed. *The Papers of George Washington, Revolutionary War Series.* Vols. 1-5. Charlottesville: University Press of Virginia, 1985-93.

Chestnut, David R. *The Papers of Henry Laurens.* Vols. 10-11. Columbia: University of South Carolina Press, 1985, 1988.

Clark, Walter, ed. *The Colonial Records of North Carolina.* Vol. 11. Winston, NC: M.I. & J.C. Stewart, Printers to the State, 1895.

Clark, William, ed. *Naval Documents of the American Revolution.* Vols. 1-4. Washington, D.C.: U.S. Government Printing Office, 1964-68.

Davies, K, ed. *Documents of the American Revolution.* Vols. 9-13. Shannon: Irish University Press, 1975-76.

Drayton, John. *Memoirs of the American Revolution from its Commencement to the year 1776.* Vols. 1-2. Charleston, SC: A. F. Miller, 1821.

Force, Peter, ed. *American Archives,* Fourth Series. Vols. 2-6. Washington, D.C.: M. St. Clair Clarke and P. Force, 1837-1846.

Force, Peter, ed. *American Archives,* Fifth Series. Vol. 1. Washington, D.C.: M. St. Clair Clarke and P. Force, 1848.

Ford, Worthington C., et al., eds. *Journals of the Continental Congress, 1774-1789.* Vols. 1-3. Washington, D.C.: U.S. Government Printing Office, 1904-37.

Gibbes, Robert W., ed. *Documentary History of the American Revolution.* Vols. 1-2. New York: D. Appleton & Co., 1853-57.

Henings, William W., ed. *The Statutes at Large: Being a Collection of all the Laws of Virginia.* Vol. 9. Richmond: J. & G. Cochran, 1821.

Hooker, J Richard, ed. *The Carolina Backcountry on the Eve of the Revolution: The Journal and other Writings of Charles Woodmason, Anglican Itinerant.* Chapel Hill: University of North Carolina Press, 1953.

Journal of the House of Delegates, 1835-36, Doc. No. 43, Richmond: Virginia State Library, 1835.

Kennedy, John P., ed. *Journal of the House of Burgesses*: 1773-1776. Richmond: Virginia State Library, 1905.

Lee, Charles. *Lee Papers,* Vols. 1-2. New York: New-York Historical Society Publication Fund, 1872.

Mays, David John, ed. *The Letters and Papers of Edmund Pendleton.* Vol. 1. Charlottesville: University Press of Virginia, 1967.

Morgan, William J., ed. *Naval Documents of the American Revolution.* Vol. 5. Washington, D.C.: U.S. Government Printing Office, 1970.

Moultrie, William. *Memoirs of the American Revolution.* Vol. 1. New York: David Longworth, 1802.

Rutland, Robert, ed. *The Papers of George Mason.* Vol. 1. Chapel Hill: University of North Carolina Press, 1970.

Saunders, William L., ed. *The Colonial Records of North Carolina,* Vols. 9-10. Raleigh: Josephus Daniels, Printer to the State, 1890.

Scribner, Robert L., and Brent Tarter, eds. *Revolutionary Virginia, The Road to Independence*. Vols. 1-7. Charlottesville: University Press of Virginia, 1973-1978.

Siebert, Wilbur H. *Loyalists in East Florida, 1774-1785: The Most Important Documents Pertaining There To. . . .* Vols. 1-2. Deland, FL: Florida State Historical Society, 1929.

Smith, Paul, ed. *Letters of Delegates to Congress*. Vol. 2. Washington, D.C.: U.S. Government Printing Office, 1977.

U.S. Census Bureau. "Estimated Population of American Colonies: 1610 to 1780," *Historical Statistics of the United States: Colonial Times to 1970*, Part 2. Washington, D.C.: U.S. Government Printing Office, 1975.

———. "Value and Quantity of Articles Exported from British Continent Colonies, by Destination: 1770," *Historical Statistics of the United States: Colonial Times to 1970*, Part 2. Washington, D.C.: U.S. Government Printing Office, 1975.

White, Rev. George. "Proceedings of the Georgia Provisional Congress, July 4–July 17, 1775." *Historical Collections of Georgia*. New York: Pudney & Russell, 1855.

SECONDARY SOURCES

Barrs, Burton. *East Florida in the American Revolution*. Jacksonville, FL: Guild Press, 1932.

Bearss, Edwin C. *The Battle of Sullivan's Island and the Capture of Fort Moultrie: A Documented Narrative and Troop Movement Maps*. U.S. Dept. of the Interior, 1968.

Brown, Richard. *The South Carolina Regulators*. Cambridge, MA: Belknap Press, 1963.

Cashin, Edward. *William Bartram and the American Revolution on the Southern Frontier*. Columbia: University of South Carolina Press, 2000.

Dean, Nadia. *A Demand for Blood: The Cherokee War of 1776*. Cherokee, NC: Valley River Press, 2012.

Dill, Alonzo T., Jr. "Eighteenth Century New Bern: A History of the Town and Craven County, 1700-1800, Part 7." *North Carolina Historical Review*, Vol. 23, No. 3, July 1946.

Dunkerly, Robert M. *Redcoats on the Cape Fear: The Revolutionary War in Southeastern North Carolina.* Jefferson, NC: McFarland & Co., 2012.

Georgia Humanities. *New Georgia Encyclopedia.* www.georgiaencyclopedia.org.

Gordon, John W. *South Carolina and the American Revolution: A Battlefield History.* Columbia: University of South Carolina Press, 2003.

Greene, Jerome. *Historic Resource Study and Historic Structure Reports. Ninety-Six: A Historical Narrative.* U.S. Dept. of the Interior, 1978.

Hatch, Charles E., Jr. *The Battle of Moores Creek Bridge.* National Park Service, 1969.

Jones, Charles C., Jr. *The History of Georgia*, Vol. 2, Boston: Houghton, Mifflin and Co., 1883.

Lambert, Robert. *South Carolina Loyalists in the American Revolution.* Columbia: University of South Carolina Press, 1987.

Marshall, John. *The Life of George Washington.* Vol. 2. Fredericksburg, VA: The Citizens Guild of Washington's Boyhood Home, 1926.

McCall, Hugh. *The History of Georgia.* Vol. 2. Savannah: Seymour & Williams, 1816.

McCrady, Edward. *History of South Carolina.* New York: Macmillan, 1901.

O'Hammon, Neal, and Richard Taylor. *Virginia's Western War, 1775-1786.* Harrisburg, PA: Stackpole Books, 2002.

Powell, William S., ed., *Dictionary of North Carolina Biography.* Vols. 1-6. Chapel Hill: University of North Carolina Press, 1979-1996.

Proctor, Samuel, ed. *Eighteenth-Century Florida: The Impact of the American Revolution.* Gainesville: University Press of Florida, 1978.

Rankin, Hugh. "The Moore's Creek Bridge Campaign, 1776." *North Carolina Historical Review*, Vol. 30, 1953.

Rankin, Hugh F. *North Carolina in the American Revolution.* Chapel Hill: University of North Carolina Press, 1959.

Searcy, Martha C. *The Georgia-Florida Contest in the American Revolution, 1776-78*. Tuscaloosa: University of Alabama Press, 1985.

Selby, John. *The Revolution in Virginia: 1775-1783*. Colonial Williamsburg Foundation, 1988.

Wirt, William. *Sketches in the Life and Character of Patrick Henry*. Philadelphia: James Webster, 1817.

Wright, James Leitch, Jr. *Florida in the American Revolution*. Gainesville: University Press of Florida, 1975.

ARTICLES

Kotlik, George, "Thomas Fletchall's Association: A Loyalist Proclamation in the South Carolina Backcountry." *Journal of the American Revolution*, June 24, 2019, Online.

Olson, Gary D. "Loyalists and the American Revolution: Thomas Brown and the South Carolina Backcountry, 1775-76." *South Carolina Historical Magazine*, Vol. 68, 1967 and Vol. 69, 1968.

Pennington, Edgar L., "East Florida in the American Revolution, 1775-1778." *Florida Historical Society Quarterly*, Vol. 9, no. 1, July 1930.

Smith, Roger. "The Failure of Great Britain's Southern Expedition of 1776: Revisiting Southern Campaigns in the Early Years of the American Revolution, 1775-1779." *Florida Historical Quarterly*, Vol. 93, No. 3, Winter 2015.

Soltow, James H. "Table V: Number of Hogsheads of Tobacco Exported from Virginia, 1745-56, 1768-69, and 1773." *The Economic Role of Williamsburg*, Colonial Williamsburg Foundation Library Research Report Series, 1956.

Troxler, Carole Watterson. "Refuge, Resistance, and Reward: The Southern Loyalists' Claim on East Florida." *Journal of Southern History*, Vol. 55, No. 4, November 1989.

Walsh, Lorena, Ann Smart Martin, and Joanne Bowen. "Table 2.7: Population and Estimated Food Requirements in 1775." *Provisioning Early American Towns, The Chesapeake: A Multidisciplinary Case Study: Final Performance Report*, Colonial Williamsburg Foundation Library Research Report Series, No. 0404, 1997.

UNPUBLISHED WORKS

Bell, Pierson J. *The Struggle for the South Carolina Backcountry, 1775-76.* Dissertations, Theses and Masters Projects, Paper 1539626534, College of William and Mary, 2007.

Posey, Thomas, *Revolutionary War Journal*, Thomas Posey Papers, Indiana Historical Society Library, Indianapolis, IN.

NEWSPAPERS

Dixon and Hunter, *Virginia Gazette*, June 10, 1775.
Dixon and Hunter, *Virginia Gazette*, June 24, 1775.
Dixon and Hunter, *Virginia Gazette*, October 28, 1775.
Dixon and Hunter, *Virginia Gazette*, June 15, 1776.
Dixon and Hunter, *Virginia Gazette*, July 20, 1776.
Dixon and Hunter, *Virginia Gazette*, November 15, 1776.
Pinkney, *Virginia Gazette, Supplement*, April 28, 1775
Pinkney, *Virginia Gazette*, May 4, 1775.
Pinkney, *Virginia Gazette*, June 1, 1775.
Pinkney, *Virginia Gazette*, June 8, 1775.
Purdie, *Virginia Gazette, Supplement*, April 21, 1775.
Purdie, *Virginia Gazette, Supplement*, April 28, 1775.
Purdie, *Virginia Gazette, Supplement*, May 5, 1775.
Purdie, *Virginia Gazette, Supplement*, June 9, 1775.
Purdie, *Virginia Gazette*, July 12, 1776.
Purdie, *Virginia Gazette*, July 14, 1775.
Purdie, *Virginia Gazette*, August 4, 1775.
Purdie, *Virginia Gazette*, November 3, 1775.
Purdie, *Virginia Gazette*, November 10, 1775.
Purdie, *Virginia Gazette*, November 17, 1775.
Purdie, *Virginia Gazette*, March 8, 1776.
Purdie, *Virginia Gazette*, March 29, 1776.
Purdie, *Virginia Gazette*, April 5, 1776.
Purdie, *Virginia Gazette*, July 25, 1776.
Purdie, *Virginia Gazette*, August 16, 1776.
North Carolina Gazette, May 12, 1775.

ACKNOWLEDGMENTS

A S WITH ALL MY BOOKS, I AM INDEBTED TO SEVERAL PEOPLE FOR their support and assistance. The good folks at Westholme Publishing—Bruce H. Franklin, Nate Best, Tracy Dungan, and Trudi Gershenov, in particular, deserve my gratitude. Bruce shepherded the whole process along, Nate, as copy editor, cleaned up all of my writing mistakes, Tracy did a fantastic job on the maps as did Trudi Gershenov for her beautiful cover design.

My wife Susan, who has enormous patience with me, deserves my gratitude, especially with this book as we spent more time than usual together in our house. Sue is an amazing spouse, mother, partner, and friend, and I am always appreciative of her support.

As with past projects, the staff and research resources at the Jamestown-Yorktown Research Library and the Rockefeller Library at the Colonial Williamsburg Foundation were very helpful. And of course, I am ever grateful to my friends and fellow Revolutionary War Reenactors, whose passion for this time period is always inspirational.

INDEX